Female Juvenile Delinquency

Female Juvenile Delinquency

Saumya Shanker

RAWAT PUBLICATIONS

Jaipur • New Delhi • Bangalore • Guwahati • Kolkata

ISBN 978-81-316-0958-3

The publication of this book was financially supported by the ICSSR. The responsibility for the facts stated, opinions expressed, or conclusions reached, is entirely that of the author and that the ICSSR accepts no responsibility for them.

ICSSR Consultant: Prof. R.S. Sandhu, Department of Sociology, Guru Nanak Dev University, Amritsar.

Published by
Prem Rawat for **Rawat Publications**
Satyam Apts., Sector 3, Jawahar Nagar, Jaipur 302 004 (India)
Phone: 0141 265 1748 / 7006 Fax: 0141 265 1748
E-mail: info@rawatbooks.com
Website: www.rawatbooks.com

New Delhi Office
4858/24, Ansari Road, Daryaganj, New Delhi 110 002
Phone: 011-23263290

Also at *Bangalore, Guwahati* and *Kolkata*

Typeset by Rawat Computers, Jaipur
Printed at Nice Printing Press, New Delhi

Dedicated to

My Father

The Inspiration of My Life

Contents

List of Tables and Figures

Tables

Figures

Preface

The common perception about delinquent behaviour of girls is that it is not a serious problem. This is because girls are more likely to commit only minor offences and have historically constituted a very small proportion of the offender population. What animates this study is not so much the number of offenders but the 'circumstances' of the girls behind that number.

During my data collection days I was regularly visiting Nirmal Chhaya and Prayas, which are institutional care setups (home) for girls in Delhi below the age of 18 years, who are either in need of care and protection (neglected) or are in conflict with law (delinquent). The interviewees were from all age groups, communities, and cultures, and I found that in most of the cases the child had to take up acts of delinquency because of the circumstances surrounding them and not out of their free will.

Society with a single stroke of judgement terms these girls as *delinquents*, and they are shunned away to institutional setups as a result and are not allowed to be a part of society as normal human beings. However, what makes them indulge in acts, which the society calls as delinquent acts, in the first place needs to be questioned.

A few of the inmates were deliberately lost by their parents or their guardians, for the despicable yet very harsh Indian reality portrays the belief that these girls would grow up to be a burden for them. They are declared a burden because a girl will bring no monetary respite to the family in hard times. Instead, they would have to provide the girl with dowry from the hard-earned money of the family. Although the child may be the most talented among all the siblings, she is neither allowed to work nor make something of herself.

Being abandoned at a vulnerable age of her childhood can be the most devastating and scarring experience that could take an entire lifetime to correct.

Many run away from home because they were being physically or sexually abused and in most cases by someone they knew. It could be a family member or a friend, but the punishment for not quietly accepting it as "fate", and choosing instead to escape the torment, earns the wrath of the society which only too quickly terms these children as *delinquents*, while the real culprits continue to lead a guilt-free life. Is that fair? No, but it certainly is the reality for these children.

A number of girls would gather around and demand that their story be heard during my visits. I was conscious of the fact that it had very little to do with me and my individual nature, and much more to do with the fact that I was very polite to them and ready to talk *with* them and not *to* them, accept them, and not judge them. Unless they have had excruciatingly tormenting experiences with their own family members, all of the girls, given a chance, would want to return to their families however bad the situation at home might be.

What is even more bizarre is the different definitions of delinquency for different social and cultural contexts in the same society. What is considered delinquent in a particular society may not be delinquent in another. Choices for some of the girls is an extravagance, as they have only known life to be governed by others, either by their families or by their not-so-progressive societies. Whereas for some these precious choices are something we take for granted. It is therefore important to take both social and cultural relativism into account.

Cultural relativism propounds that there is no ultimate standard of good or evil and every judgement about right and wrong is a product of society. Therefore, any opinion on morality or ethics is subject to the cultural perspective of each person. Delinquent behaviour therefore cannot be understood apart from the cultural and social context in which it occurs. Generalizations about delinquent behaviour must refer to the cultural and subjective values of those who engage in it. Cultural and social variations not only affect the definition of delinquency but also help in determining the degree of seriousness which is measured by the severity of punishment imposed. Cultural and social perspective can help us understand why certain actions are considered right or wrong by a particular section of society.

This book has been divided into nine chapters. Chapter 1 gives an overview on female juvenile delinquency and focuses on its occurrence. The chapter also explains the concepts and definition of female juvenile delinquency. Chapter 2 deals with the review of literature pertaining to the study and the methodology applied for the study. Chapter 3 outlines the various theories on juvenile delinquency. Chapter 4 dwells upon both the national and international perspectives regarding this issue. It offers a statistical look at female delinquency at the international, national, and local levels. Chapter 5 analyses the socio-economic profile of the respondents. Determinants of juvenile delinquency among the girls have been examined in Chapter 6 along with nine case studies. Chapter 7 takes an incisive look into the institutional treatment of female juvenile delinquents and condition of the homes where these girls are staying and the respondents' perspective on delinquency and their aspirations for the future. Chapter 8 highlights the coping mechanisms adopted by the state and the society in handling female juvenile delinquency. Chapter 9, the concluding chapter, presents a holistic view of preventing delinquency and provides recommendations for further course of action.

Maybe the number of cases studied are not statistically significant, but, hopefully, the present work will throw new and incisive light on this social problem which affects the future of the girl child and in turn the society in ways more than one. This study will also provide an interface with the present and future social policy framework and contribute to knowledge in this uncharted territory. Let us now proceed toward understanding in detail what are the various concepts and definitions of delinquency which that have come about so far and currently circulating in the field.

Saumya Shanker

Acknowledgement

In completion of this study my foremost thanks and regards go to my supervisor Dr Renuka Singh for her continuous moral and intellectual encouragement. Her richness in ideas and emphatic understanding gave me the much-needed insight that enabled me to carve out a suitable framework for the study.

My primary acknowledgement goes to my father, late Mr Gauri Shanker, who was the biggest inspiration of my life. It was his dream to see me complete my doctoral research, and I am extremely thankful to God that I am able to fulfil this dream of my father.

My in-laws Shri R.B. Ram and Madhuri Devi have always given me the right guidance and encouragement in difficult as well as in happy situations. It goes without saying that their support has meant a lot to me. I shall always be indebted to my husband Siddharth Priyadarshi to whom 'Thank you' is not enough. Without his love and support this work could have never been completed. He would always cheer me up whenever I was down and behind schedule.

Furthermore, my utmost thanks also goes to my brother, Siddharth Shanker, who would always push me to complete my doctoral research and was always around to provide me with all the support that I needed in the most difficult times of my life.

This work would have never seen the light of the day without the support from my mother, Sanghmitra Shanker, and my sister-in-law, Sunita Shanker. They never failed in giving utmost love, time, and affection to my six-month-old baby boy, Ishu, thus giving me enough time and space to complete my PhD.

Credit also goes to my little brother Sambhavya Shanker who, as a National Law School student, gave me valuable insights into the legal concept of crime and delinquency.

I also acknowledge with gratitude all the help and cooperation extended by the teachers and office staff of my centre. I also thank the non-teaching staff of JNU and the staff of both the shelter homes covered under this study for their valuable help during the work.

Finally, I sincerely hope I have succeeded in understanding the subject of my study at least partially, if not completely, for complete knowledge is always elusive.

Saumya Shanker

1

Female Juvenile Delinquency

An Overview

"Delinquency" as a concept and definition in India has varied sociocultural implications attached to it. Western theories have very limited practical utility, but since all the definitions are based on them this has very serious ramifications. Besides, delinquency when referred to women makes its meaning all the more vague and obscure. Owing to the pluralistic cultural profile of India, drawing a uniform definition of delinquency among women is indeed a difficult task. For instance, in a conservative family, women found to be drinking and smoking may be termed as delinquent. On the other hand, in a progressive family, this is only a part of normal social behaviour and may be characterized as 'social drinking'. It similarly applies to the case of love marriage. There are many such disparities prevalent in Indian society as to what 'Delinquency' may mean and how is it perceived by the girl children themselves.

The important factors that are mainly responsible for the causation of juvenile delinquency and antisocial behaviour are (1) economic factors, (2) personality factors, and (3) environmental factors. Poverty may not be a direct cause of delinquency but its effects on the child may be disastrous. A feeling of inadequacy and frustration and emotional insecurity play a dominant role in giving rise to antisocial behaviour.

Whether antisocial behaviour develops or not depends on what happens to the child in its infancy and childhood. In the early years, the basic personality pattern of the child is laid down for good or bad by the emotional stability provided by its parents. Every child born has a right to be wanted, loved, and understood. As it grows, it desires to have increasing love, affection, and care from the mother, father, and other members of the family. If these needs are not adequately met during this crucial period of a child's life, dissatisfaction and hostility creep in and agitation begins to take root in its impressionable mind. The consequences of such an adverse situation lead to results which can be disastrous for both the child and the society.

A number of sociological theories explain delinquent behaviour as a consequence of inequalities within the social structure, inapt social surroundings (leading to faulty learning behaviour), and economic disparity. In these theories, deviance is seen to be related to social disadvantages.[1] These social inequalities and disadvantages imposed implicitly and explicitly promote the emergence of adaptive behaviour patterns among emotionally scarred individuals that block their access to various resources attainable through legitimate means for others but not to them and thus leads to an attitudinal shift in their thinking that it is alright to use illegitimate means to acquire these resources which are denied to them through legitimate means. A.K. Cohen in his book *Delinquent Boys: The Culture of the Gang* has stressed the importance of status frustration as a motivation factor in individual deviant acts. Others see crime and delinquency as behaviours accepted within the normal value systems of certain disadvantaged groups without this status frustration element. In both cases, the definition of deviance itself is seen as part of the mechanism that imposes separate normative behavioural values for different sets or classes of people through which those in control restrict others. This is evident in social control procedures to which those committing particular acts are more likely subjected to and get labelled as deviant if they come from lower social class groups.[2] Some studies have shown delinquency to be related to social status when official delinquency is considered, but others have found no such association. On balance, the evidence suggests that the occupational status of a family is not generally related to deviance or disorder on its own, although the relationship is more consistently found when persistent offending is considered and when class is associated with other indicators of disadvantage.

Truly speaking, no child is born antisocial or delinquent. Delinquency is acquired through the learning process. Sutherland's theory of "differential association" explains criminal behaviour as a product of learning in interaction with other persons, principally within intimate personal groups.[3] In other words, techniques relating to the commission of crime are learnt through association with criminals alone. The delinquent behaviour of a child is often the reflection of his or her surroundings as well. Children follow certain behaviour patterns by imitating their parents and are affected by what their parents do than by what they say. It has a strong influence on their impressionable minds, and, it is their early association with their parents determines their ideas about what is right and wrong. Freud termed this sense of right and wrong as superego, that is, conscience.

The factors that give rise to antisocial tendencies of a child at the initial stage are wrong upbringing, neglect and lukewarm attitude of parents, unhappy home, feeling of insecurity, lack of recreational facilities, abject poverty, unwholesome surroundings, and so on. For want of basic needs in the family, the child moves out and strives to satisfy the unmet needs by resorting to antisocial activities. Thus, the child gradually gets exposed to nefarious elements like gang influence, vagrancy, homosexuality, indecent film shows, pornographic literature, lure of easy life, and so on. One of these factors or a combination of some of these factors leads a child toward adverse direction and ultimately impels him or her to take to antisocial activities.

Economic factors often play an important role to indirectly give rise to the problem of delinquency and antisocial tendencies. Owing to abject poverty, unemployment, underemployment, social ostracism, and conflicts among different sections of people at the rural levels, a large-scale migration of people takes place from rural to urban areas, thus swelling the enormous floating population. They settle down in undesirable areas without adequate amenities, which leads to formation of slums with an unfavourable environment. A strange culture prevails without any social norm. In other words, there is total "anomie", that is, normlessness.

Emile Durkheim opined that antisocial activities thrive in such a state of anomie. The social control system ceases to remain in the strange atmosphere of slums in cities. In fact, the rural regulatory functions of the normal social order break down upon migration of people to urban slums. This situation results in social disorganization. The rural societies are small in size and have strong group solidarity, conventional behaviour, traditional ways, and use informal social control rather than formal codes of law to control personal behaviour. Village forums are utilized for resolving most of the problems related to social and personal control. There is no nonconforming behaviour because the aspiration of people is generally culturally prescribed and the ways of realizing them socially structured. In such a milieu, there may be little motivation toward deviant behaviour.

In urban slums there is extreme weakening of family and neighbourhood controls, and those children who have not acquired life organizations based on habits of conventional behaviour are easily duped by the baneful influences of gangs and other nefarious groups. Thus, the regulatory functions of the collective order break down upon migration to urban slums and a state of de-regulation, normlessness, and anomie prevails. Unlike the rural small-group life, the urban area can be seen as an assortment of strangers. This situation gives rise to indiscipline, moral degradation, obstinacy, and waywardness among slum-dwelling youth. Thus slums become a fertile ground and proves tempting for the confused youth to resort to antisocial activities. What is worse, they often fall prey to the manipulations of unscrupulous persons for vicious ends.

In developing countries like India, the problems of rural-urban drift, poverty, and deprivation have adversely affected a substantial segment of the youth population. The recent trends of youth unrest due to frustration, communication gap, social inequality, illiteracy, lack of opportunities for gainful employment, and so on have also accentuated the problem of juvenile deviance and maladjustment. It India, tradition, religion, and age-old value still exert a considerable influence on everyday life. However, an adverse trend is now noticeable in all these spheres of life. The age-old tradition of respect, obedience, and faith has hardly any influence over the young generation of today. There is a tendency among this substantial segments of the youth population to refuse to heed to the advice and commands of their parents, guardians, or teachers. The old saying, *Gururbrahmaa Gururvishnuh Gururdevo Maheshwarah, Gurursaakshat Parabrahma Tasmai Shreegurave Namah*, no longer holds good. It is now discarded as an obsolete idea.

The social phenomena play a vital role in delinquency causation. Sociologists across the world have made extensive studies on juvenile delinquency from socio-economic and cultural points of view. According to them: (1) family conditions, (2) neighbourhood influence, (3) peers influence, (4) school environment, and (5) economics factors, are some of the predominant social factors that play a dominant role in the formation of the behaviour patterns of a child. So Grant S. McClellan holds the view that "no child is born into the world to be bad or good. He is as bad or as good as we make it possible for him to be."[4] Through the process of socialization the child develops its personality and acquires the values of the family and other groups. It gradually learns to perform certain social roles satisfactorily, first in the family and then in other groups. Thus, the family becomes the primary socializing agent while other groups like neighbourhood group, peer group, school group, and so on play the secondary socializing roles.

In fact, family lays down the foundation of personality development and emotional attachment. The attitude of parents is, therefore, an important criterion in the formation of behaviour pattern of a child. Parents' indifference often leads to lack of attachment between the child and the parents, and this then leads to a failure in generating a close emotional relationship between the parents and the child. As a result, the child develops a feeling of isolation, gets into in bad company, and gradually gets involved in antisocial activities. As usual, a child develops propensities of delinquency after its association with delinquent friends and other unscrupulous antisocial elements in the neighbourhood. W.C. Reckless has aptly stated, "Companionship is unquestionably the most telling force in male delinquency." Similarly, Breckenridge and Abbot opine that delinquents generally concentrate in a particular area which may be called as "Delinquent Neighbourhood." As a matter of fact, the main problem is the problem of unhealthy family life without any scope for the child to fulfil his or her social, emotional, and economic aspirations. In such a situation, he seeks to achieve his ends by resorting to any means fair or foul.

The home environment may also be detrimental for the smooth development of the child due to a number of adverse factors. In some cases sudden death of a parent, poor economic condition, addiction of parents to drugs and alcoholism, constant conflicts in the family, defective parental discipline, and so on lead to an unhappy home and hamper proper upbringing of a child. In such situations, the child becomes frustrated, resentful, and hostile and moves out of the home and takes to antisocial activities through his or her association with bad companions in schools or other places. The family tradition and culture in which the child is brought up at the early stage of his life have a great influence on every sphere in his later life.

Like the family, which plays a dominant and primary role in socialization of the child, the school also has a very important role in moulding the personality of the child. It provides the most important opportunity to a child for the development of his social attitude. The child gets the first exposure at the school with the outside world, which was hitherto unknown to him or her. The school reinforces the family's social training received by the child. Therefore, children not going to school may fall victim to delinquency as they are left vulnerable because of the lack of social control and discipline. Missed opportunity of going to school also pushes away the possibility of the child to achieve the desired life goals through legitimate means.

In lower-class families, parents are generally reluctant to send their children to schools. A child becomes an asset to the family as he or she grows up. Even at the age of seven or eight years, he or she can look after many domestic chores like grazing cows, carrying food for the members of the family engaged in cultivation in the field, and so on. The parents' indifference toward their children at the early impressionable age encourages them to discontinue their studies even if they are initially admitted to schools. The number of school dropouts in rural areas is, therefore, comparatively high. In fact, the lack of discipline at home, laxity in parental control over the growing child, remote control by unscrupulous persons over the child, double standards of conduct practiced by elderly persons, unremitting exposure to violence, generation gap, and so on are important factors that lead to children becoming disobedient and demonstrating deviant traits, eventually becoming antisocial and juvenile.

The determination of the boundary between desirable and undesirable social behaviour is not a legal matter alone in terms of what is or is not socially acceptable behaviour, as it is also a question of social, economic, and political factors in different population groups. Religion plays a major role is determining what is desirable or undesirable and lawful or unlawful behaviour. The development of civil and criminal laws is deeply rooted in religious traditions. All major religions and sects of the world have established rules and codes of conduct that have been codified into law during the evolution of nation-states.[5] For example, Hinduism in India provided a cultural foundation to the development of Indian law and its legal systems before and after the influence of the British.[6]

Similarly, caste and delinquency are also linked to each other. Even though the ideology and structural hierarchy of the historical caste system have lost their vigour, they can help to explain this linkage. Under the hierarchical caste system, elders in families and castes disciplined family and caste members. The higher-caste elders disciplined members of lower castes. The lower castes through the process of Sanskritization try and immolate the socially appreciated and socially approved behaviour of higher castes. Children were reared to fit into the family, caste, and higher-caste expectations and norms.[7] Failure to conform to these expectations not only involved social criticism and sanctions against those who refuse to conform but also against their group members to force them to assume collective responsibility for the behaviour of the rebelling group members. Consequently, every family taught children the norms and rules they should abide by and maintain separateness from other families and groups to keep family matters private and to avoid harmful outside influences.

Similarly, every caste group saw to it that its families and individual members behaved in a disciplined manner, as the reputation of the caste depended on their behaviour. The attachment of children to family, caste, elders, and conventional groups and their impact on them help to explain the general conforming nature of children in India.[8]

There exists also a relationship between class and delinquency. Most delinquent acts are committed by juveniles who are poor. There is a difference between the poor committing offence in India and a developed, rich nation like America. Unlike in America, most of the property crimes committed by poor children in India are due to hunger and utter poverty.[9] However, in urban areas some children from affluent classes commit offences out of greed and a desire for fashionable goods and a high life. Such crimes often occur in shopping centres and malls.[10]

Here media and films come to play a very important role in influencing the young minds. In general in recent times, films in general depict intolerance and violence which have lasting effects on the impressionable minds of young children. Sometimes children may develop a sense of curiosity and seek to put into practice whatever they have witnessed in cinema halls and over televisions at home. Films like *Oye Lucky, Lucky Oye*, *Bluffmaster*, *Bunty Aur Babli*, and so on show slick, suave, polished and lovable crooks who outsmart the cops and people and lead a very rich and sophisticated lifestyle. *Oye Lucky, Lucky Oye* is a story of Lucky Singh who plays a loveable thief, of whom even the Delhi police are extremely fond. His modus operandi is to outsmart the people, chowkidars, and policemen with his sharp mind and wit. He is an aspiring individual who loves good things in life and is generally enamoured by the lifestyles of the rich and affluent Delhi families. Lucky, a gawky 15-year-old lower-middle-class Sikh kid, rises to become one of the most wanted master thieves of India with tens of millions worth loot, a glamorous lifestyle, cars, women, and a fan following. Lucky's journey develops him into a flamboyant playboy who now wants more than just the riches. Now he needs the respectability and the social standing of a city gentleman.

Bluffmaster on the other hand is the story of a slick, suave, and polished con artist, who prides himself on the art of swindling the rich and powerful of their millions and is charming enough to woo the nice, gorgeous girl next door.

Bunty Aur Babli too is a story of two ambitious thugs who wants to live a rich and successful life in the city. There's little support at home because their parents fail to understand their dreams. Therefore, they decide to leave town and try their luck in the city. They decide to travel around from city to city, conning unsuspecting victims and making heaps of money at the same time. However, instead of committing the crimes under their own names, Rakesh and Vimmi, use the alias Bunty and Babli. Their capers are hugely successful and the pair becomes notorious in the media. The crimes committed by them seem way too easy and the couple never consider the consequences either. Such movies goad the young minds to resort to unfair means for reaching their desired goals. The easy flow of things and convenient escape from the police makes it look like a cakewalk and the children are led to believe that they can get away with indulging in antisocial activities. In the minds of these youth the definitions favourable to the violation of laws supersedes the definitions unfavourable to the violation of law.

The novel *Crime and Punishment* by Fyodor Dostoyevsky also gives an excellent account of a man's inner struggle to dominate his conscience. An everyday, average man with aspirations of greatness sets himself above common morality and tries to prove that he can commit murder without punishment, external or internal. The story revolves around Rodion Raskolnikov, a student living in poverty, struggling to make ends meet. He is obsessed with the idea of great, "extraordinary" people who have the right to overstep human laws in order to make a difference, to help the society. Some are doomed to live miserable lives because they are unable to think and rise above the rules, but others are bigger than that. Determined to find out whether he is one of "the great," Rodion carefully plans and commits a murder. The story tracks the consequences and mental anguish of his encounter with the police and his own condemning sense of right and wrong.

We thus see that the greater sense of independence, equality, personal importance, and living a good life, and as a whole individual aspirations, are gradually disintegrating traditional group attachments and constrains.[11] The conditions that have contributed to lower delinquency rates in India are bound to weaken eventually under the impact of modernization. The abilities of the family, communities, and castes to control and keep their members in line are now weakening with the development of egalitarian views introduced as the foundation for the laws of the land and those arising from modernization.

As these modern forces become stronger, they will have serious consequences for delinquency. In the context of these changes, anomie theory of Durkheim[12] and Merton[13] become pertinent. Crime and delinquency are bound to increase as group structures weaken, causing social controls to decline and socialization to become impaired, and as a growing desire for "good life" cannot be achieved because of limited means to earning a livelihood and lack of economic opportunities.[14]

We must accept that violence does not suddenly "happen" at the age of 16 or 17 years. It is part of a long developmental process that begins during the childhood. Many children mature in an atmosphere of violent relationships between men and women, husbands battering wives, and women assaulted by boyfriends and other males or being at the receiving end of the physical punishment. These children come to adopt the same attitudes and practices in dealing with peers and, eventually, their own families as their elders did. This is known as the social learning approach. Children will model their behaviour according to the reactions they receive from others, either positive of negative; the behaviour of those adults with whom they are in close contact, especially parents; and the behaviour of characters they view on television and movies. If children observe aggression by parents and see that aggressive behaviour is approved and rewarded, they will likely react violently during a similar incident. Eventually, children will master the techniques of aggression and become more confident that their behaviour will bring tangible rewards.[15]

By implication, social learning suggests that children, who grow up in a home where violence is a way of life, may learn to believe that such behaviour is acceptable and rewarding. Even if parents tell children not to be violent and punish them if they are, children will start to model their behaviour on the observed acts of violence committed by their parents. Thus, children are more likely to follow what their parents do than what their parents say. The family may serve as the training ground for violence because the child perceives physical punishment as the norm during conflict situations within or outside the family context.[16]

The environment that the parents provide to the children determines their attitudes toward the problems in life. Grossly maladjusted parents, single-parent families, or where there is the physical absence of parents are breeding grounds for deviants. Children who are closely supervised by their parents are less likely to engage in risky behaviour.[17] It is scarcely realized that neglect can emanate from a variety of sources. Because of the increase in the number of dual-career families (both parents working) the concept of "Latchkey" children is also fast-surfacing in the urban/metro regions of India. It is feared that children belonging to families where parental supervision is absent are more likely to develop deviant behaviour and become delinquent. Some psychologists believe that as children become more materialistic and are not taught the values of love, honesty, caring, and sharing they could pose problems for others.[18]

Glaring economic inequalities make children feel neglected and craving for more goodies and gadgets that others have and they don't. Conspicuous consumption plays its own role in making youngsters feel "neglected or left out." Sociologically, the conflict between culturally accepted values and the socially structured difficulties in living up to them exert pressure on children to gravitate towards deviant and disrupted behaviour. This also provides a potential for the formation of subgroups alienated from the rest of the community even though they still notionally form of the mainstream social groups and communities.

The enormity of the problem of juvenile delinquency and antisocial propensities has been causing serious concern all over the world. Even in developed countries, this problem has already assumed an alarming proportion. In a developing country like India, its ugly head has already surfaced. However, in India, the annual statistics on juvenile crimes published in "Crime in India" do not indicate the seriousness of the problem; as such, the issue is that the magnitude of the problem of juvenile delinquency cannot be correctly assessed as of now. Juvenile deviance and infractions at rural levels are even now dealt with informally by the family, community, and religious organization without taking recourse to legal remedies because traditional social control system is still prevalent in this country, particularly in rural areas.

Moreover, people in general in far-flung rural areas are not aware of the existence of a separate juvenile justice administration for exclusively dealing with the cases of juveniles and its efficacy to promote juvenile welfare and reformation. As a result, juvenile trivial offences are not reported to the police. In spite of this fact, the only official source of statistics "Crime in India" published by the National Crime Records Bureau, Ministry of Home Affairs, Government of India, can provide an indication of the recent trends and dimensions of the problem. In addition to these IPC crimes, juveniles are also involved in offences under various Special and Local Laws, such as Arms Act, Narcotic Drugs and Psychotropic Substance Act, Gambling Act, Excise Act, Prohibition Act, Explosives and Explosive Substances Act, Immoral Traffic (Prevention) Act, Indian Railways Act, Registration of Foreigners Act, Protection of Civil Rights Act, Indian Passport Act, Essential Commodities Act, Terrorists and Disruptive Activities Act, Antiquity and Art Treasure Act, Child Marriage Restraint Act, Indecent Representation of Women (Prohibition) Act, Copyright Act, and so on.

Occurrence of Female Juvenile Delinquency

The plight of girl child is another story altogether compared to the trials boys go through in the mainstream society and in the family context. As far girls, they are socialized to be less expressive of their desires, less aggressive in pursuing their interests, and more submissive to and sacrificing for the needs of the family. To bring this about they are highly dominated by adult supervision and control. Social and physical separation of sexes occurs from the early years. Almost always marriages are arranged within their own castes; there is practically no dating, and even talking with members of the opposite sex is highly discouraged in most of the families. For the most part, girls are not left alone at home specifically after early evening. Virginity before marriage is important. The severity and sincerity may differ in urban and rural scenarios. Thus because of the teaching, controlling, and supervising girls experience throughout their formative years, including during childhood, teen years, and later adulthood up until the time they get married, they become overly conscious and particular about their acts and behaviour. This excess control is one of the reason for lower level of delinquency among girls compared to boys.

Admittedly, delinquent behaviour is not a phenomenon that is confined only to the males. But if current figures are any indication various institutions and agencies coping with the delinquents have males as a major part of their inmates. What does this signify? Does it mean that females are less prone to indulge in delinquency? Does it signify that the female persona is more malleable and positively responsive to social control, both formal and informal? Could one say that the female's preoccupation with domestic chores keeps them away from entering the domain of delinquency? Could one say that cases of female delinquency are less prone to be reported and published? Or can it be attributed to something else?

As there is low occurrence of girls indulging in crime, most of the studies on juvenile delinquency in India has focussed primarily on boys while relatively little attention has been paid to girls who commit delinquent acts. Here again the girls get the backseat. The problem of female juvenile delinquency cannot be ignored.

The dearth of study on female delinquency has left a void in our knowledge of the disparities in female and male delinquency, the changing nature and scope of female delinquent behaviour, the differences between adult and juvenile female crime, the characteristics of female criminals and delinquents and the factors and causes of female deviances, and the scope and dynamics of life of girls as female inmates in juvenile and adult correctional facilities.

Consider a situation where a young, abused girl runs away from home at the age of 13 and fails to seek state assistance out of fear that she will be returned to abusers. Once she runs out of money, she may begin stealing. Within a year she may fall into prostitution and may begin using drugs at the age of 16 and soon get arrested. How is the Juvenile Justice System to handle such a case? Before the court she is a juvenile who has committed theft, prostitution, and drug abuse, but in reality she is the one who has suffered enormous abuses and in turn needs the state and society to protect her.

More attention needs to be given to the female juvenile delinquents and separate specific mechanisms need to be developed and implemented in order to provide more effective and meaningful support. They also need to be protected from further social stigma resulting from the tag of juvenile delinquents given to them. Even our justice system is grappling with the question, "Should these young offenders be treated as delinquents or victims?"

Female delinquency has long been overshadowed by male delinquency in terms of incidence, magnitude, seriousness, research, and recognition. As a result, we know relatively little about the modern female delinquency: motivations, diversity, complexities, incarceration, and victims. This is not to say that female delinquency has gone virtually unnoticed through the years. Female delinquencies, similar to male delinquency, are heterogeneous in nature. Equally, female offenders are neither easily nor singularly characterized; in fact, the female offender population varies widely on account of several key factors, such as age, race, ethnicity, family and economic background, and the kinds of delinquent behaviours demonstrated.

This book examines the participation of girls in delinquent activities. It is written to promote a greater understanding and knowledge of girls' crime, its dimensions, its distinctness from male crime, situational and social variables that affect and influence delinquency, delinquent girls' aspirations for the future, and coping mechanisms to deter female delinquency. This study offers a multifaceted exploration of female delinquency: Who are they? Where do they come from? What is the socio-economic profile of female juvenile delinquents? What are the kinds of delinquent acts they commit? What are the elements/causal factors that prompt and perpetrate girls' delinquency?

This book will also provide an interface between the present and future social policy framework and contribute to knowledge in this uncharted territory. Let us now proceed toward understanding in detail the different concepts and definitions of delinquency developed and proposed by researchers and regulatory authorities and policymakers in this area.

Notes

1. Rutter, Michael (1980), *Developmental Psychiatry*, London, American Psychiatric Press, p. 86.
2. Ibid.
3. Bhattacharyya, Kanta Sunil (2000), *Juvenile Justice: An Indian Scenario*, New Delhi, Regency Publications, p. 64.
4. Ibid., p. 67.
5. Barton, J.H., Gibbs, J.L., Li, V.H., and Merryman, J.H. (1983), *Laws in Radically Different Cultures*, St Paul, MN, West Publishing Co., pp. 5–6.
6. Friday, P.C. and Ren, X. (ed.) (2006), *Delinquency and Juvenile Justice System in the Non-Western World*, New York, Criminal Justice Press, p. 37.
7. Dumont, L. (1970), *Homo Hierarchicus*, Chicago, University of Chicago Press, p. 9.
8. Friday and Ren, *Delinquency and Juvenile Justice System*, p. 33.
9. Vincentnathan, S.G. (1985), Caste, Class and Crime: India and the United States, *Comparative Social Research: Vol. 3. Deviance*, Greenwich, CT, Jai Press, p. 114.
10. Chowdhary, S. (2003), Keeping Them at Bay, *The Hindu*, May 14, http://www.thehindu.com/thehindu/mp/2003/05/14/stories/2003 3051400360200.htm
11. Mines, M. (1988), Conceptualizing the Person: Hierarchical Society and Individual Autonomy in India, *American Anthropologist*, 90, 568–579.
12. Durkheim, E. (1951), *Suicide*, New York, Free Press, p. 248.
13. Merton, R. (1938), Social Structure and Anomie, *American Sociological Review*, 3, 672–682.
14. Friday and Ren, *Delinquency and Juvenile Justice System*, p. 38.
15. Larry, S.J. and Brandon, W.C. (2008), *Juvenile Delinquency Theory, Practice and Law* (10th ed.), Wadsworth, IL, p. 95.
16. Ibid., p. 95.
17. Menon, S. (2000), *Young Criminals: Crime and Punishments in Juvenile Delinquency*, New Delhi, Kanishka, pp. 6–7.
18. Friday and Ren, *Delinquency and Juvenile Justice System*, p. 30.

2

Review of Literature and Methodology

Delinquency as a non-conformist behaviour on the part of a child not only manifests issues like personal disorganization but also symptomatizes a state of social breakdown. The problem in its entirety seldom comes to surface, given that most of its affects occur in settings that are beyond the reach of law enforcement agencies. The nature of the problem varies from culture to culture and within the same culture from time to time. Just like the term *crime*, the term *delinquency* has also become a part of routine, everyday vocabulary. Yet there is no clarity over what exactly what does the term imply and its exact meaning.[1] The definition of the term *crime* and the term *delinquency* differs, and it is very difficult to find out a precise definition of the concept.

The term *juvenile delinquency* has been differently interpreted, but generally it refers to a large variety of behaviours of children and adolescents that the society does not approve, and use of admonishment, punishment, or preventive and corrective measures to curtail such deviant acts is justified in public interest. The term *juvenile* has been derived from its Latin original *Juvenis*, which means *young*. The term *delinquency* has been derived from two terms "do" (away from) and "liquere" (to leave). It was apparently used in times to refer to the failure of an individual to perform a task or duty. The term *delinquent* describes a person guilty of an offence against the customs.

Review of Literature on Definition of Juvenile Delinquency

Delinquent behaviour could be analysed from different angles, including the legal and social standpoints. The legal definition of delinquency is that it is a "behaviour against the criminal code committed by an individual who has not reached adulthood" (Bartol, 1999).[2] However, numerous definitions of the term are in vogue, and interpretations are many and go well beyond the scope of this one-sentence definition. In some states, the legal definition also includes in its scope "status offending," which is not behaviour against adult criminal code but behaviour prohibited only for juveniles. For example, running away, violating curfew laws, and truancy, all qualify as status offences. Therefore, from a legal standpoint, a juvenile delinquent is one who commits an act against the criminal code and who is adjudicated by an appropriate court/board. In India, the legal definition is restricted to persons younger than age 18 (16 years in the case of heinous crimes), but the maximum age of an individual who is legally held as a juvenile delinquent varies from country to country.

The social definition of delinquency consists a wide array of typical acts of deviant youth which are considered inappropriate, such as aggressive behaviour, truancy, petty theft, vandalism, drug abuse, and sexual promiscuity. The behaviour may or may not come to the attention of the law enforcement; in fact, it often does not. If the law enforcers apprehend and contain minor-age individuals committing misdemeanours, it is not unusual for them to refer such social delinquents to community social service agencies or to juvenile justice courts/boards. However, these youth do not qualify for the legal definition of delinquency unless they are found at a court/board hearing to have committed the crime for which they are charged.

Nevertheless, from the social point of view, delinquency means any type of behaviour that is not socially accepted. The difficulty regarding the exact or precise meaning, once again, arises due to the fact that legal and moral standards differ in different countries. Bela Dutta Gupta rightly observes, "What appears to be delinquent behaviour in USA might not be considered so in other society where there is an institutionalized indulgence in certain behaviour patterns."[3] According to Cyril Burt, "when anti-social tendencies of a child appear so serious that he/she becomes or ought to become, the subject of official action," he or she is marked as a delinquent child.[4]

Paul W. Tappan, an eminent criminologist, has also given a definition of delinquency:

> Delinquency is an act, course of conduct or situation which might be brought before court adjudicated whether in fact it comes to be treated there or by other resources or indeed remains untreated. The juvenile delinquent is a person who has been adjudicated as such by a court of proper jurisdiction though he may be no different, until the time of court contract and adjudication, at any rate, from masses of children who are not delinquents.[5]

However, Sophia M. Robinson does not depend on legal action because for her delinquency means "any behaviour which a given community, at a given time, considers in conflict with its best interests, whether or not the offender has been brought to court."[6]

The second United Nations Congress on Prevention of Crime and Treatment of Offenders held in 1960 declared, "By juvenile delinquency should be understood the commission of an act which, if committed by an adult would be considered a crime."[7]

Ruth Cavan proposed that

> A delinquent child is one who, by habitually refusing to obey the reasonable and lawful commands of his parents or other persons of lawful authority, is deemed to be habitually uncontrolled, habitually disobedient or habitually wayward or who habitually is a truant from home or school, or who habitually so deports himself as to injure or endanger the moral, health or welfare of himself of others.[8]

The definition of juvenile delinquency from a sociological point of view, for the purpose of this study, can be defined simply as a tendency or characteristic of an individual who demonstrates non-normative or antisocial behaviour. However, it is also true that social norms differ from country to country; therefore, what is offensive in one country may not be so in another. In spite of these differences, there exist some common rules, cutting across geographical barriers or countries, which define what is, and is not, socially acceptable conduct or behaviour.

Review of Literature on Factors of Delinquency

John Bowlby states, "The more complete the deprivation in early years the more isolated and asocial the child."[9] Moreover, the need for acceptance is closely related to the need for affection. The child must not feel that he or she is unwanted, rejected, or neglected. Especially, "Neglect is not merely failure to provide the physical needs, the clothing, shelter and medical care needed. Failure to provide proper supervision leadership and guidance within the home is a more serious form of neglect."[10] An unwanted child reveals "characteristics of instability and general lack of self-control," and being deprived of affection he or she may "resort to stealing, exhibitionism, lying or other forms of behaviour in an effort to adjust to such conditions."[11]

According to Ponnaian (1992),[12] home is the cradle of human personality, and children are what home environment makes them. Kadushin and Martin (1988)[13] have explored the parent–child network and how it moulds children's behaviour. Should the parent–child interaction be uncongenial, children are bound to tilt towards antisocial attitudes and behaviour. This is what has been emphasized by Lane and others (1987).[14] They report a positive relationship between child maltreatment and juvenile delinquency.

Edwin H. Sutherland discovered certain characteristics prevalent in homes "from which delinquent children come most frequently."[15] These are (1) criminality, immorality, intoxication, and so on among prevalent among family members; (2) separation, divorce, or desertion in the family; (3) overcrowding at home; (4) defective discipline due to ignorance, blindness, and so on the part of parents or substitute parents; (5) negligence on the part of parents; (6) unsympathetic behaviour of parents or adult family members; (7) frequent displays of anger and excitement by adult family members; (8) rigorous or severe treatment of minors in the name of discipline; and (9) poverty.

Next to family, companionship and peer-group relationship exert a decisive influence on the antisocial behaviour of children. Both Ponnaian (1992) and Thilagaraj (2000) have explored this aspect in depth.[16] Wilson and Herrenstein (1985) have also taken an incisive look into some of basic the issues that are directly related to children's antisocial behaviour.[17] According to them, peer groups supply their members with attitudes conducive to crime. Another dimension of, or causal factor for, antisocial behaviour in recent times is the process of urbanization. Bose (1992)[18] highlights the problems of disadvantaged children in urban India. Khan and Dassi (1997)[19] look into the situation of children in urban slums.

Harjit S. Sandhu points out some forms of behaviours as delinquent and suggests to make juvenile law in order to prohibit delinquency. These are "running away from home, absenting oneself from school, wandering about railroad yards, visiting places where liquor is used, indulging in sexual promiscuity, associating with criminals or other deviants and smoking cigarettes."[20] Thus, Sandhu wants to impose a much wider concept of juvenile delinquency and antisocial behaviour that incorporates all and every form of juvenile misbehaviour.

Review of Literature on Female Delinquency

A number of theories tied to social and economic forces have been proposed in explaining female criminality. Role or opportunity theorists posit that females are most likely to engage in criminal behaviour when legitimate avenues for reaching social goals are closed and pursue illegitimate avenues open to them. The criminality and delinquency of females is therefore directly related to female socialization and opportunities, and conversely, the lack of either of these elements.[21] In a study of delinquent girls and differential opportunities, Susan Datesman and associates found that perception of blocked opportunity was more closely related to female delinquency than it was to male delinquency.[22]

Crime and delinquency statistics are held by most observers to be relatively accurate indicators of real and substantial differences in criminality between sexes. Most sociologists would argue that girls and women are markedly less deviant than males, owing to restrictions imposed upon females that curtail their involvement or movement within the larger society. Women are less inclined to indulge in law-breaking because of the sex–role socialization they undergo right from birth. They also have relatively few opportunities to engage in criminal or delinquent acts.[23]

When it comes to girls we can imagine closer ties to parents, but that closeness gives rise to bitter infighting due to close parental supervision. Also, broken homes and parental fighting seem to have a more significant adverse effect on girls than on boys; another major factor is the difference between the two sexes in relation to the level of pressure exerted by peer groups. For boys, gang membership is not only more frequent but also brings them closer to those already exhibiting delinquent tendencies. In a general sense, public talks about delinquency or youth crime usually refer to males. This situation should come as no surprise. Even within academia, the study of "delinquency" has, until recent years, focussed mostly on male delinquency. "The delinquent is a rogue male," wrote Albert Cohen in his influential book on gang delinquency in 1955.[24]

However, once a girl is identified as "easy," she comes under even greater pressure from boys to provide sexual favours. Reiss identified a vicious cycle of status loss, promiscuity, further status loss, aggravated promiscuity and so on in which adolescent girls get caught. Even if the sexual acts are consensual, parents belonging to lower-income may press charges of rape against boys whom they find dallying with their daughters. They do this to salvage public reputation of their girls. In contrast, it is common for middle-class parents to try to cover up their daughters' misbehaviour.

We know from what little research exists on teen daughters' relationships with parents that compared with sons daughters are given less freedom to go out of home, are not given chores that need them to go out, when they are allowed to go out it is only for very brief periods and they are expected to return home earlier, and are certainly not allowed to choose their own activities, be it personal recreation or educational goals.[25] This means, as girls approach puberty parents begin to monitor them more closely, precisely when they demonstrate a desire for freedom, subtle or overt, and lesser dependence on parents in decision-making. Clashes between daughters and parents may be more likely during late adolescence. Much of the family disharmony is an outgrowth of the long-standing sexual double standard that tacitly encourages male sexual exploration and totally curtails female sexuality.

During the early 1900s, more male theorists emerged trying to explain why young women committed crimes. These women were said to be tomboys who were trying to assume a male role (Beirne, 2004),[26] suffered from penis envy (Freud, 1924),[27] and even camouflaged their appearances to overcome their feelings about what they considered shortcomings, such as lack of penis or menstruating, and their desire to be as strong as their male peers. These theories and many more were some of the main paradigms of the 1900s.

Sociologist William Thomas was among the first to relate female criminality to social environment. Thomas criticized anthropologists for their "assumption of the inferiority of women and their subsequent failure to distinguish between congenital and acquired characteristics."[28] He postulated that gender differences in intellectual functioning were not a reflection of biological differences but social influences.

W.I. Thomas argues in *The Unadjusted Girl* (1923)[29] that as women have greater capacity to love than men they suffer more when they do not receive social approval and affection. The "unadjusted girls" are those who use their sexuality in a socially unacceptable way to get what they want out of life. He saw female criminals as a product of innate instincts in conjunction with influences within the social environment. Thomas developed a dynamic goals–means conflict theory in which he proposed that every human (particularly prostitutes) had four basic desires: security, recognition, new experience, and response. It was the desire for new experience and response that Thomas believed most influenced female criminality. "A women entered prostitution to satisfy a desire for excitement and response; as a women, prostitution in one form or another was the most likely avenue to satisfy those needs."[30]

Thomas's work was criticized for its liberal paternalism and unproven assumptions. "He believed in manipulating people's life for their own good to conform to social norms that were not necessarily universal. His theories were sexist in that females were identified as offenders thorough sexual behaviour."[31]

Otto Pollak's *Criminality of Women* (1950) was considered a definitive work on female crimes during the postwar years. Pollak, a sociology professor, analysed data from a comprehensive survey of American, British, German, and French literature. Ho posited that female crime was primarily sexually motivated with the exception of crimes of passion. Pollak further postulated that the incidence of crime among women was probably equal to that of men were it not for the "masked" and "hidden" female criminality.[32] Thus, he contended that women's criminality was inadequately reflected in official statistics, giving such examples as shoplifting, illegal abortions, domestic thefts, and prostitute-perpetrated thefts of customers.

Pollak was influenced by Lombroso's and Freud's theories, and according to him,

> Women are particularly addicted to crimes that are easily concealed and rarely reported. The traditional social roles assigned to women (for instance, homemakers, caretakers of children, or the sick) are ideal for hiding crimes such as sexual offences against children, which leaves no physical evidence and even less suspicion. Women are more deceitful than men in their commission of crimes.[33]

Recent studies have supported Pollak's views with regard to more lenient treatment of women in the criminal justice system. However, other findings reject the argument, contending in some instances that females are treated more harshly than males in the criminal and juvenile justice system.[34]

According to Ghosh (1984),[35] if a woman behaves towards a man in such a manner that she goads him to commit a crime, of which either she herself or somebody else is the victim, she is morally and indirectly answerable for the crime. And if she uses the natural influence of her sex to compel a man to commit a crime she is also to be held morally accountable and accomplice to such an act of crime. And it is in this manner that women enter far more extensively into crime than is shown by statistics. Thus, there are many cases where women are answerable for crimes committed by men.

Many believe that female criminality is by and large a reflection of economic need or necessity rather than the need for fulfilment of sexual desires. In a review of literature on the etiology of female criminality, Dorie Klein found that poor and Third World women "negate the notions of sexually motivated crime"; instead, they engage "in illegal activities as a viable economic alternative."[36] Indeed studies show that most female offenders tend to be economically disadvantaged and undereducated.

It has also been found in researches that except in the area of prostitution, India's female crime rate is low and underreported. B.K. Nagla in *Women, Crime, and Law*[37] tried to come up with some of the reasons for the low female juvenile crime rates, which include the following:

1. Female roles are more clearly defined.
2. Females are more closely supervised.
3. Females receive greater protection.
4. Females have more opportunity for household employment.

Young women in India are concerned with different social things than boys are. While boys struggle with power and status, girls struggle to keep their relationships with others from going bad.

When their relationships go wrong, girls could act delinquently. "Masking" is a term that Nagla used when studying female crime in India. Indian officials believe that the female criminals are hard to detect because they always "mask" themselves "behind the roles they enact in society."

Review of Literature on Female Juvenile Delinquency

Albert Reiss provided some insights into female delinquency[38] and is of the view that sexual favours are frequently employed by girls who lack peer-group status as a means for acquiring the attention of boys. He pointed out that adolescent girls across all social classes use their ability to attract boys to derive much of their social standing among peers of both sexes. Those girls who are disadvantaged in this competitive struggle, due to physical unattractiveness, social clumsiness, or other liabilities, may have to offer more to boys in order to receive increased attention.

Girls get into trouble more quietly. In most cases, they were victims themselves before they became offenders (Prescott, 1998).[39] When girls are angry, frightened, or unloved, they are more likely to strike inward or hurt themselves more instead of hurting others. They may indulge in drug abuse, prostituting their bodies, starving, or even mutilating themselves (Belknap, 1996).[40] Because girls in crisis are more likely a threat to their own well-being, they may not seem dangerous to society. As a result, their needs or problems often go undetected or overlooked or undertreated (Chesney-Lind, 1988).[41] Girls in trouble have been an afterthought of a juvenile justice system that is in essence designed to deal with only boys. Girls who break the law may not be perceived as a danger to society because, traditionally, they have come into contact with the courts for nonviolent-status offences such as curfew violations, running away, or unruly behaviour (Chesney-Lind, 1988).[42]

Sheldon and Eleanor Glueck's work in the field of female criminality was based on a detailed study of 500 delinquent girls in Massachusetts in 1934. The Gluecks followed the girls from childhood through parole, tracing their backgrounds and social histories as well as comparing their physical and psychological traits. They concluded that female delinquency was a result of biological and economic factors. They found that an extremely high percentage of delinquent girls came from abnormally large families where criminal behaviour was intergenerational. Many of these girls were believed to be mentally defective and had been arrested primarily for illicit sexual behaviour.[43] Their findings were attacked as being methodologically sexist and influenced by biases. For example, they routinely examined the sexual histories of their subjects.

Professionals in the juvenile justice field now report that in many instances of offence, young women may be acting out as a means of self-protection in response to life-threatening conditions. The underlying cause of female juvenile delinquency has been reported to be family problems, including sexual and/or physical abuse they experienced at home. It is not surprising, therefore, that most female juvenile offenders report that their first arrest was for running away from home to avoid physical and sexual abuse.

Abuse is a primary cause for running away from home, a status offence that is often a girl's first involvement with the juvenile justice system. Studies indicate that sexually abused female runaways are more likely to engage in delinquent activities (e.g. substance abuse, theft, and prostitution) than non-abused female or male runaways. According to Chesney-Lind, when seeking help most girls ask for help to deal with consequences than for the causes of abuse.[44]

Although female offenders have been called "the forgotten few" (Bergsmann, 1989),[45] they are fast becoming too many and their problems have become too serious to ignore. Myriad social and emotional issues and risk factors are involved with female juvenile offenders in the juvenile justice system. Despite the multiplicity of their problems, female juvenile offenders and at-risk girls respond positively when placed in a caring environment. To address the needs of this population, it is necessary to develop and implement innovative community-based programmes that provide comprehensive, gender-specific prevention, treatment, and rehabilitative care that includes case management and follow-up for at-risk and delinquent girls.[46]

Gaps in Existing Literature

Review of literature thus indicates that further research on the role of families of delinquent girls is necessary to determine whether future measures should include penalization of the parent of a delinquent or developing and implementing income-generation programmes to benefit the parents of delinquent girls hailing from poor families. The difference in the male-to-female ratio in child delinquency focuses attention primarily on boys, but the gradual increase in the female child delinquent has become a real cause for concern in the present times.

This detailed review of female juvenile delinquency literature has also brought to light that most of the concepts discussed in the context of female delinquency, such as the feminist theory, reflect that females are less prone to delinquency or breaking the law due to the sex–role socialization they undergo right from birth. As a result, female juvenile delinquency is not a very extensively researched topic. Literature on female delinquency remains a substantially neglected area.

The limited studies that are there are mostly of Western countries whose sociocultural conditions are vastly different from the Indian situation. The studies and theories of criminology among females in India often limit themselves to women above the age of 18 years. Mostly all the studies on crime among women in India concentrate on the singular issue of "prostitution." Others issues that may be associated with delinquency of a girl below the age of 18 years are usually neglected.

This study thus attempts to fill up exiting gaps in the literature by throwing light on the determinants of female juvenile delinquency in India. This study also highlights the aspirations of a female delinquent in the larger society, which in turn may help policymakers in carving out a girl child–friendly interventions keeping in mind the abusive circumstances in which they were raised and the constant negligence of their desires and goals by their parents.

Methodology

For any research effort to be successful, it is imperative that researchers choose appropriate methods and tools designed to specifically enhance the efficacy of the study and the robustness and accuracy of the findings. The following were identified were identified primary areas of concerns before embarking on a study and the tools and techniques developed and used should necessarily focus foremost on these.

Study Area

This study was conducted in Delhi, and the respondents consisted of girls below the age of 18 years staying in the homes under the Juvenile Justice (Care and Protection of Children) Act, 2000. These institutions included the Observation Home for Girls

(Nirmal Chhaya) and Shelter Homes for Girls (Prayas Tughlakabad Institutional Area).

Study Universe

All registered and willing residents of both homes were interviewed, and as many as 200 girls expressed their willingness to participate. The individual female juvenile delinquent at both homes was the unit of analysis.

Sample Selection

By using the census method a total of 200 girls at both homes were selected. As many as 50 respondents were selected from Prayas Institute of Juvenile Justice and 150 respondents were chosen from the Observation Home for Girls, Nirmal Chhaya Complex, Jail road, New Delhi.

Study Objectives

The objectives of this study are as follows:

1. to identify factors that might prompt females to adopt delinquent behaviour. An exploratory study like this holds the promise of highlighting various issues that are hitherto unknown.
2. to study parental attitudes towards the girl who has committed an offence, existence of gender discrimination in family, and specific acts responsible for the inmate to be labelled as *delinquent*. The socio-economic background of inmates, nature of their socialization, and parental expectations were also taken into account.
3. to identify the personal aspirations of the study participants.
4. to highlight the coping mechanisms adopted by the society and the initiatives taken at the international and national levels towards preventing girl child delinquency.

Tools and Techniques Used in Data Collection

In a study of this nature, a vast amount of information is required. This may include both official/secondary data and firsthand/primary data. Entry into these homes/shelters is the biggest task in order to elicit firsthand information from respondents.

Nirmal Chhaya Observation Home for Girls is a government home/shelter that houses juveniles in conflict with the law (in other words delinquent girls) and has been established as per provisions of

Juvenile Justice (Care and Protection of Children) Act, 2000. Being a government home it comes under the direct control of the Department of Social Welfare. Appointment was thus sought with the Secretary-cum-Director of Social Welfare, G. Narender Kumar. He extended his support and directed me to Ram Chander, who was the concerned authority to grant permission. On informing him about my topic of research he was very keen and expressed his interest to help me further with the research process. He felt that there was a dearth of such research work and the information collected will be very useful even for the Government. Within three weeks I received the permission letter from the Department of Social Welfare.

Similarly, Prayas Shelter for girls, also a place set up under the purview of Juvenile Justice (Care and Protection of Children) Act, 2000, is an institution for girls in need of care and protection as envisaged under the said act. Here too permission was taken from Amod Kanth, Secretary, and Rajib K. Haldar, Executive Director, to conduct the study and obtain access to official records.

Due to the sensitivity of the subject, eliciting participants' response and clearly ascertaining their opinion was an uphill task. In this connection, the choice of data collection has been the interview method. Based on the objectives of the study an interview schedule was prepared that encompassed questions related to all information required for the research.

It addition, the data were supplemented by non-participant observation, and in-depth case studies were also conducted through one-on-one discussion between the researcher and the respondents. The purpose of one-on-one discussion with children was to elicit actual information from them regarding what they thought about the subject of the study.

Care was taken to adhere strictly to the ethical guidelines in order to ensure that children did not experience any psychological trauma while they shared their past experiences and how they ended up in the shelter (*see Annexure for Ethical Guidelines*).

The official records and files of 10 girls from Prayas and 25 from Nirmal Chhaya were studied for the purpose of getting an idea about the personality of respondents and also to identify the right way to ask and elicit accurate responses/information from the respondents. By reading files, a general profile of the children was developed, which included info on family background and reasons for their stay in the shelter.

Going through the files we realized that the schedule had some overlapping questions and that very important questions were missing. The schedule was thus revised to remove overlaps and incorporate the missing questions. With the revised schedule, we embarked on the formal process of data collection.

Data Analysis

The study has generated a large amount of information. Handling of all the firsthand information or primary data was a difficult task. Interview schedules were edited and checked for accuracy and consistency. Likewise, codes were developed and open-ended questions were coded. All data were entered into the computer, and, subsequently, one-way tables were prepared. Furthermore, a lot of tables were converted into diagrams to highlight trends. Quantitative and qualitative material, including "observations of the interviewer," has been utilized to prepare select "case studies." The names of the respondent/subjects remain confidential.

Notes

1. Chandana, S. (1987), *Juvenile Delinquency in India*, Delhi, Daya Publishing House, p. 21.
2. Bartol, C. and Bartol, A.M. (2004), *Introduction to Forensic Psychology*, London, Sage, pp. 102–103.
3. Bela, G.D. (1964), *Contemporary Social Problems in India*, Calcutta, Vidyodaya Library, p. 122.
4. Burt, C.L. (1915), *The Young Delinquents*, London, University of London Press, p. 15.
5. Tappan, P.W. (1949), *Juvenile Delinquency*, New York, McGraw Hill, p. 30.
6. Robinson, S.M. (1961), *Juvenile Delinquency: Its Nature and Control*, New York, McGraw Hill, p. 11.
7. Bhattacharyya, C.D. (1972), *Sociology*, Calcutta, Vidyodaya Library, p. 628.
8. Caven, R. (1961), The Concept of Tolerance and Contra-culture as Applied to Delinquency, *Sociological Quarterly*, 2, 243.
9. Bowlby, J. (1952), *Maternal Care and Mental Health*, Geneva, WHO, p. 47.
10. McClellan, G.S. (1956), *Juvenile Delinquency*, New York, Wilson Publishers, p. 47.

11. Garrison, K.C. (1959), *Growth and Development*, New York, Longmans Green and Co., p. 420.
12. Ponnaian, M. (1992), *Criminology and Penology*, New Delhi, Pioneer Books, pp. 67–68.
13. Kadushin, A. and Martin, J.A. (1988), *Child Welfare Services*, New York, MacMillan, pp. 11–17.
14. Lane, T.W. and Davis, G.E. (1987), Child Maltreatment and Juvenile Delinquency: Does a Relationship Exist? In D.J. Burchard and N.S. Burchard, *Prevention of Delinquent Behaviour*, Newbury Park, CA, Sage, pp. 122–138.
15. Sutherland, E.H. (1939), *Principles of Criminology*, Chicago, University of Chicago Press, p. 157.
16. Thilagaraj, R. and Priyamvadha, M. (2000), Deviance among Street Children, *Indian Journal of Criminology*, 28(1), 41–44.
17. Wilson, J.Q. and Herrenstein, R.J. (1985), *Crime and Human Nature*, New York: Simon and Schuster, pp. 59–67.
18. Bose, A.B. (1992), The Disadvantaged Urban Child in India, in *UNICEF: Innocenti Occasional Papers: The Urban Child Series*, 1, Florence, Italy, pp. 56–73.
19. Khan, M.Z. and Dassi, A. (1997), Children in Urban Blight in Delhi: Problems and Social Intervention, *Contemporary Social Work*, 14, 39–50.
20. Sandhu, H.S. (1977), *Juvenile Delinquency: Causes Control and Prevention*, New York, McGraw-Hills, p. 2.
21. Flowers, R.B. (1995), *Female Crime, Criminals, and Cellmates: An Exploration of Female Criminality and Delinquency*, Jefferson, NC, McFarland, p. 70.
22. Datesman, S.K., Scarpitti, F.R., and Stephenson, R.M. (1975), Female Delinquency: An Application of Self and Opportunity Theories, *Journal of Research in Crime and Delinquency*, 12, 120.
23. Gibbons, D.C. (1968), *Society, Crime and Criminal Careers*, Englewood Cliffs, NJ, Prentice Hall, pp. 104–105.
24. Cohen, A. (1955). *Delinquent Boys: The Culture of the Gang*, New York, Free Press, p. 140.
25. Komorosky, M. (1953), *Women in the Modern World*, San Francisco, Jossey-Bass, pp. 67–76.
26. Beirne, P. (ed.). (2004), *The Chicago School of Criminology 1914–1945: The Gang: A Study of 1,313 Gangs in Chicago* (Frederic Milton Thrasher), London, Taylor and Francis, p. 224.
27. Freud, S. (1924), *The Dissolution of the Oedipus Complex: Standard Editions of Freud's Works*, London, Hogarth, pp. 320–321.

28. Mann, C.R. (1984), *Female Crime and Delinquency*, Tuscaloosa, AL, University of Alabama Press, p. 57.
29. Thomas, W.I. (1923), *The Unadjusted Girl with Cases and Standpoint for Behavior Analysis*, Boston, Little Brown and Company, pp. 37–38.
30. Pollock, J. (1978), *Early Theories of Female Criminality*, in L.H. Bowker, *Women, Crime and the Criminal Justice System*, Lanham, MD, Lexington Books, p. 45.
31. Ibid.
32. Flowers, *Female Crime, Criminals, and Cellmates*, p. 69
33. Flowers, R.B. (1987), *Women and Criminality: The Women as Victim, Offender and Practitioner*, Westport, CT, Greenwood Press, p. 97.
34. Carol, T.E. (1973), Discriminating Sentencing of Women Offenders, *American Criminal Law Review*, 11, 353–372.
35. Ghosh, S.K. (1984), The Aiders and Abettors of Crime, in *Women in Changing Society*, New Delhi, Ashish Publishing, pp. 95–96.
36. Klein, D. (1973), The Etiology of Female Crime: A Review of Literature, *Issues in Criminology*, 8, 6.
37. Nagla, B.K. (1991), *Women, Crime and Law*, Jaipur, Rawat Publications, p. 120.
38. Reiss, A.J., Jr. (1960), Sex Offences: The Marginal Status of the Adolescent, *Law and Contemporary Problems*, 25, 309–333.
39. Prescott, L. (1998), *Adolescent Girls with Co-occurring Disorders in the Juvenile Justice System*, New York, Policy Research, Inc., pp. 2–6.
40. Belknap, J. (1996). *The Invisible Woman: Gender, Crime and Justice*, Belmont, CA, Wadsworth, pp. 3–21.
41. Chesney-Lind, M. (1988), Girls and Status Offences: Is Juvenile Justice Still Sexist? *Criminal Justice Abstracts*, 20(1), 144–165.
42. Ibid.
43. Flowers, *Female Crime, Criminals, and Cellmates*, p. 68.
44. Chesney-Lind, M. (1995), Girls, Delinquency and Juvenile Justice: Toward a Feminist Theory of Young Women's Crime, in Barbara R. Price and Natalie J. Sokoloff (eds), *The Criminal Justice System and Women*, New York, McGraw-Hill, pp. 71–88.
45. Bergsmann, I.R. (1989), The Forgotten Few: Juvenile Female Offenders, *Federal Probation*, 53(1), 73–78.
46. Schwartz, I.M., William, B. and Frank, O. (1991), Keeping Kids Out of Secure Detention: The Misuse of Juvenile Detention Has a Profound Impact on Child Welfare, *Public Welfare*, 49(2), 20–26.

3

Juvenile Delinquency

Conceptual Framework

Sociologists study the interrelationships between individuals, socio-economic groups, social processes, and societal structures. They have long examined the association between societal factors and criminal causation, focussing on the effects of societal factors on individual and collective behaviour. Sociological theories are not strongly deterministic in that they tend to explain predispositions toward criminal deviance and, therefore, allow for some degree of free will.

Beginning in the 1920s, the Chicago School of Sociology (centred at the University of Chicago) pioneered modern sociological research. A great deal of research and a number of theories since that time have been developed and continue to be developed, to improve our understanding of the relationship between society and human deviance. Several elements are commonly present in sociological explanations of delinquency and crime:

1. socio-economic conditions and pressures shape individual and collective behaviour.
2. Inequality and deprivation are associated with delinquency and criminality.
3. Subcultural norms are often at odds with accepted norms of society creating tensions that can result in subcultural conflict with the greater society.
4. Delinquency and crime are associated with underclass conditions such as poverty, neighbourhood degeneration, low

educational achievement, inadequate housing, and family dysfunction.

The topic of juvenile delinquency is a fertile area for construction of sociological theory. Three major sociological traditions, including structural functionalism, symbolic interactionism, and critical theory, contribute to the explanation of delinquency and have been the inspiration behind the present study to contribute to the explanation of delinquency.

Sociological Theories on Juvenile Delinquency

Structural-Functional Theories

Structural-functional theories regard delinquent behaviour as the consequence of strains or breakdowns in the social processes that produce conformity. These theories focus on institutions such as the family and school that socialize individuals to conform their behaviour to values of the surrounding society and on the ways in which these institutions can fail in this task. Wide agreement or consensus is assumed about which behaviours are valued and disvalued in society. Under the structural-functional theories we will deal with

1. Anomie theory
2. Subcultural theory
3. Social control theory

Anomie Theory

Emile Durkheim, a French sociologist, introduced the concept of anomie in his book *The Division of Labor in Society* published in 1893. He used anomie to describe a condition of deregulation that was occurring in society. This meant that rules on how people ought to behave with each other were breaking down and thus people did not know what to expect from one another. Anomie, simply defined, is a state where norms (expectations on behaviours) are confused, unclear, or not present. It is normlessness, Durkheim felt, that led to deviant behaviour. In 1897, Durkheim used the term again in his study on suicide, referring to a morally deregulated condition. Durkheim was preoccupied with the effects of social change.

Anomie thus refers to a breakdown of social norms and is a condition where norms no longer control the activities of members in society. Individuals cannot find their place in society without clear rules to help guide them. Changing conditions as well as adjustment of life leads to dissatisfaction, conflict, and deviance. He observed that social periods of disruption (economic depression, for instance) brought about greater anomie and higher rates of crime, suicide, and deviance. Durkheim felt that sudden change caused a state of anomie. The system breaks down during times of major changes in the social or economic environment, for example, when a society experiences great prosperity or great depression, with both leading to anomie.[1]

Such a perspective of suicide, and deviant behaviour in general, does not imply that such phenomena are pathological entities. Working from the assumptions that behaviour do not persist unless these entities perform some social function, and since deviant behaviour is a persistent entity, Durkheim thus conceived of these phenomena as normal entities and studied then in terms of their functions in maintaining the existing social order. In his classic essay, "The Normal and the Pathological," Durkheim contends that crime and deviance are present in all societies. Such behaviour serves the following functions for the society: (1) it functions as a boundary maintenance mechanism—it defines the boundaries of right conduct; (2) it also functions to reconfirm the solidarity of society—it reemphasizes the norms and values of society, strengthening collective sentiments against infringement of the norm; and (3) deviance and criminal behaviour functions to initiate social change. According to him, "Where crime exists, collective sentiments are sufficiently flexible to take on new form, and crime sometimes helps to determine the form they will take. How many times, indeed, it is only an anticipation of future morality—a step towards what will be."[2]

Robert King Merton also adopted the idea of *anomie* to explain deviant behaviour. While Durkheim contended that anomie resulted from social deregulation and, thus, took as his major focus the analysis of breakdowns in the social order, Robert Merton, by contrast, introducing a class variable, focussed his theory on the imperfections in the social order, specifically the inconsistencies between cultural goals and the means of achieving them.

Merton's essay, "Social Structure and Anomie," centres around this idea of "structured strain," which means that the general forces and pressures in the social system push individuals into deviation. Merton used the concept of anomie to develop "strain theory," defining it as the discrepancy between common social goals and the legitimate means to attain those goals. In other words, an individual suffering from *anomie* would strive to attain the common goals of a specific society yet would not be able to reach these goals legitimately because of the *structural* limitations in society. As a result the individual would exhibit *deviant behaviour*.

According to Merton, social life is comprised of two elements[3]: (1) the social situation, that is, sets of relationships among individuals, and (2) the cultural situation, that is, socially approved goals to which people aspire and the institutional means for achieving such goals. Anomie, for Merton, arises not as a result of social deregulation but from a disjunction between socially approved goals and the institutional means of achieving them. While both the goals and means are prescribed by culture, when society overemphasizes the goals in proportion to the means (or when the means becomes inaccessible for certain social classes) a state of anomie or demoralization results which expresses itself in deviant behaviour of various forms, so contends Merton.

Merton outlined a number of ways individuals adapt when faced with inadequate means of attaining their goals. Wherever approved means to approved goals are not available, Merton argues that the following deviant adaptations may emerge[4]:

Type 1. Adaptation in this case means demonstration of "conforming behaviour." Such an adaptation occurs where culturally approved goals and means of achieving them are pursued successfully.

Type 2. Adaptation here means 'innovation', which occurs when the culturally approved goals are accepted but the institutionalized means are absent. Merton states, "[innovation] ... occurs when the individual has assimilated the cultural emphasis upon the goal without equally internalizing the institutional norms governing ways and means of its attainment." This adaptation is common to the lower social and economic classes.

Type 3. Here adaptation means "ritualism," which occurs when culturally approved goals are not accepted but the institutionalized means are. The ritualist, who is perhaps frequently a member of the lower middle class has given up all hopes of achieving societal goals but clings, nevertheless, to the institutionalized means of achieving them.

Type 4. In this case, adaptation is "retreatism," which occurs when both socially approved goals and approved means are rejected.

The retreatist is a social outcast and is termed as a vagrant, tramp, alcoholic, and so on.

Type 5. Adaptation refers to "rebellion" in this case; rebellion occurs when both the approved goals and means are rejected and new goals and means take their place. Specifically, this adaptation represents an organized struggle for social change, to "introduce a social structure in which the cultural standards of success would be sharply modified and provision would be made for a closer correspondence between merit, effort and reward."

Subcultural Theory

In criminology, subcultural theory emerged from the work of the Chicago School on gangs and developed through the symbolic interactionism school into a set of theories arguing that certain groups or subcultures in society have values and attitudes that are conducive to crime and violence. The primary focus is on juvenile delinquency because theorists believe that if this pattern of offending can be understood and controlled, it will break the transition of a teenage offender into a habitual criminal. Some of the theories are functionalist; they assume that criminal activity is motivated by economic needs, while others posit a social class rationale for deviance. Group-based adaptations to the failure to attain success goals involve the delinquent subculture.

Culture is all that is transmitted socially, rather than biologically, representing the norms, customs, and values against which behaviour is judged by the majority. A subculture is a distinctive culture within a culture, so its norms and values differ from the majority culture but do not necessarily represent a culture deemed deviant by the majority. A subculture is distinguished from a counterculture that operates in direct opposition to the majority culture.

Cultural transmission theory and social disorganization theory posit that in the poorest zones of a city certain forms of behaviour become the cultural norm transmitted from one generation to the next, as part of the normal socialization process. Successful criminals are role models for the young, demonstrating both the possibilities of success through crime and its normality. Subcultural theory proposes that those living in an urban setting are able to find ways of creating a sense of community despite the prevailing alienation and anonymity. The cultural structure is dominated by the majority norms, which forces individuals to form communities in new and different ways.

The use of subcultural theory to explain deviant behaviour was first developed by Albert Cohen (1955),[5] who wished to explain why most delinquent acts were not motivated by money as the anomie model suggests. He concluded that delinquency was a result of the pressures of all dominant values. As working-class male adolescents in the inner city fail in school, they begin to feel that they cannot achieve in society by legitimate means and experience a social "status frustration."

The features of Cohen's theory of subculture include:

1. *Anti-utilitarian*. In many cases, there is no profit motive in thefts or other crimes. The main intention is to foster peer bonding through sharing the experience of breaking the laws.
2. *Collective reaction formation*. The gang inverts the values of majority culture, deliberately pursuing the mirror image of the American Dream.
3. *Malice*. Many acts of vandalism and property damage are motivated by spite, contempt, and personal intention to injure.
4. *Short-termism*. The gang lives for the moment, looking for instant gratification.
5. *Group autonomy*. Everything is aimed at consolidating group loyalty.

Cohen suggests that children of the underclass and potential members of a delinquent subculture first experience a failure to achieve when they enter school. When assessed against a "middle-class measuring rod," these children are often found lacking in several aspects, which in turn results in a growing sense of "status frustration." Underclass children are simply not prepared by their earliest experiences to meet with middle-class expectations. The delinquent subculture therefore emerges as an alternative set of criteria or values that underclass adolescents can meet.

Another influential work on delinquent subculture was written by Richard Cloward and Lloyd Ohlin, *Delinquency and Opportunity: A Theory of Delinquent Gangs*.[6] They argued that different types of delinquent subcultures can be linked to different types of communities. Thus, not only can one imagine the pressures toward delinquency and crime from a structural perspective but one can also assess the form of subculture on the basis of the local social structure in each community.

Like Cohen, Cloward and Ohlin also focussed on delinquent gangs that are typically found among adolescent males in the lower-class areas of large urban centres. Those in the lower class often find opportunities for success are blocked for the and experience strain. This strain leads to the formation of delinquent subcultures that eventually lead to delinquent behaviour. They further elaborated upon three delinquent subcultures and suggested that the route to delinquency involved one of three subcultures:

1. *Criminal subcultures.* This is the manifestation of Merton's anomie theory, in which adolescents use crime for material gain. This subculture usually forms in areas where exists an established organization of adult crime that provides an "illegitimate opportunity structure" for youth to learn the "tricks of the trade."
2. *Conflict subcultures.* When an illegitimate opportunity structure is not available, delinquents often form conflicting gangs out of frustration arising from the lack of opportunity structures.
3. *Retreatist subcultures.* Retreatist subcultures, which involve drug use and hustling, are generally found among "double failures"—those who cannot find acceptance in either legitimate groups or the two other subcultures.

Walter Miller (1958,[7] 1959[8]) agreed with Cohen that there was a delinquency subculture but argued that it arose entirely from the lower-class way of life. There was a clear distinction in values between the two social classes. Whereas the middle class is achievement and social goal oriented, Miller thought that lower-class parents were more concerned with ensuring that their children stayed out of trouble, for example, sons avoiding fights and daughters avoiding pregnancy. Boys were expected to be tough and street-smart, which gave them an incentive to join a gang. Given that their ordinary lives were boring, the excitement of crime was a welcome relief, bringing a sense of autonomy by denying the social controls imposed by the state.

For the middle class, the most important institutions are family, work, and (for the child) school. For the lower class another institution plays a crucial role—the same-sex peer group or gang is more important than family, work, or school because it offers a sense of belonging and a way to achieve status that they cannot easily achieve in mainstream society. Thus, delinquency was not a reaction against middle-class values but rather a means of living up to their own cultural expectations for toughness and smartness. Indeed, the gang only recruited the most "able" members, so membership of a gang confirmed high status. It was simply unfortunate that the state had decided that many gang activities were criminals.

Social Control Theory

Social control theory is a major theory of deviant behaviour, although it has been utilized primarily in the study of delinquent behaviour in contrast with other traditional theories of deviance. The key difference between social control theorists and traditional theorists is that traditional theorists ask, "Why do people commit deviant acts?" and social control theorists ask, "Why don't they do it?"[9] Social control theorists begin with the assumption that we all find deviance attractive, enticing, lucrative, and so on. Why is it then that most people do not engage in deviant behaviour? Why don't they break the law and become criminals?

As Hirschi explains in *A Control Theory of Delinquency*,[10] the answer lies in the bonds or ties we have with conventional society. If these bonds are weak or broken, we will be free to deviate from the norm. At the level of individuals, to have neither goals nor means is to be uncommitted and thus uncontrolled. He argues that the absence of control is all that is really required to explain delinquent behaviour.

There are other types of controls (besides commitment to conformity) that may also operate in the realm of social life: involvement in school and other activities; attachments to friends, school, and family; and belief in various types of values and principles. According to Hirschi, delinquent behaviour is inversely related to the presence of these controls. Alternatively, just as these controls accumulate, so too does conformity. Again, Hirschi's point is that no special strain between goals and means is necessarily required to produce delinquent behaviour; all that is required is the elimination of the constraining elements of the social bond.

It is our lack of ties to conventional society that lead to deviance and delinquency. Control theory has four essential elements[11]: (1) attachment, (2) commitment, (3) involvement, and (4) belief.

The first bond, *attachment*, refers to one's interest in others. One's acceptance of social norms and the development of social conscience depend on attachment for other human beings. Hirschi views parents, schools, and peers as important social institutions for a person. Attachment takes three forms—attachment to parents, attachment to school, and attachment to peers. While examining attachment to parents, Hirschi found that juveniles refrain from delinquency due to the consequences that the act would most likely produce, thus putting such a relationship between the parents and the child in jeopardy. In some respect, we can argue that this acts as a primary deterrent to engaging in delinquency.

The second bond is that of *commitment*, which involves time, energy, and effort placed on conventional lines of action. In other words, the support of and equal partaking in social activities tie an individual to the moral and ethical code of society. Hirschi's control theory holds that people who build an investment in life, property, and reputation are less likely to engage in criminal acts which will jeopardize their social position. A lack of commitment to such conventional values will cause an individual to partake in delinquent or criminal acts.

The third bond is *involvement*. This addresses a preoccupation in activities that stress the conventional interests of society. Hirschi argues that an individual's heavy involvement in conventional activities doesn't leave time to engage in delinquent or criminal acts. He believes that involvement in school, family, recreation, and so on insulates a juvenile from potential delinquent behaviour that may be a result of idleness.

The final bond, *belief*, deals with assents to society's value system—which entails respect for laws and the people and institutions that enforce such laws. Hirschi argued that people who live in common social settings share similar human values. If such beliefs are weakened, or absent, one is more likely to engage in antisocial acts. Also, if people believe that laws are unfair, this bond to society weakens and the likelihood of committing delinquent acts rises.

Symbolic-Interactionist Theories

Early versions of symbolic-interactionist theories focussed on how adolescents acquired these meanings and definitions of behaviours or social conduct from others, especially peers; more recently, theorists have focussed on the role of official control agencies, especially the police and courts, in imposing these meanings and definitions on adolescents. The significance of this difference in focus will become apparent as we consider the development of the symbolic-interactionist tradition. Under this section, a detailed discussion will address the following:

1. Differential association theory
2. Labelling theory

Differential Association Theory

The first explicit statement of the theory of differential association appeared in the 1939 edition of *Principles of Criminology* by Edwin Sutherland, and in its fourth edition, he presented his final theory. In 1939 Sutherland published the third edition of his book, *Principles of Criminology*, a work that had a major impact on the fields of deviance and criminology. He termed his theory "differential association." He anticipated an emphasis of the symbolic-interactionist perspective with his early use of the concept of differential association. He argued that people violate laws only when they define such behaviour as acceptable and that there is an explicit connection between people and their ideas (i.e. definitions).

So, for example, in his book *White Collar Crime* he wrote that delinquent behaviour is "learned in association with those who define such behaviour favourably and in isolation from those who define it unfavourably, and that a person in an appropriate situation engages in such criminal behaviour if, and only if, the weight of the favourable definitions exceeds the weight of the unfavourable definitions."[12]

Later Sutherland and Cressey wrote an essay titled "The Theory of Differential Association." In their essay, they maintain that "deviance is a group product, the result of an excess of definition unfavourable to violation of the law."[13] Furthermore, such definitions are learned in a normal learning process with other individuals who are in the process of communication. The chief source for learning criminal behaviour occurs within small, intimate groups. This learning process includes techniques of committing the crime and the specific direction of motives, drives, rationalizations, and attitudes. The efficiency of this learning process is a function of the frequency, duration, priority, and intensity of differential association. In sum, deviance involves a learning process that one person passes on to others; people who develop deviant careers differentially associate with others who condone deviant/illegal activities.

Sutherland's theory of differential association was elaborated and refined in various editions of Sutherland's highly influential textbook *Principles of Criminology* (later coauthored with Donald Cressey), and the following nine propositions came to light.[14]

1. Criminal behaviour is learned.
2. Criminal behaviour is learned in interaction with other persons in a process of communication.
3. The principal part of the learning of criminal behaviour occurs within intimate personal groups.
4. When criminal behaviour is learned, the learning includes techniques of committing the crime, which are sometimes very complicated, sometimes simple, and the specific direction of motives, drives, rationalizations, and attitudes.
5. The specific direction of motives and drives is learned from the definitions of legal codes as favourable or unfavourable.
6. A person becomes delinquent because of an excess of definitions favourable to violation of law over definitions unfavourable to violation of the law.
7. Differential associations may vary in frequency, duration, priority, and intensity.
8. The process of learning criminal behaviour by association with criminal and anti-criminal patterns involves all of the mechanisms that are involved in any other learning.
9. While criminal behaviour is an expression of general needs and values, it is not explained by those needs and values, since non-criminal behaviour is an expression of the same needs and values.

In summary, Sutherland believed that an individual's associations are determined in a general context of social organization (for instance, family income as a factor of determining residence of family, and in many cases delinquency rate is largely related to the rental value of houses); thus, differential group organization as an explanation of various crime rates is consistent with the differential association theory.[15]

Labelling Theories

Beginning in the 1950s with the work of people like Becker (1963) and Lemert (1951), the symbolic interactionist approach to deviance began to focus on the way in which negative labels get applied and on the consequences of the labelling process. Edwin Lemert,[16] for example, made a distinction between primary deviance and secondary deviance. Primary deviance is rule-breaking behaviour that is carried out by people who see themselves and are seen by others as basically conformists. People break rules in all kinds of circumstances and for all kinds of reasons, such that Lemert thought sociology can't possibly develop any general theories about primary deviance. As for secondary deviance, according to Lemert it occurs when a negative label gets applied so publicly and so powerfully that it becomes part of that individual's identity.

These dramatic negative labelling become turning points in that individual's identity; thus, he or she is apt "to employ his or her deviant behaviour or a role based upon it as a means of defence, attack, or adjustment to the problems created the subsequent societal reaction."[17] Having been processed by the juvenile justice system and labelled a delinquent, or harassed by the police as a gang member, the individual takes on that label as a key aspect of his or her identity.

The way labels are applied is likely to have important consequences for the delinquent. The degree to which youngsters are perceived as deviants may affect their treatment at home and at school. Parents may consider them a detrimental influence on younger brothers and sisters. Neighbours may tell their children to avoid the "troublemaker." Teachers may place them in class reserved for students with behaviour problems, minimizing their chances of obtaining higher education. The delinquent label may also affect the attitudes of society in general, as youthful offenders are often subjected to sanctions ranging from mild reprimands to incarceration.

As the negative feedback of law enforcement agencies, teachers, and other figures strengthens their commitment, delinquents may come to see themselves as "screw-ups." Thus, through a process of identification and sanctioning, re-identification, and increased sanctions, young offenders may transform into delinquents. They are no longer children in trouble: they are "delinquents," and they accept the *delinquent* label as personal identity. This process is called self-labelling.[18]

Howard Becker on the other hand noted that the process of segregation creates "outsiders,"[19] who are outcast from society and then begin to associate with other individuals who have also been cast out. When more and more people begin to think of these individuals as deviants, they respond to them as such; thus, the deviant reacts to such a response by continuing to engage in the behaviour society now expects from them. This "Labelling Theory," propounded in *Outsiders: Studies in the Sociology of Deviance* (1963), is perhaps Becker's most important and influential contribution to sociology. The label of *deviant* is applied to an individual when others observe their behaviour and react to it by labelling that person as *deviant*. No particular act is inherently deviant until a group with socially powerful statuses or positions label it as such. In Becker's terminology, those who take the lead in getting a particular behaviour negatively labeled (or in getting a negative label removed) are called moral entrepreneurs.

When kids who have been rejected by society violate the criminal law, they may be given official labels, applied in "ceremonies," for example, during trials or expulsion hearing in schools, that are designed to redefine the deviant identity.[20] The effect of this process is a durable negative label and an accompanying loss of status. The labeled deviant becomes a social outcast who is prevented from enjoying higher education, well-paying jobs, and other societal benefits. Because this label is "official," few question the accuracy of the assessment. People who may have been merely suspicious earlier would now feel justified in their assessment.

The labelling process helps create a self-fulfilling prophecy. If children continually receive negative feedback from significant others such as parents, teachers, and others whose opinion they take to heart, their behaviour will begin to conform to the negative expectations and they will become the person others perceive them to be. The self-fulfilling prophecy leads to damaged self-image and an increase in antisocial behaviour.[21] Labelling creates a deviant identity. Those exposed to negative sanctions experience both self-rejection and lower self-esteem. Self-rejection by self-fulfilling prophecy attitudes results in both a weakened commitment to conventional values and the acquisitions of motives to deviate from social norms.

Critical Theory

Critical theory of delinquency argues that deviance is a product of inequalities created in all societies. These inequalities are endemic to socio-economically hierarchical societies, which allow many members of society to prosper yet prevents many members from participating in this prosperity. Three critical theories of delinquency are examined in this section:

1. Conflict theory
2. Foucault's discourse theory
3. Feminist theory

Conflict Theory

Conflict theory of causation hypothesizes that social tensions and conflict are indelible features of society. Conflicts arise between dominant groups and subordinate classes, races, genders, political groups, ethnic groups, and other defined outsiders in the society. The fundamental characteristic of these tensions is that they often pit the haves against the have-nots, with the latter being labeled as *criminals* or *insurgents* during the conflict. Because such tensions are indelible, they can be best controlled by social institutions rather than completely eradicated. In practice, this means that the have-nots must be coerced to obey the laws and rules of those in power. From this perspective, laws and rules are simply instruments of control used by the ruling elites to maintain control of key institutions and, thereby, shut out others who might challenge the authorities of the elites. The focus of conflict theory is on the entire economic and political system and the socio-economic tensions theoretically created by this system.

An early group-conflict theory. George Vold was the first to write explicitly about a group-conflict theory of delinquency. He began with the assumption that criminality involves both human behaviour (acts) and the judgements or definitions (laws, customs, or mores) of other as to whether specific behaviour is appropriate and acceptable or inappropriate and disreputable.[22] Of the two components, Vold regarded judgements and definitions as more significant. His salient interest was in how groups impose their value judgements by defining the behaviours of others as illegal.

Vold regarded delinquency as a "minority group behaviour." For example, he argues that "juvenile gang ... is nearly always a 'minority group', out of sympathy with and in more or less direct opposition to the rules and regulations of the dominant majority, that is, the established world of adult values and powers."[23] In this struggle, the police are seen as representing and defending the values of the adult world, while the gang seeks the symbolic and material advantages not permitted under the adult code. At the root, Vold argues, exists the problem of intergenerational value conflict, with adults' control and authority prevailing through their control of the legal process.

Karl Marxist conflict theorists argue that those who own the means of production (e.g. factories, businesses) have the greatest power. This group—the capitalist class—uses its power for its own advantage. Capitalists work for the passage of laws that criminalize and severely sanction the "street" crimes of lower-class persons but ignore or mildly sanction the harmful actions of business and industry (e.g. pollution, unsafe working conditions). And capitalists act to increase their profits; for example, they resist improvements in working conditions and they attempt to hold down the wages of workers. Those economically powerful use the laws and the state to protect their interests. Economic powerlessness translates into political powerlessness.

In response to the expropriation of their labour and the exploitation of their potential in commercialized relationships, criminals come to recognize their true objective interests and engage in proto-revolutionary action to bring about the end of capitalism and the start of socialist or guaranteed freedom from want and misery. Here's what Marx said about criminals "The proletariat created by the breaking up of feudalism and the forcible expropriation of people from the soil could not possibly be absorbed by the newly-created capitalist manufacturers. At the same time, the proletariat could not suddenly adapt to the discipline of their new conditions, and so were turned into beggars, robbers, and vagabonds, partly from inclination, but in most cases from the stress of circumstances. Hence, by the end of the 16th century, the whole of Europe engaged in a bloody war against vagrancy, and legislation was created to treat them as criminals. It was also assumed that their criminal behaviour was voluntary and the result of free will, when in actuality it was because they could not adapt to the new economic conditions."[24]

Marxists explain crime in several ways. Some draw on strain theory, arguing that workers and unemployed people engage in crime because they are not able to achieve their economic goals through legitimate channels. Also, Marxists argue that crime is a response to the poor living conditions experienced by workers and the unemployed. Some draw on control theory, arguing that crime results from the fact that many workers and the unemployed have little stake in society and are alienated from governmental and business institutions. And some draw on social learning theory, arguing that capitalist societies encourage the unrestrained pursuit of money. Marxist theories, then, attempt to explain both class and societal differences in crime.

A recent effort to answer behaviour questions with the insights from conflict theory is an "integrated structural Marxist theory" proposed by Colvin and Pauly (1983).[25] This theory integrates elements of control theory and Marxian theory. The theory is comprehensive, and only some of its most striking features can be outlined here. These features include Marxian focus on working-class parents experiences' of coerciveness in the workplace, which Colvin and Pauly suggest lead to coerciveness in parenting, including parental violence toward children. In turn, Colvin and Pauly argue that such children are more likely to be placed in coercive control structures at school and to enter into alliances with alienated peers. All of these experiences make delinquent behaviour more likely, including the violent and instrumental kinds of delinquents that may be precursors of adult criminality.

Discourse Theory

Michel Foucault, the French philosopher, was the most influential of the postmodern philosophers of the twentieth century. *Discipline and Punish* (1975) is considered Foucault's most important and lasting work. This book shows how Foucault arrived at his major theme of power and domination. It lays out Foucault's thoughts on how the elite in society dominate and control the rest of society. Foucault believed no societal advancements have occurred since the Renaissance and only technology has grown, further enslaving the human spirit. Foucault theorized the reason the prison system has lasted so long is it benefits the ruling social class. He believed the ruling class used criminality as a way of preventing confrontations that could lead to revolution. According to Foucault, the dynamic groups of the lower social class commit crime. By committing crimes, they were calling for a change in the social system and rebelling against the social elite. The ruling class used the law as a means to diminish the power of these uprisings.

According to Foucault, "It would be hypocritical or naive to believe that the law was made for all in the name of all; that it would be more prudent to recognize that it was made for the few and that it was brought to bear upon others; that in principle it applies to all citizens, but that it is addressed principally to the most numerous and least enlightened classes."[26]

The legal systems segregated the most dynamic of the lowest social class from the rest of society, then forced them together as a group of outcasts, thus rendering them politically harmless. Foucault also stated by marking this group as criminals they are easier to supervise and keep disorganized by keeping the members flowing in and out of the prison system. He gave people a new way to view the prison system. In his book, Foucault describes the history of prisons. He explained why prisons continue to be popular even when they are not successful. Foucault believed prisons serve a greater purpose than just incarcerating criminals. He described how prisons really enslave everyone to a life of government-imposed discipline.

Foucault believed the dominant class used the delinquent class as a means of profiting themselves and said that "Delinquency, controlled illegality, is an agent for the illegality of the dominant groups. The setting up of prostitution networks in the nineteenth century is characteristic in this respect. Police checks and checks on the prostitutes' health, their regular stay in prison, the large-scale organization in the prostitution milieu, its control by delinquent-informers etc. made it possible to canalize and to recover by a whole series of intermediaries the enormous profits from a sexual pleasure. An ever-more insistent everyday moralization condemned to semi-clandestineity and naturally made expensive; setting a price for pleasure, in creating a profit from repressed sexuality and in collecting this profit, the delinquent milieu was in complicity with a self-interested Puritanism: an illicit agent operating over illegal practices."[27]

He was concerned with the way in which criminology as a discipline grows at the same time as a whole new apparatus of crime control is brought into being. The whole professions of criminology, he suggests, is there not really to solve the problem of crime but to extend and organize power and surveillance.

Always a radical and critical thinker, he saw dramatic ruptures with the past and suggested that these modern developments are not signs of simple "enlightened" progress, often backed up by institutions. Thus, criminology is a discourse that invents or produces its own set of ideas and languages about the criminal as an object to be studied, backed up by many institutions such as the prison and the courts. Power works its way distinctly through this discourse to help shape the whole society's view of crime. "Knowledge" in this view may act as a way of keeping people under control.

Many of Foucault's ideas challenge common sense. Whereas we like to see criminology as a science that studies and helps us understand crime, Foucault sees it as a discourse that extends surveillance and power relations. Whereas prisons are conventionally understood to combat crime, he sees them as mechanisms for extending crime.[28]

Feminist Theories

Feminist theories focus on gender differences in power as a source of crime. Most theories of crime were developed with males in mind; feminists argue that the causes of female crime differ somewhat from the causes of male crime.

Gender differences in crime are said to be due largely to gender differences in social learning and control. Women are socialized to be passive, subservient, and focussed on the needs of others. Furthermore, women are more closely supervised than men, partly because fathers and husbands desire to protect their "property" from other men. Related to this, women are more closely tied to the household and to child-rearing tasks, which limits their opportunities to engage in many crimes.

Some women, of course, do engage in crime. Feminist theories argue that the causes of their crime differ somewhat from those of male crime, although female crime is largely explained in terms of strain theory. Meda Chesney-Lind and others[29] argue that much female crime stems from the fact that juvenile females are often sexually abused by family members. This high rate of sexual abuse is fostered by the power of men over women. Abused women frequently run away, but they have difficulty surviving on the street. They are labelled as delinquents, making it difficult for them to obtain legitimate work. Juvenile justice officials, in fact, often arrest such women and return them to the families where they were abused.

Furthermore, these women are frequently abused and exploited by men on the street. As a consequence, they often turn to crimes like prostitution and theft to survive. Theorists have pointed to still other types of strain to explain female crime, like the financial and other difficulties experienced by women trying to raise families without financial support from fathers. The rapid increase in female-headed families in recent decades, in fact, has been used to explain the increase in rates of female property crime. It is also argued that some female crime stems from frustration over the constricted roles available to women in our society.[30]

Hagan (1989) on the other hand attempts to explain large and persistent gender differences in delinquency by taking power relations into account through his power-control theory.[31] Power relations in the family are the starting point of this theory. The cornerstone of the theory is the observation that, especially in more patriarchal families, it is mothers who control daughters on a level that is more rigorous than the kind of control fathers exert on sons usually. A result of this intensified mother–daughter relationship is that daughters become less inclined to take what they perceive as greater risks of involvement in delinquency. Police and other processing agencies act on stereotypes that extend these gender differences in officially recorded delinquency. Power-control theory generally predicts that in more patriarchal families, sons will be subjected to less maternal control, develop stronger preference for risk taking, be more delinquent, and more often be officially labelled for being so.[32]

Parents' class position, as defined through their work experiences, influences the delinquent behaviour of their children.[33] When fathers occupy the traditional role of sole breadwinner and mothers have only menial jobs or remain at home to handle domestic affairs, the paternalistic or patriarchal family is indicated. Here the father's experience of control over others or being controlled is reproduced in the household. His focus is directed outward toward his instrumental responsibilities, while the mother is left in charge of the children, especially daughters. Sons are granted greater freedom as they are prepared for the traditional male role symbolized by their fathers. Daughters are socialized into the cult of domesticity under the close supervision of their mothers, preparing them for lives oriented toward domestic labour and consumption while sons are encouraged and allowed to "experiment" and take risks. Daughters in this scenario are closely monitored so that participation in deviant or delinquent activity is unlikely.

According to Siegel[34] the egalitarian family is characterized by little difference between the mother's and father's work roles, so that responsibility for childrearing is shared. Here neither child (i.e. neither the boy nor the girl) receives the close supervision present over girls in the paternalistic family. Middle-class aspirations and values dominate: mobility, success, autonomy, and risk taking. Daughter's deviance now mirrors their brother's. This pattern seems to hold true for single-parent (female-headed) households; even within the working/lower class. Here, without the presence of the father, the mother's supervision over her children is not as intense as in the paternalistic family and, in fact, children of both sexes may be encouraged to experiment with risk taking, instrumental roles. He said that "middle-class girls are the most likely to violate the law because they are less closely controlled than their lower-class counterparts. And in homes where both parents hold positions of power, girls are more likely to have the same expectations of career success as their brothers. Consequently, siblings of both sexes will be socialized to take risks and engage in other behaviour related to delinquency. Power-control theory, then, implies that middle-class youth of both sexes will have higher crime rates than their lower-class peers."[35]

Morash and Chesney-Lind[36] argue that a better explanation of female deviance, especially their lower rates of participation, would focus on the nurturing relationships developed during socialization, leading them toward more prosocial behaviours. Female deviance becomes a product of the "sexual scripts" within patriarchal families that make it more likely for them to become the victims of both sexual and physical abuse. If they run away, the juvenile court supports parental rights and returns them to the home.

Out of the various theories on juvenile justice discussed in detail in the chapter, this study subscribes to:

1. Hirschi's social control theory and
2. Meda Chesney-Lind's feminist theory of crime.

According to Hirschi's social control theory, delinquency has a direct link to the bonds or ties we have with conventional society. If these bonds are weak or broken, a juvenile may deviate from the norms of the society. He argued that the absence of control may result in delinquent behaviour. Control theory has four essential elements: (1) attachment, (2) commitment, (3) involvement, and (4) belief.

The present study substantiates the above theory that once child's attachment, commitment, involvement, and belief in the conventional social institutions such as family are weak or broken then the child may take up acts of delinquency. A number of respondents of this study reported that since they were abused by their parents they did not feel attached to them. Their belief in this conventional social institution was broken and therefore they ran away from home which is considered to be a delinquent act.

Meda Chesney-Lind argues that much female crime stems from the fact that juvenile females are often sexually abused by family members. Abused females frequently run away. They are labelled as delinquents, making it difficult for them to obtain legitimate work.

Juvenile justice officials, in fact, often arrest such females and return them to the families where they were abused.

A similar trend was observed in this study. Most of the respondents opted to run away from the abusive situations in their homes and as a result came in direct contact with the juvenile justice system. Despite the abusive situations at home, Child Welfare Committees attempt to rehabilitate them to bring them back to their families. During the course of my data collection in one of the homes a group of young girls were rescued from Mumbai Bar Club, and it came to light that a village in Agra (the name of the village is deliberately not being mentioned here so as to conceal the identities of the girls in question) encourage and train their young daughters to enter the trade of bar dancing. They send their daughters to Mumbai and live on the earning sent by them. Given such circumstances, sending these girls back to such families should not be an option worthy of consideration by the juvenile justice officials.

Notes

1. Larry, R.T. and Herman-Kinney, N.J. (2003), *Handbook of Symbolic Interactionism*, Lanham, MD, Altamira, pp. 696–697.
2. Durkheim, E. (1950), *The Rules of Sociological Methods*, trans. and ed. S.S. Solovay and J.H. Mueller, New York, Free Press, p. 71.
3. Merton, R. (I957), *Social Theory and Social Structure*, New York, Free Press, p. 154.
4. Ibid., pp. 155–160.
5. Cohen, A. (1955), *Delinquent Boys*, New York, Free Press, pp. 24–32, 121–137.
6. Cloward, R. and Ohlin, L. (1960), *Delinquency and Opportunity*, New York, Free Press, pp. 31–47.
7. Miller, W. (1958), Lower Class Culture as a Generating Milieu of Gang Delinquency, *Journal of Social Issues*, 14, 5–20.
8. Miller, W. (1959), Implications of Urban Lower-Class Culture for Social Work, *The Social Service Review*, 33, 219–236.
9. Herman, N.J. (1995), *Deviance: A Symbolic Interactionist Approach*, Dix Hill, New York, p. 36.
10. Hirschi, T. (1969), *Causes of Delinquency*, Berkeley, University of California Press, pp. 162–186.

11. Burfeind, J.W. and Bartusch, D.J. (2005), *Juvenile Delinquency: An Integrated Approach*, Sudbury, MA, Jones and Bartlett, pp. 380–386.
12. Bhushan, B. (1989), *Dictionary of Sociology*, New Delhi, Anmol, p. 74.
13. Sutherland, E. and Cressey, D.R. (1966), *Principles of Criminology* (7th ed.), Philadelphia, Lippincott, p. 43.
14. Sutherland, E. (1974), *Criminology*, Philadelphia, Lippincott, pp. 75–76.
15. Ibid., p. 77.
16. Lemert, E. (1967), *Human Deviance, Social Problems, and Social Control*. Englewood Cliffs, NJ, Prentice Hall, p. 40.
17. Lemert, E. (1951), *Social Pathology*, New York, McGraw Hills, p. 76.
18. Ibid., p. 78.
19. Becker, H.S. (1963), *Outsiders: Studies in the Sociology of Deviance*, New York, Free Press, pp. 9–10.
20. Garkinkel, H. (1956), Conditions of Successful Degradation Ceremonies, *American Journal of Sociology*, 61, 420–424.
21. Ross, M. (1992), Reflecting Appraisals, Parental Labeling and Delinquency: Specifying a Symbolic Interactionist Theory, *American Journal of Sociology*, 57, 1577–1611.
22. Borgatta, E. and Borgatta, M. (1991), *Encyclopedia of Sociology* (Vol. 2), New York, Maxwell Macmillan, p. 1031.
23. Vold, G. (1958), *Theoretical Criminology*, New York, Oxford University Press, p. 211.
24. Marx, Karl (1867), *Capital* (Vol. 1), London, Lawrence and Wishart, p. 734.
25. Colvin, M. and Pauly, J. (1983), A Critique of Criminology: Towards an Integrated Structural-Marxist Theory of Delinquency Production, *American Journal of Sociology*, 89(3), 512–552.
26. Foucault, M. (1975), *Discipline and Punish: The Birth of the Prison*, New York, Pantheon, p. 276.
27. Ibid., pp. 279–280.
28. Carrabine, E., Lee, M., South, N., Cox, P., and Plummer, K. (2008), *Criminology: A Sociological Introduction* (2nd ed.), New York, Routledge, p. 113.
29. Chesney-Lind, M. (1995), Girls, Delinquency and Juvenile Justice: Toward a Feminist Theory of Young Women's Crime. In *The Criminal Justice System and Women* (ed. B.R. Price and N.J. Sokoloff), New York, McGraw-Hill, pp. 71–88.
30. Moretti, M.M., Odgers, C.L., and Jackson, M.A. (2004), *Girls and Aggression: Contributing Factors and Intervention Principles*, New York, Kluwer, p. 170.

31. Adler, F. (1992), *New Directions in Criminological Theory*, New York, Routledge, pp. 381–398.
32. Borgatta and Borgatta, *Encyclopedia of Sociology*, p. 1032
33. Hagan, J., Gillis, A.R., and Simpson, J. (1987), Class in the Household: A Power-Control Theory of Gender and Delinquency, *American Journal of Sociology*, 92, 788–816.
34. Siegel, L. (1992), *Criminology* (4th ed.), St. Paul, MN, West Publishing, p. 270.
35. Ibid.
36. Morash, M. and Chesney-Lind, M. (1991), A Reformulation and Partial Test of the Power Control Theory of Delinquency, *Justice Quarterly*, 8, 347–377.

4

International and National Perspective

Juvenile delinquency is the broad-based term given to juveniles who commit crimes. Juveniles are defined as those people who haven't reached adulthood or the age of majority. What defines adulthood or the age of majority in a court system may be predetermined by law of that particular country. Delinquency can be defined as the committing of those things considered crimes by the state. Thus, juvenile delinquency can cover anything from small crime—a student who cuts school repeatedly is delinquent—to very serious crimes like felony theft and murder.

When a child, anyone under the age of majority, commits a crime, most frequently they are tried and sentenced through a court system separate from that which tries adults. There are also confinement centres, specifically designed for children who commit serious crimes. These are often called juvenile detention centres or observation homes in the context of India.

It is often within the court's province to determine the degree of risk the juvenile poses to society and the degree of benefit incurred by incarceration. Juvenile court judges may have greater license, especially with very young children, to find alternative means of rehabilitating a child and preventing future delinquency. They may recommend court-appointed therapy, house arrest, or a variety of measures short of incarceration. In many cases, records of children who commit crimes are expunged when a child reaches the age 18, especially if no other crimes have been committed.

This has advantages and disadvantages. A juvenile who has committed very serious crimes may continue a pattern of criminal behaviour of which an adult court will be unaware of. The advantage is that having been successfully rehabilitated, they won't be discriminated against based on a previous arrest, sentencing, or incarceration record.

There are many schools of thought as to the primary factors that contribute to juvenile delinquency. Many of these are tied to nature–nurture arguments. It is certainly the case that children who are neglected, abused, or impoverished are statistically more likely to fall into delinquency patterns. Although this may be statistically relevant, it fails to account for the delinquency of those who have good and loving parents and suitable living circumstances.

The common observation that crime runs in the family suggests that the tendency for involvement in crime is inherited. Despite evidence of intergenerational criminality, the role of genetic influences in criminal behaviour has been heavily discounted and, for the most part, ignored by social scientists. Genetic contributions are often misunderstood and sometimes distorted. Identification of genetic contribution does not reduce behaviour to a gene level, nor does identifying the role of genetics in criminal behaviour imply that there is a crime gene.[1] Moreover, a genetic predisposition toward criminal behaviour does not mean that an individual is destined to become criminal, regardless of environmental conditions. Rather, the study of behavioural genetics seeks to estimate the relative contributions of heredity and environment on individual traits, such as impulsivity, aggressiveness, and negatively.[2] Whether these traits are given in full expression in the form of delinquent and criminal behaviour depends on environmental conditions. The gene-based evolutionary theories acknowledge that there is no crime gene.

Although genetic makeup may play a factor in juvenile delinquency, it may only establish a predilection toward delinquent behaviour, whereas nurturance or lack thereof may create circumstances necessary to cause this delinquent behaviour. Furthermore, knowledge of early-onset mental illness helps determine suitable rehabilitative efforts for juvenile delinquents. Consideration can be given to a juvenile's reasonable ability to control his or her own behaviour, based on factors like mental illness, drug use, and upbringing. Key to determining the best rehabilitation in juvenile delinquency trials is the attempt to understand why a child was delinquent and what circumstances contributed to this delinquency.

In many societies, one common way chosen to attack the problem of juvenile delinquency is to create programmes that help prevent children from committing crimes. These programmes may focus on avoiding drug use or gang involvement or may focus on early education, therapeutic help for families, help to the impoverished, or a variety of other things. With unclear answers on a single cause for juvenile delinquency, these programmes may have some success, but probably won't reach all children who might commit a crime. Society is sometimes horrified by the seemingly random acts of relatively "normal" children that are so heinous they do not bear repeating (e.g. 2012 Nirbhaya Rape Case of New Delhi, India). Although delinquency prevention is admirable, it isn't universally successful. Yet preventing some juvenile delinquency through intervention and education is better than allowing it to occur.

For many young people today, traditional patterns guiding the relationships and transitions between family, school, and work are being challenged. Social relations that ensure a smooth process of socialization are collapsing; lifestyle trajectories are becoming more varied and less predictable. The restructuring of the labour market, the extension of the maturity gap (the period of dependence of young adults on the family), and, arguably, the more limited opportunities to become an independent adult are all changes influencing relationships with family and friends, educational opportunities and choices, labour market participation, leisure activities, and lifestyles.

It is not only developed countries that are facing this situation; in developing countries as well there are new pressures on young people undergoing the transition from childhood to independence. Rapid population growth; unavailability of housing and support services; poverty, unemployment, and underemployment among youth; decline in the authority of local communities; overcrowding in poor urban areas; disintegration of families; and ineffective educational systems are some of the issues young people must deal with.

Youth nowadays, regardless of gender, social origin, or country of residence, are subject to individual risks yet they also have access to new opportunities—some beneficial and some potentially harmful—to fulfil personal aspirations. Quite often, advantage is being taken of illegal opportunities as young people commit various offences.

Statistical data indicate that in virtually all parts of the world, with the exception of the United States, rates of youth crime rose in the 1990s. In Western Europe, one of the few regions for which data are available, arrests of juvenile delinquents and underage offenders increased by as much as 50% between the mid-1980s and the late 1990s. The countries in transition have also witnessed a dramatic rise in delinquency rates; since 1995, juvenile crime levels in many countries in Eastern Europe and the Commonwealth of Independent States have increased by more than 30%.

Many of the criminal offences are related to drug abuse and excessive alcohol use.[3] According to the UN's *World Youth Report* (2004) on juvenile delinquency the sharpest increase in the rate of juvenile violence in most Western European countries occurred in the mid-1980s or early 1990s. In some countries, the official figures indicated a staggering increase in the range of 50–100%. In England and Wales, for example, approximately 360 of every 1,00,000 youth aged 14–16 years were convicted or cautioned by the police for violent crimes in 1986; by 1994, that figure had increased to approximately 580 per 1,00,000.

In Western Germany in 1984, the number of 14–18-year-olds suspected of violent crimes was approximately 300 per 1,00,000; by 1995, that figure had more than doubled to approximately 760 per 1,00,000. Rates in the former East Germany were even higher at 60–80%. The results of a number of studies indicated that the victims of violent crimes committed by juveniles were mostly other juveniles. For example, in the Netherlands in 1995, young people 15–17 years of age were 4 times more likely than adults (25 years or older) to be the victims of assault.

It must be noted that in most countries the crime rate among adults has either remained stable over the years or increased moderately. In no country has the increase in the adult crime rate parallelled that of juveniles. Thus, the rise in violent crime among juveniles derives only partially from overall crime trends.[4] Within developed countries there are groups of impoverished and needy people suffering from relative deprivation. In recent years some countries have reduced their social services, placing the weakest strata of the population in an even more vulnerable position. Poverty has increased, and the problems of homelessness and unemployment have reached alarming dimensions.

In most EU countries the rise in juvenile crime has corresponded to observed increases in poverty and unemployment rates among vulnerable groups.[5] According to the *World Youth Report* (2003), the overall crisis in Eastern Europe and the Commonwealth of Independent States deriving from the transition to market-based economies has contributed to an increased tendency toward criminal behaviour, owing mainly to the weakening of the primary institutions of socialization (e.g. family, public education system, recreation services, work collectives, and informal peer environment) and to personal alienation. Juvenile delinquency in the region is most often related to the unemployment of both young people and parents, poverty in the family, or pressures on overworked parents to successfully maintain the traditional guardianship of children.

These challenges and other socio-economic pressures have intensified in the past decade, affecting the behaviour of children and youth. The impact of pathological behaviours in the family, educational negligence, negative patterns of conduct conveyed by parents or guardians, and the lack of leisure alternatives is also considerable. In Slovakia, only about 8% of young people are members of youth associations. There may be a reluctance to join such groups, in which participation was virtually mandatory under past regimes.

In many countries of the former Soviet Union, the collapse of public educational organizations has undermined efforts to prevent juvenile delinquency. For most adolescents there are no opportunities for involvement in associations or clubs. Many social services in the region have been eliminated during the transition period, and those still operating face chronic financial problems. The low wages paid to social service employees give them little incentive to work with adolescents. Alienated from society these young people often become involved in delinquent groups.

In Africa, delinquency tends to be attributed primarily to hunger, poverty, malnutrition, and unemployment, which are linked to the marginalization of juveniles in the already severely disadvantaged segments of society. As a result of rapid population growth, young people in Africa will soon constitute two-thirds of the region's population. Every year about 7,90,000 people enter the labour market, while the economy generates fewer than 60,000 jobs. One half of all households in Africa are living in poverty. Many of the urban poor live in slum and squatter settlements with overcrowded, unhealthy housing and lack of basic services. It is here that the majority of urban youth and children live. One of the most serious problems is the great number of street and orphaned children, whose numbers have been growing as a result of continuous and multiple armed conflicts, the advent of HIV/AIDS, and the breakdown of a centuries-old way of living and social structure. Juvenile crime and delinquency are on the rise, a trend also linked to the rapid and dramatic social, political, and economic changes that have taken place in Africa in recent decades. The principal offences committed by young people are theft, robbery, smuggling, prostitution, drug abuse, and drug trafficking.[6]

In the Arab world, the problems associated with juvenile delinquency vary from one country to another. Some countries have experienced socio-economic difficulties, while others have become prosperous. In the latter group, delinquency may occur in connection with migrants seeking employment or may be linked to factors such as continued urbanization, sudden affluence, rapid changes in economy, and increasing heterogeneity of population.[7] The conflict between traditional Arab-Islamic values and newer, often imported values appears to be a common problem throughout the region.

In Asian countries, juvenile crime and delinquency are largely urban phenomena. The most noticeable trends in the region are the rise in the number of violent acts committed by young people, increase in drug-related offences, and the marked growth in female juvenile delinquency. The financial crisis that hit some countries in East and South-East Asia in the late 1990s created economic stagnation and contraction, leading to large-scale youth unemployment. For millions of young people, this meant a loss of identity and opportunity for self-actualization.[8]

Some countries are facing great difficulty because they are located near or within the "Golden Crescent" or the "Golden Triangle," two major narcotics-producing areas of Asia. Traffickers actively involve adolescents and youth in serving this industry, and many of them become addicted to drugs because of their low prices and easy availability.[9] Another major problem is human trafficking.

A close relationship between growing affluence and delinquent behaviour has been established in many countries. Rapid industrialization and consequential urbanization have loosened the hold of traditional means of social control on the behaviour and conduct of individuals, more so among juveniles. In developing countries, the socio-economic transition coupled with the impact of consumerism has led to the emergence of a peculiar phase of social adolescence characterized by new notions and attitudes toward life and values of life. The process is more traumatic for teenage girls than boys, as they have not only to adjust to the changing social situations but are also faced with the uncertainties of the their position as women in an urbanized structure.

International Perspective: Female Juvenile Delinquency

Increasing involvement of women in various walks of life and decreasing disparity between sexes in terms of socially defined roles were recognized as factors correlated to the increase in female criminality in many countries. It was further noticed that while the proportion of women in the total criminal population still remains relatively small, the rate of crimes committed by them is rising faster compared to male counterparts.

In September of 2000, the National Institute of Justice (NIJ) published a research on women and young women in the American justice system. The research showed a steady rise in crime among women since the 1980s, identifying a firm link between abuse and criminal behaviour. An alarming 75–95% of girls (aged 14–18 years) in the justice system are former victims of abuse.[10] Such abuse often results in a very low sense of self-worth for young women. These young women, suffering from a degraded opinion of their value as people, are more likely to engage in damaging behaviours. The majority of crimes young women commit, according to the Office of Juvenile Justice and Delinquency Prevention (OJJDP), are simple assault and illegal substance abuse. Young women are more likely than young men to commit the status offence of running away and to become involved in prostitution and commercialized vice.

The NIJ reported that the average age a young woman becomes involved in prostitution is 14. Because many of the young women who commit crime have experienced abuse, the justice system is grappling with the question, "Should these young offenders be treated as delinquents or victims?"

Moore and Hagedorn authored a research on female gangs in America. This study outlined the most common reasons for female youth to join a gang. What was often found was that the majority of the women who had been labelled as an official gang member had joined as refugees. This majority left their homes as a way of escaping problems such as physical, sexual, and mental abuse often perpetrated by the male parent. Girls also join gangs while searching for friendship, solidarity, self-affirmation, and a sense of new possibilities as well as economic and family pressures.[11]

Most gangs are either all-male or co-ed. When male gang members of co-ed gangs were asked about the role female gang members play, they replied that the girls were in fact not members of the gang but "possessions"[12] of the gang. Unfortunately, this may be the case in some situations; however, when many of the male gang members are incarcerated it is the girls who take over the responsibility of running the gang activities, which is a sure sign of a regular gang member. It was these events, which initially occurred in the 1970s, that led to the formation of all-female gangs. The girls who usually leave their co-ed gangs do so because of disappointment. They believe that they can in fact support what they need to support by handling "gang activities" on their own. The "gang activities" with which the majority of girls are involved are drug related. This is the most common offence.[13]

Some reasons why women leave their gang completely is because of events like pregnancy. They realize that choosing the gang as a "family" in which to raise their child is indeed an unhealthy choice. Unfortunately, because of constant changes in the welfare system, it becomes increasingly difficult for women to leave their gang "family" because of the financial support the "family" provides for them.

The world of female juvenile crime has been underreported and avoided for years. Across the globe it is possible to see there are few programmes in existence that focus on and help with reforming juvenile young women. Because men have dominated our juvenile justice systems, today's girls are being subjected to the same kind of rehabilitative measures that target male offenders, which is unfair because women commit different kinds of crimes and often for different reasons. Chesney-Lind in *The Female Offender* states, "major efforts to reform the way the Juvenile Justice System handles youth were crafted with no concern for girls and their problems within the system."[14]

However, according to a study by Poe-Yamagata E and J.A. Butts[15] for the U.S. Department of Justice, Office of Juvenile Justice and Delinquency Prevention, for Crime in the United States 1983, 1988, and 1993 presented in Federal Bureau of Investigation reflects that during the decade 1983–1993, arrests of female juveniles increased by 31% (compared to 21% for boys; see Table 4.1). Between 1989 and 1993, the relative growth in juvenile arrests involving girls was 23%, more than double the 11% growth measured for boys.

Table 4.1

Female Proportion of Juvenile and Adult Arrests 1983, 1988, and 1993

Most Serious Offence	*Female Proportion of arrests of Persons Under Age 18*			*Female Proportion of Arrests of Persons Age 18 or Older*		
	1983	*1988*	*1993*	*1983*	*1988*	*1993*
All Arrests*	21%	22%	24%	16%	17%	19%
Violent Crime Index	11	11	13	11	11	13
Murder/Non-negligent Manslaughter	11	7	6	14	13	10
Forcible Rape	1	2	2	0	1	1
Robbery	7	7	9	8	9	9
Aggravated Assault	16	15	18	13	13	15
Property Crime Index	20	20	24	24	26	27
Burglary	7	7	10	7	9	10
Larceny-theft	27	26	31	31	32	33
Motor Vehicle Theft	11	10	14	8	10	10
Arson	10	10	12	14	16	17
Weapons Offence	6	7	8	8	8	8
Drug Abuse Offence	16	12	11	14	16	17

*Includes offences not detailed below.

Sources: Federal Bureau of Investigation. Crime in the United States 1983, Crime in the United States 1988, and Crime in the United States 1993 from Poe-Yamagata E and J.A. Butts (1996), *Female Offenders in the Juvenile Justice System: Statistics Summary*, Washington DC, Diane Publishing, p. 4.

Although females were responsible for a greater proportion of juvenile (24%) than adult (19%) arrests in 1993, the female proportion of arrests for most index offences was comparable between juveniles and adults (Table 4.1). However, there were variations across offence categories. The female proportion of juvenile arrests was larger than the female proportion of adult arrests for aggravated assault and motor vehicle theft. By contrast, girls were responsible for a smaller proportion of juvenile than adult arrests for murder and arson.

Nonetheless, the female proportion of arrest among both juveniles and adults increased between 1983 and 1993. Although

Figure 4.1

Juvenile Proportion of Arrests by Sex 1993

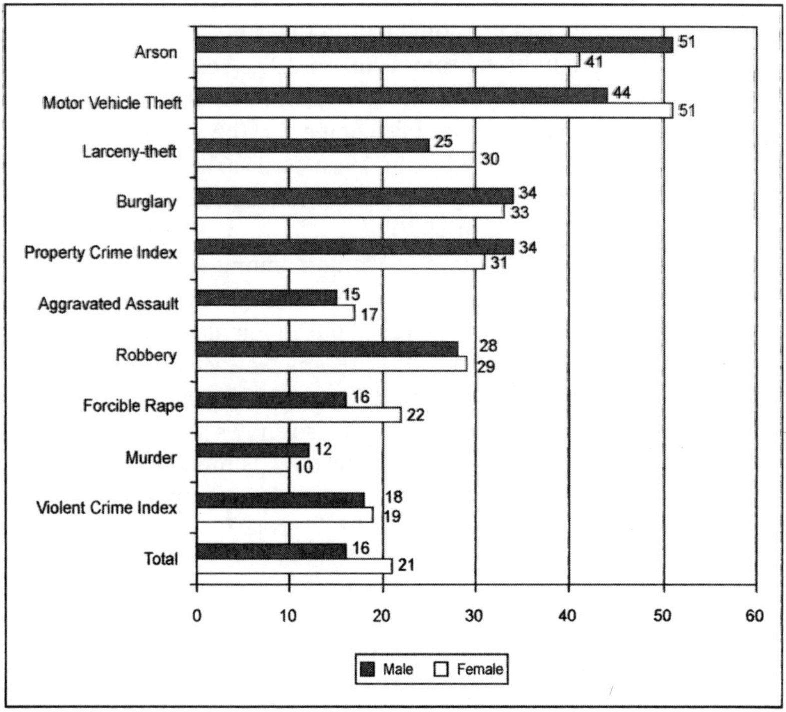

slight variation existed among offences, changes in the female proportions of juvenile and adult arrests were similar for Violent Crime Index and Property Crime Index Offences.

Variations also occurred across offence categories in the overall proportion of female and male arrests that involved juveniles. In 1993, 21% of all female arrests involved youth under the age of 18 compared with 16% of male arrests (Figure 4.1). Juveniles were responsible for 19% of female arrests and 18% of male arrests for Violent Crime Index offences in 1993. The youth proportion of female arrests for Property Crime Index offences was slightly lower than the corresponding proportion for male arrests (31% vs. 34%).

While certain aspects of juvenile delinquency are universal, others vary from one region to another. As a rule, cultural contexts are important in understanding the causes of juvenile delinquency and developing culturally appropriate measures to deal with it.

The initial survey conducted by the Secretariat of United Nations on the situation of female criminality reveals that the increasing crime rate among women in most of the countries is indicative of a new universal phenomenon. In the United States, the arrest among female population from 1960 to 1972 rose nearly 3 times faster than among male population. The criminal statistics of Japan indicate that the proportion of women in the total number of offenders increased from 9.8% in 1962 to 13.6% in 1972. In the Federal Republic of Germany, the rate of female offenders increased from 15.4 in 1963 to 17.1 in 1970.

In Canada, the proportion of women among offenders charged with indictable offences rose from 7% in 1960 to 14% in 1969. Norwegian statistics record a sudden spur in female criminality from 4% in 1958 to 10% of total crime at present. New Zealand reported a dramatic increase in female crime rate after 1960. The rate of female criminality in the developing countries also shows an upward trend.

In Brazil, there has been an increase by as much as 89% in the absolute numbers of offences among women as compared with an increase of 43% among men, from 1957 to 1971. In India, 27,891 women were arrested under the Indian Penal Code in 1972 as against 16,303 in 1971. A few social systems, however, present exceptions to this universal trend of increase in female criminality.

In Poland, a steady decline in female crime rate has been witnessed after 1951. The proportion of women among prisoners in that country has sharply fallen from 25.9% in 1951 to 11.4% in 1972. However, most of the countries participating in the Fifth United Nations Congress confirmed the increasing incidence of female criminality and expressed a growing awareness and concern about this problem.

A study was conducted in China to examine the current behaviours and social service needs among Chinese male and female juvenile delinquents in Hong Kong.[16] The findings were published in an article in *Children and Youth Services Review*. Semi-structured interviews were conducted with 398 (183 girls and 215 boys) Chinese juvenile delinquents between 12 and 18 years of age in Hong Kong. Findings revealed that a majority of the participants had engaged in delinquent behaviours and that girls had demonstrated higher rates of delinquent behaviours in many salient areas. Results also revealed that more than 50% of participants needed assistance with the continuation of studies, job placement, academic studies, provision of social activities, and vocational training.

The most common delinquency that female juveniles in China are arrested for is sexually promiscuous behaviour. The sex trade is a huge operation in China that involves even minor girls aged 10 or 11 years. According to Irving Epstein, "females were particularly difficult to reform because, once incarcerated, they saw themselves as irreparably ruined, like a broken vase."[17] Epstein also attempted to find the reasons behind female delinquency in China. He thought it could be related to the Cultural Revolution, poor parenting, unsympathetic teaching, unhealthy peer influences, and the Western media.[18]

In Europe, the nineteenth century formed a crucial watershed in the evolution of models of male and female juvenile criminality. At the cessation of the French wars in 1815 there was a widespread belief that juvenile crime was on the rise. A number of factors—population rise, urbanization, and poverty—inter-reacted, leading to this increase. Concerns had been expressed about delinquents in previous centuries; however, it was expressed vociferously only from the 1810s that consistent representation and inquiries started to appear.[19] The most characteristic anomaly of these chronicles was the almost invisible figure of the female juvenile offenders. Indeed, when the girls were considered it was from the confines of narrow descriptive categories, which stereotyped them as either prostitutes or flash girls.[20]

These flash girls or prostitutes however had a very crucial role to play in the demonstration of masculinity and maturity by young men and boys. The presence of female company was seen as the mark of complete transition from the image of immaturity associated with boyhood to maturity or manliness associated with full adulthood, and the boys apparently sought this transition.[21] There was a general inference that these female seductresses tended to be older than the boys with whom they consorted. Tentative findings from sampled indictments derived from the Middlesex criminal registers between 1797 and 1847 suggest that girls entered the criminal justice system when slightly older. Thus 45% of juvenile females were aged 16, as opposed to 34% of juvenile males.[22] This pattern changed overtime. However, since much "sexual corruption" presumably took place outside the justice system there is one practical way to assessing the relative ages of girls. These girls were clearly defined in their gender roles. The children were not portrayed merely as boys and girls herding together; rather, they were boy thieves and girl prostitutes.[23]

Australia's juvenile female crime has barely been identified and there is little help for young female offenders. The most common acts that cause young girls to become involved with the law are running away, simple assault, disorderly contact, and underage drinking. Because there are few girls involved with the justice system, officials are not sure how to handle them or recognize their problems. Girls in Australia are often stereotyped as aggressive. When girls fight among one another police often end up as victims. Alder also focussed on the attitudes of the girls involved in the justice system, and she found that "girls are described as 'verbally aggressive', 'hysterical', 'manipulative', 'dishonest', and 'untrusting'." Sexuality and changing bodies often trouble adolescent girls. Such changes in physical and mental makeup create confusion in the young girl's head, forcing them to experiment with "acting up" or indulge in rebellion which could result in delinquency.[24]

Female crime is on the rise in New Zealand even though girls constitute only 14% of the total number of people arrested. In the *New Zealand Herald*,[25] Jan Corbett states, "Rotorua's youth aid officer, sergeant Jim Harvey, says that while boys are still committing most of the juvenile violence, the worst attacks in the past 2 years have been committed by packs of girls." This evidence is comparable with Japan where girls are also acting in groups. Girls are also acting more violently in schools, physically fighting instead of passing nasty notes as they once did. Many people in New Zealand have tried to come up with reasons for the increase in female juvenile crime. Some blame feminism as the cause and believe that it has "allowed girls to express their anger, rather than turning it in on themselves."[26]

A close relationship between growing affluence and delinquent behaviour has been established in the sociological surveys many countries. Rapid industrialization and, consequently, urbanization, has loosened the hold of traditional means of social control on the behaviour and conduct of individuals, more so among the troubled youth population who demonstrate the propensity to become juveniles and become juveniles eventually. In developing countries, the socio-economic transition coupled with the impact of materialism has led to the emergence of a peculiar phase of social adolescence characterized by new notions, attitudes toward life, and a different set of life values and sensibilities. The process is more traumatic for teenage girls than for boys, as they have to adjust not only to the changing social situations but also experience the uncertainties of their position as women in an urbanized social space. This social space marks the erosion of power of traditional social institutions or systems of control, such as family or community, which though oppressive at their core provided a semblance of control and safety for women and acted as a major deterrent to resorting to deviant behaviour.

National Perspective: Female Juvenile Delinquency

The current dynamics of Indian society reflect a wide range of cultural variations, socio-economic developments, and technological changes, and the problem of juvenile delinquency assumes a peculiar character in the Indian context. Although juvenile delinquency is generally known as an urban phenomenon, the extent of its presence in rural areas remains largely unreported. The assumption is that most of the so called unreported cases are death and solved by the informal control mechanisms of the traditional society system. There is, however, a growing awareness that the processes of rapid industrialization, urbanization, and modernization have brought as their offshoot an unprecedented erosion of social values, making the children more vulnerable to committing delinquent acts than ever before.

As long as there are social tensions arising from social disparities and caste prejudices in the rural milieu, the children and adolescents of underprivileged groups are especially prone to social maladjustment. Despite the fact that constitutional provisions have made people much more conscious of their rights and obligations, the rural society still tends to cling to a social hierarchy that renders individuals in the lower strata liable to be socially handicapped, emotionally disturbed, and morally insecure. When a person is not fully assured of a social status deserved by him or her as a human being, his or her capacity to fulfil social obligation is seriously impaired. Such a situation not only inhibits the growth of community consciousness in rural areas but also induces a sense of frustration among those deprived of an equal sharing of sociocultural and economic opportunities. The resultant distortion in social values may be closely associated with a high incidence of social vices among the underprivileged people. Children and adolescents are apparently the worst victims of such social disabilities.

In the wake of rapid industrialization, a large number of families migrate from rural areas to industrial centres in search of gainful occupation. Completely cut off from their cultural moorings, they struggle hard to secure a place in the urban community. Faced with social deprivation and neglect they either float about or cluster around overcrowded localities, unhygienic surroundings, and socially unhealthy environment, encountering a situation termed by sociologists as "social marginality." In this process, children of families coming from rural areas suffer more than adults. They are seriously disadvantaged in adjusting and competing with urban children, both culturally and economically. It is, therefore, not surprising that a large segment of children in correctional institutions consists of those who are born and brought up in such families.

In the Indian context, there are innumerable factors causing delinquency among girls, and any attempt to prevent and control them has to be related to the overall situation and the larger issues confronting our country and society. Table 4.2 gives a clear picture of the stark difference between juvenile boys and apprehended girls under the Indian Penal Code and Special and Local Laws during the period 1992–2002.

Table 4.2

Crime in India (a Report by NCRB, Government of India)

Year	*Incidence of Juvenile Crimes*	*Incidence of Total Cognizable Crimes*	*Percentage of Juvenile Crimes*	*Total Juveniles Apprehended*	*Boys Apprehended*	*Girls Apprehended*	*Percentage of Girls*
1994	8,561	16,35,251	0.5	17,203	13,852	3,351	19.5
1996	10,024	17,09,576	0.6	19,098	14,068	5,030	26.3
1998	9,352	17,78,815	0.5	18,923	13,974	4,969	26.2
2000	9,267	17,71,084	0.5	17,982	13,854	4,128	26.2
2002	18,560	17,80,330	1.0	35,779	33,551	2,228	6.2
2004	19,229	18,32,015	1.0	30,943	28,878	2,065	6.7

Source: Crime in India 2004, NCRB, Ministry of Home Affairs, Government of India.

In the Indian context, the analysis of the juvenile crimes presents a very peculiar situation, particularly in relation to the total number of crimes reported. The share of girls among those detained for juvenile offences is much less than that of boys. India has witnessed an increase both in crimes committed by children and those committed against them. There has been a 7.9% increase in crimes committed by children between 2003 and 2004, with more children being apprehended for arson, theft, and cheating.

The number of children in conflict with law has increased from 17,203 in 1994 to 30,943 in 2004. The crimes committed by juveniles have also seen an increase in the same period from 8,561 to 19,229. While part of this increase in juvenile crimes may be attributed to the inclusion of boys aged 16–18 years in the definition of child in the revised juvenile justice law of 2000, the fact remains that the rate of juvenile crimes is fairly high and more and more children in the 16–18 years age group are coming in conflict with law.

Keeping the above statistics in mind and the present stage of socio-economic development in the country, an effective strategy for delinquency control may have to emphasize a high priority for not only those apprehended as delinquents but also for children who show the propensity to be delinquents. As it is often very difficult to draw a line between a delinquent and a potential delinquent, just on the basis of an overt behaviour, the intervention measures must cover all the phases of juvenile maladjustment. Although an ounce of prevention is always considered better than a pound of cure, the problems of those who have already come in conflict with law can hardly be deferred for better times. The various constitutional and legal provisions attempt to imbibe a comprehensive scheme for the care and treatment of both the delinquent and the potential delinquent, but their implementation is still to reach its efficient best. If the tide of delinquency is to be stemmed in time, a multisided action to deal with the problem in its various dimensions is urgently called for. In the present context, therefore, prevention and cure must go hand in hand, which undoubtedly requires a much greater effort than what has been witnessed in the recent years.

Preventive action against juvenile delinquency in the Indian setting obviously necessitates a greater thrust on ameliorating adverse socio-economic conditions that influence the child. A multipronged or holistic approach needs to be devised to cover all the facets of the child's environment: home, school, and neighbourhood. Studies on children in correctional institutions show abundant evidence that lack of emotional support from parents or guardians is a major causal factor behind juvenile maladjustment and consequently deviant behaviour. A delinquent child is very often the product of a socially unhealthy family. The institution of joint family in urban areas has weakened considerably given the stresses and strains of modern life. It is, therefore, imperative that the community and the state supplement, and if necessary substitute, the resources available with the family for the wholesome growth and development of children.

Similarly, the school environment and teacher–pupil relationship is of vital importance in the emotional development and social maturation of growing children. Explicit demonstration of double standards by adults in the family or in a public space like school in the context of personal discipline and the discriminating behaviour that children face in the public space, given the limitations of their families' socio-economic status in relation to education, recreation, and sociocultural opportunities, are not only highly demoralizing for disadvantaged children but are also responsible for creating an acute sense of frustration and antisocial reactions among such children. Unsatisfactory conditions in home or school are largely conducive to truancy and vagrancy, which often precede delinquency. Lack of proper care and control over the child heavily contributes to the formation of street gangs as a substitutive device for need satisfaction. It is only when a child is emotionally deprived and socially devalued that he or she finds solace in the company of a street gang which gives him or her an identity and sense of belongingness. The child's quest for excitement, lure of adventure, and love of pleasure hasten the process of social alienation and indoctrination into criminal behaviour. These children need to be weaned away skilfully from the gang activities by engaging them in such socially constructive activities that are equally exciting, stimulating, and adventurous.

The level and form of juvenile delinquency reflect more faithfully the changes in Indian social structure, cultural values, and shifts in standards discipline and civilized behaviour than adult crime does. There is much less juvenile delinquency in India than in most of the Western industrialized countries, including the United States. In a study it was found that in 1978 juvenile offenders contributed to only 3.3% of all the crimes committed under Indian Penal Code. In the same year, American juveniles committed as much as 21.4% of all the violent crimes and 45.5% of property crimes.[27]

Although delinquency may be comparatively a minor problem in India, more recent figures show that it has been rising steadily. Its rate of growth is greater than that of general criminality.[28] The figures for arrested juveniles revealed that during the period 1976–1980, more than 80% of them were in the 16–21-year age group. Female representation in juvenile crime varied from as low as 4.6% in 1981 to 7.7% in 1984.[29] This shows that the proportion of female involvement in juvenile delinquency is much less than that is witnessed or reported in developed industrialized countries where female offenders constitute as much as one-third of the total population of juvenile delinquents.

In India, female juvenile delinquency is still largely conditioned by economic insecurity, social deprivation, and emotional disturbances. Family feuds, domestic quarrels, and destitution continue to play a significant part in causing criminality among rural girl children. In urban areas, they are charged for a variety of offences such as riots, thefts, murder, kidnapping, abduction, and cheating. It may, however, be pointed out that official statistics are considerably influenced by the extent to which laws are enforced in a particular area and, thus, do not always present the phenomenon as it actually exists in society.

Some studies on deviant behaviour among girls provide significant indications of changing forms and patterns of female criminality. Women offenders are playing a more independent and aggressive role in various types of economic offences. They are now more prominently involved in the commission of sex offences and other forms of antisocial activities, such as alcoholism, drug abuse, and gambling. As the scope and range of their participation in social life is fast expanding, the nature and magnitude of criminal behaviour among women is assuming new forms and dimensions.

Crime Profile and Patterns of Criminality in National Capital Territory (NCT), Delhi

Incidence of Crimes in Delhi[30]

Out of 1,764,629 cognizable IPC crimes reported in Crime in India 1999, the NCT of Delhi registered 58,701 such crimes, which constituted 3.3% of the all-India total (see Table 4.3). This displays a clear trend of decline in the crime rate from the previous year when incidents of crime reported in Delhi was 64,882 or 3.6% of the all-India crime rate. However, the crime rate in NCT of Delhi is overwhelmingly high in comparison to the six other union territories. NCT's crime rate comprises 88.8% of the overall number 66,092 acts of crime reported for the union territories.

Table 4.3

Crime Scenario in NCT, Delhi

Rate of IPC Crimes in 1999	
For all-India	178.9 Per Lakh
For NCT of Delhi	431.6 Per Lakh
Delhi's Rank in Criminality	First
Total Number of Cognizable Crimes Committed under IPC	
All-India	17,64,629
NCT of Delhi	58,701
Delhi's Percentage in all-India Total	3.3
All Union Territories (UT)	66,092
Delhi's Percentage in all-UT Total	88.8
Delhi's Percentage Change in 1999 Compared to 1998	–0.34
Violent Crimes	*Number of Incidents*
All-India	2,38,081
All UTs	4,843
NCT of Delhi	4,289 (88.6% of UT Total)
Share of Violent Crimes to Total IPC Crimes	
All-India Percentage	13.5
NCT of Delhi Percentage	7.3

Source: Crime in India, 1999.

The rate of crime, that is, incidence of crime per lakh (1,00,000) of the population, for Delhi in 1999, was highest in the country at 431.6 per lakh as compared to all-India rates of 178.9 per lakh (Table 4.3). In 1998, the crimes under IPC for Delhi were reported at 58,701. Thus, there is a 0.3% decline in figures reported for 1999 compared to the previous year, 1998, when the number reported was 64,882.

Thus, just as any other metro region in the country, NCT of Delhi too is a state with a high crime rate. However, the incidence of rise in crimes should be viewed under the context of high population density, high rate of marginalization, and vast influx of the migrant population. Considering the nature and pattern of crimes it is significant that the incidence of violent criminality is relatively low in Delhi, constituting only 7.3% as against the national average of 13.5% (Table 4.4).

Table 4.4

Violent Crimes in Delhi

Type of Crime	*Years*				
	1996	*1997*	*1998*	*1999*	*2000*
Murder	518	575	649	654	588
Attempt to Commit Murder	512	506	612	581	595
Culpable Homicide not Amounting to Murder	82	78	96	–	–
Rape	484	544	438	408	446
Kidnapping and Abduction	1,250	1,266	1,333	–	–
Dacoity	32	37	65	63	69
Preparation and Assembly for Dacoity	21	16	36	–	–
Robbery	609	625	823	727	758
Riots	236	211	195	199	210
Arson	87	47	65	–	–
Dowry Death	132	148	126	–	–
Total	3,963	4,053	4,438	–	–

Source: Madhava Menon, N.R. and Banerjea, D. (2002), *Criminal Justice India Series: National Capital Territory of Delhi*, New Delhi, Allied Publishers, p. 8

Table 4.4 shows that the incidence of murder, which was steadily increasing from 1996 and rose to 654 in actual numbers in 1999, has suddenly dropped to 588 in 2000. However, the figures reported for attempt to commit murder, dacoity, robbery, and riots have shown an increase from 1999 to 2000. In all, we may say that the incidence of violent crimes seem to be on the rise in 2000 over 1999.

Crimes against Women

As for crimes against women, statistics presented in Table 4.4 show a decrease since 1997. Although women may be subjected to any crime such as murder, robbery, clearing, theft and so on, there are certain crimes that are specifically directed against women and characterized as crimes against women. These are classified under two categories (Madhava and Banerjea, 2002):

1. Crimes identified under that Indian Penal Code
   (i) Rape (Section 376, IPC)

- (ii) Kidnapping and abduction for different purposes (Sections 363–373, IPC)
- (iii) Homicide for dowry, dowry deaths, or their attempts (Section 302/304B, IPC)
- (iv) Torture, both mental and physical (Section 498A, IPC)
- (v) Molestation (Section 354, IPC)
- (vi) Sexual harassment* (Section 509, IPC)
- (vii) Importation of girls (up to 21 years of age; Section 366B, IPC; *referred in the past as eve-teasing)

2. The crimes identified under the Special Local Laws (SLL)
   Some acts with special provisions enacted to safeguard women and their interests are:
   - (i) Employees State Insurance Act, 1948
   - (ii) Plantation Labour Act, 1951
   - (iii) Family Courts Act, 1984
   - (iv) Special Marriage Act, 1954
   - (v) Hindu Marriage Act, 1955
   - (vi) Hindu Succession Act, 1956
   - (vii) Immoral Traffic (Prevention) Act, 1956
   - (viii) Maternity Benefit Act, 1961 (amended in 1955)
   - (ix) Dowry Prohibition Act, 1961
   - (x) Medical Termination of Pregnancy Act, 1971
   - (xi) Contract Labour (Regulation and Abolition) Act, 1976
   - (xii) Equal Remuneration Act, 1976
   - (xiii) Child Marriage Restraint (Amendment) Act, 1979
   - (xiv) Criminal Law (Amendment) Act, 1983
   - (xv) Factories (Amendment) Act, 1986
   - (xvi) Indecent Representation of Women (Prohibition) Act, 1986
   - (xvii) Commission of Sati (Prevention) Act, 1987.

Table 4.5 shows clearly that the "Incidence" of total cognizable crimes against women in Delhi has been on a constant decrease since 1997. Also, the percentage contribution of crimes against women in Delhi to the all-India total of crimes against women has come down to 1.8% in 1999 from 2.2% reported for 1997. Similarly, the rate of cognizable crimes against women in Delhi has come down to 17.9% in 1999 from 21.9% reported for 1997, although it is still higher than the all-India rate of crimes against women, which stood at 13.8% in 1999 (Madhava and Banerjea, 2002).

Table 4.5

Incidence of Crimes Committed against Women in NCT of Delhi

No.	*Description*	*Year*					
		1997		*1998*		*1999*	
		Delhi	*India*	*Delhi*	*India*	*Delhi*	*India*
1	Incidence of Total Cognizable Crimes	2,725	1,21,265	2,556	1,31,338	2,428	1,35,771
2	Percentage Contribution to All-India Total	2.2	100	1.9	100	1.8	100
3	Percentage of Cognizable Crimes	21.9	12.7	19.6	13.5	17.9	13.8
4	Rank	2	—	3	—	4	—

Source: Madhava Menon, N.R. and Banerjea, D. (2002), *Criminal Justice India Series: National Capital Territory of Delhi*, New Delhi, Allied Publishers, p. 12.

Going by the number of individual crimes, incidence of rape has decreased considerably to 402 in 1999 as compared to 544 in 1997. Along with it, most of the crimes in other categories have also shown a decline: Incidence of dowry deaths have come down to 122 in 1999 from 148 in 1997; incidence of molestation, down to 588 in 1999 from 675 in 1997; incidence of eve-teasing, down to 146 in 1999 from 185 in 1997; incidence under the Immoral Traffic (Prevention) Act, down to 78 in 1999 from 117 in 1997; and incidence of cruelty by husband and relatives, down to 88 in 1999 from 113 in 1997.

The only aberration seen is in the increasing number of the incidence of kidnapping and abduction for various purposes. It was 925 in 1997, 978 in 1998, and 986 in 1999. However, rate per lakh for the kidnapping and abduction cases has declined from 7.4 in 1997 to 7.3 in 1999. Out of the total number of crimes committed against women in all UTs (2,774), Delhi alone has a share of 2,428 in 1999 and a share of 1.8% of the all-India total of 1,35,771 in 1999 (Table 4.4).

Crimes against Children

As for crimes against children, there is no separate classification of offences categorized as "offences against children" under the Indian Penal Code. The Indian Penal Code and the various protective and preventive Special and Local Laws specially mention the offences wherein children are the victims. Such offences are construed as crimes against children and can be categorized under two broad heads:

1. Crimes under the Indian Penal Code
   - (i) Foeticide (Section 315 and 316, IPC)
   - (ii) Infanticide (Section 315, IPC)
   - (iii) Abetment of suicide (Section 305, IPC)
   - (iv) Exposure and abandonment (Section 317, IPC)
   - (v) Kidnapping and abduction for varied purposes (Sections 360–369, IPC)
   - (vi) Procuration of minor girls (Section 366A, IPC)
   - (vii) Selling of girls for prostitution (Section 372, IPC)
   - (viii) Buying of girls for prostitution (Section 373, IPC)
   - (ix) Rape
   - (x) Unnatural offences
2. Crimes punishable under Special and Local Laws
   - (i) Immoral Traffic (Prevention) Act
   - (ii) Child Marriage Restraint Act
   - (iii) Child Labour (Prevention) Act

Table 4.6

Incidence of Crimes Committed against Children in NCT of Delhi

No.	*Description*	*Year*					
		1997		*1998*		*1999*	
		Delhi	*India*	*Delhi*	*India*	*Delhi*	*India*
1	Incidence of Total Cognizable Crimes	338	5,980	358	5,788	403	4,957
2	Percentage Contribution to All-India Total	565	100	6.19	100	8.13	100
3	Rate of Cognizable Crimes	2.71	0.63	2.75	0.60	2.96	0.50
4	Rank	1	—	2	—	4	—

Source: Madhava Menon, N.R. and Banerjea, D. (2002), *Criminal Justice India Series: National Capital Territory of Delhi*, New Delhi, Allied Publishers, pp. 7–13.

Table 4.6 shows us that crimes against children in Delhi are on the rise. In 1999, the incidence of total cognizable crimes against children rose to a total of 403 from a total of 338 in 1997 (Table 4.6). Figures of kidnapping and abduction are on an alarming rise; compared to 21 incidences reported for 1997, 104 incidents reported for 1998 and 156 for 1999 show a steep increase in this category of crime. The rate of incidence of these cases has also increased to 19.7 per 1,00,000 as reported for 1999 from the figure reported for the year 1997 at 3.4 per 1,00,000.

Juvenile Justice System in Delhi

Juvenile Justice Administration in Delhi has been fairly well developed and up-to-date. Right from early 1960s the Union Territory of Delhi had an exclusive Children Act, 1960. The act later served as the model for the Juvenile Justice Act, 1986. In consonance with the exclusive legislation the Delhi administration provided for an elaborate juvenile institutional network such as Observation Home at Feroz Shah Kotla and Majnu-ka-Tila and Children's Court and Child Welfare Board at Kingsway Camp and Feroz Shah Kotla and Children's Home and Special School. With the enactment of the Juvenile Justice Act, 1986, the juvenile institutions underwent the changes envisaged under the new act.

Enforcement of the Juvenile Justice (Care and Protection of Children) Act, 2000

The act came into force in Delhi with effect from April 1, 2001. According to the law the two streams of institutions for adjudication and custodial care have been constituted in Delhi. Thus, for children in conflict with law the Juvenile Welfare Board has been constituted in terms of Section 4 and is functioning at the Kingsway Camp, Poor House Complex, in Northwest Delhi. The Child Welfare Committee located at the Feroz Shah Kotla Children Complex has been reconstituted for children in need of care and protection. The NCT of Delhi has in all 14 juvenile institutions for catering to the justice, custody, care, and protection needs of various categories of children.

1. Observation Home for Boys I, Delhi Gate
2. Observation Home for Boys II, Magazine Road
3. Observation Home for Girls, Nirmal Chhaya
4. Children Home for Boys I, Alipur
5. Children Home for Boys II, Alipur
6. Children Home for Girls I, Nirmal Chhaya
7. Children Home for Girls II, Nirmal Chhaya
8. Children Home for Boys I, Lajpat Nagar
9. Children Home for Boys II, Lajpat Nagar
10. Children Home for Boys (Beggar), Narela

11. Special School for Boys, Magazine Road
12. Home for Mentally Retarded Children, Avantika
13. School and Home for Mentally Retarded for Girls and Women
14. Institution for Severely and Profoundly Mentally Retarded Children and Adult, Avantika.

Table 4.7 gives details about juvenile institutions, total inmate population, institution-wise population, and gender- and category-wise breakups.

Table 4.7

Juvenile Institutions in Delhi

No.	*Institutions*	*Number of Inhabitants (2000–2001)*
1	Observation Home for Boys I, Delhi Gate	1,743*
2	Observation Home for Boys II, Magazine Road	879
3	Observation Home for Girls, Nirmal Chhaya	562
4	Children Home for Boys I, Alipur	1,706
5	Children Home for Boys II, Alipur	1,442
6	Children Home for Girls I, Nirmal Chhaya	1,419
7	Children Home for Girls II, Nirmal Chhaya	427
8	Children Home for Boys I, Lajpat Nagar	1,029
9	Children Home for Boys II, Lajpat Nagar	993
10	Children Home for Boys (Beggar), Narela	1,115
11	Special School for Boys, Magazine Road	64
12	Home for Mentally Retarded Children, Avantika	1,413
13	School and Home for Mentally Retarded	
	– Girls	258
	– Women	894
14	Institution for Severely and Profoundly Mentally Retarded	
	– Children	874
	– Adults	960

*Figure indicates overall total number of juvenile population provided shelter throughout the year, that is, compound total.

Key factors like overpopulation, high rate of immigrations, slums (*jhuggi-jhopari*), and homeless survivals do contribute to crimes in Delhi. The rise in the privileged class deviance evidenced in the high-profile crimes is a normal phenomenon in any metropolitan city today.[31] The NCT is no exception to the cultural transformation associated with the modern, rich, and upwardly mobile society. The only difference is that Delhi is not only a trade or business centre but also the political capital of the nation, and, therefore, such incidents of crimes attract media coverage and exposure. However, it is significant that the crimes Delhi, despite being a well-established business or trade centre and despite economic forces overshadowing the political scenario, are not yet an organized activity. We still do not have the underworld or mafia groups operating in the crime scene as in Mumbai. The pressure of civil society, against the incidence of crimes, in the form of *dharna*, boycott, and *gherao* can be incorporated into formal measures, particularly in dealing with crimes like dowry demand, bride burning, wife beating, child abuse, and so on. There have already been some incidents of effective *dharna* by the members of the NGOs and the local community against dowry torture in East and West Delhi.[32] The need is to accord such measures some amount of official recognition and governmental support.

Notes

1. Burfeind, J. and Bartusch, D.J. (2010), *Juvenile Delinquency: An Integrated Approach* (2nd ed.), Sudbury, MA, Jones and Bartlett, p. 127.
2. Ibid.
3. United Nations Department of Economic and Social Affairs (2004), *Juvenile Delinquency, World Youth Report 2003: A Global Situation of Young People*, New York, United Nations, p. 189.
4. Ibid., p. 199.
5. Ibid.
6. Ibid., p. 198.
7. Ibid., p. 199.
8. Ibid., p. 198.
9. Ibid., p. 199.
10. Beth, R.E., Kay, T., and Cathy, W.S. (2000), *Research on Women and Girls in the Justice System: Plenary Papers of the 1999 Conference on Criminal Justice Research and Evaluation—Enhancing Policy and Practice Through Research* (Vol. 3), Washington, DC, NIJ Publications, p. 29.

11. Moore, J. and Hagedorn, J. (2001), *Female Gangs: A Focus on Research*, Washington, DC, Office of Juvenile Justice and Delinquency Prevention, p. 2.
12. Ibid., p. 3.
13. Ibid., p. 6.
14. Chesney-Lind, M. (1997), *The Female Offender: Girls, Women, and Crime*, London, Sage, p. 10.
15. Poe-Yamagata, E. and Butts, J.A. (1996), *Female Offenders in the Juvenile Justice System: Statistics Summary*, Washington, DC, Diane Publishing, pp. 2–8.
16. Davis, C., Tang, C., and Ko, J. (1998), Exploring Current Behaviors and Social Service Needs for Chinese Juvenile Delinquents in Hong Kong, *Children and Youth Services Review*, 20(8), 733–745.
17. Epstein, I. (1987), Psychological and Behavioral Attributes of Juvenile Delinquents in the People's Republic of China, *Asian Thought and Society*, 12, 268.
18. Ibid., p. 267.
19. Arnot, M.L. and Usborne, C. (1999), *Gender and Crime in Modern Europe*, London, Taylor and Francis, p. 77.
20. Ibid.
21. Ibid., p. 83.
22. Ibid.
23. Ibid., p. 84.
24. Baines, M. and Alder, C. (1996). Are Girls More Difficult to Work with? Youth Workers' Perceptions in Juvenile Justice and Related Areas, *Crime and Delinquency*, 42, 467–485.
25. Corbett, J. (1999), Women Lash Out More Readily: Crime Stats, *The New Zealand Herald*, August 21, http://www.fact.on.ca/newpaper/nz990821.htm
26. Ibid.
27. Heiland, H.-G., Shelly, L.I., and Katoh, H. (1992), *Crime and Control in Comparative Perspectives*, New York, Walter de Gruyter, p. 194.
28. Ibid.
29. Ibid.
30. Madhava Menon, N.R. and Banerjea, D. (2002), *Criminal Justice India Series: National Capital Territory of Delhi*, New Delhi, Allied Publishers, pp. 7–13.
31. Ibid., p. 16.
32. Ibid.

5

Socio-economic Profile of Respondents

An understanding of the social background of the key informants is a prerequisite for getting at the problem of juvenile delinquency in its different manifestations. This chapter focuses on some of the personal characteristics of the socially delinquent girl child. Such a description is essential to understanding the realities of the respondents' social life, their cultural antecedents, as well as their social and personal background, including demographic markers such as age, caste, education, religion, and so on.

However, before proceeding to the socio-economic and demographic profile of the respondents let us first understand some important aspects of delinquency in India. India is a traditional society having several distinctive features marking different regions of the country as distinct, religiously and culturally unique from one another. Culture is important, but ritual aspects of religion enjoy equal amount of significance. Similarly, caste structure and norms are equally important. Yet another important factor that needs to be kept in mind is the importance of family system to both children and grown-ups in the family. The exceedingly repressed position of women in India presupposes their low delinquency rates in at least two ways: (1) they are subjected to almost continuous family control and (2) such seamless reinforcing of control through age-old cultural and traditional norms perpetually limit their opportunities to deviate from familial control and tradition or to associate with others who transmit and reinforce delinquent orientations and skills.[1]

Growing up in India involves learning to be dependent on members of one's group or community, accommodating the group interests, and living in harmony by adhering to group norms and expectations. In the socialization process, the child is made to submit to group expectations, including that of his or her parents and significant others, through various means. Childhood is prolonged and even adult children do not break away from their family or group life. Mothers breastfeed longer, children are made comfortable and appeased, and yet are also disciplined by deprivation of food and affection and by infliction of physical punishment.[2] The child is not only kind to the adults but also values and respects them yet fears them.

The sense of personhood and independence that are well inculcated in Western children are discouraged in India. The Indian child does not develop as much of a separate entity from others as does the child in the West and often has a weak and fragile ego. Usually, children are not much praised for their achievements and are not allowed to develop self-importance.[3] Consequently, when children grow up and become adults they still seek the counselling of elders on important matters in their lives. What is expected of children by adults is, therefore, well learned and mechanically complied with. Children do not openly seek to be different, rebellious, or dangerous in defying parental and social expectations to assert themselves or to gain self-importance. Dependence on others, their teachings, and their control have made Indian children more social and compliant and less deviant and delinquent.

Among the historical conditions that have paved the way for submission to group standards in India, caste and family occupy a very important position. For instance, in Tamil Nadu historically people made a distinction between family life (inside life), known as *agam*, and social life (outside life), known as *puram*. In accord with this distinction, it was important to conceal inappropriate and shameful behaviour of family members from outsiders because the outside public arena could be extremely critical and unforgiving.[4] When children misbehaved in public, any adult who witnessed it intervened to advise and discipline the children and report serious matters to their parents, a practice that continues even today. If parents were present, they would punish their misbehaving children in front of others to clear themselves from the blame and shame.[5] Similarly, the caste ensures that the families behaved in a disciplined manner so that the reputation of the caste is not negatively affected by the act of family members. The abilities of the family, the caste, higher castes, and communities to control and keep their members in line are now weakening with the development of egalitarian views arising from modernization and which have been given legal sanctity to be held as the foundation of the laws of the land.

However, the vestiges of societal hierarchies imposed by both religion and caste are so deep that children are forced to continue to depend on elders and submit to them. This in turn promotes learning behaviour that are socially expected and the child earning the adage as a person of good character and having a good name in the community. Elders and children interact closely and so they do what is needed to save children from delinquency. In India, families experience extreme shame and stigma over the delinquency of their children. When Indian children engage in deviant or delinquent behaviour, they tend to experience deep depression and develop self-hate. The strong attachments they develop over the course of life to their parents and kin bring forth shame and social stigma if they do something to disappoint the family and elders in some way that is considered deviant, which in some cases even leads to suicidal tendencies and suicide.[6]

These factors are especially important for controlling delinquency among girls in India. Girls are socialized to be less expressive of their desires, less aggressive in pursuing their interests, and completely submissive in order to put family first and their personal desires and aspirations behind and sacrifice for the family. Their inferior status within family is perpetually reinforced by repressive adult supervision and control mechanisms.

Social and physical separation of sexes has been in existence for thousands of years in an ancient country like India. Marriages are arranged within caste by parents, and in a traditional society like India usually there is no dating or romantic relationships in girls' lives; sometimes even talking with boys is highly discouraged or frowned upon. For the most part, girls are not left alone at home and discouraged or restricted from going out of the house after dark. Virginity before marriage is important; as a result, delinquency has a much lower rate of incidence among girls than among boys.

Women gradually become fatalistic as they are forced to play a passive role, fulfilling their "womanly" duties in the traditional family hierarchy. Society does not encourage them to fulfil their personal desires, and marriage becomes more of a social imperative where the main objective is the performance of *dharma* (tradition and in a stricter sense 'righteousness' in line with the age-old religious traditions and customs) and the propagation of the family tree as well as that of the group. It is through their role as wife and mother that women achieve status in the family and community. Still society respects and treats them better if they give birth to sons.[7]

For women, marriage imposes strenuous socialization. Not only do their social background and lifestyle change, they are also literally raised by their husbands, if not the entire family, be that of their husbands' or their parents. The family proves to be a protective institution, yet it is not one devoid of strain-filled, controlling interpersonal relationships. Women are forced to accommodate the family's needs and their husbands' wishes, demands, and narcissistic desires.[8] In the lower and middle classes, the women tolerate abuse, battering, and extramarital affairs because they give first priority to the children's welfare. In the upper class, this situation is slightly different. Women are imprisoned by the need to preserve their family's sanctum sanctorum. The mother–child bond intensifies whenever there is conjugal aloofness or the husband engages in extramarital relationship. This probably explains in part why mothers in India invest so much emotionally in their children, particularly their sons.

However, under the impact of modernization the above dynamics have distinctly changed. The conditions that have contributed to lower delinquency rates in India are bound to weaken eventually under the impact of modernization. A greater sense of independence, equality, personal importance, and living a good life are gradually disintegrating traditional group attachments and constrains.[9] As these modern forces become stronger, they will have serious consequences for female delinquents. In the context of these changes, anomie theory of Durkheim and Merton becomes pertinent. Crime and delinquency are bound to increase as group structures weaken, causing group controls to decline and socialization to become impaired, as the growing desire for "good life" cannot be achieved because of limited means and lack of economic opportunities.

More often than not, these sociocultural factors are found to have a direct or indirect bearing on the problem of child neglect and delinquency. Attention in this study has been focussed on the social background, family environment, schooling-education, and so on of the respondents.

Sociodemographic Background of Respondents

This section takes a close look at the social and demographic aspects of children. A total number of 200 girls were interviewed, out of which a large number were in the age group of 10–15 years (66%). The highest percentage of respondents were aged about 11 years (13%), and the lowest portion of respondents were aged between 7 and 8 years (1.5%).

It is noteworthy to mention here that most of the respondents have come in contact with the juvenile justice system for running away from abusive situation at home (will be discussed in detail in the next chapter). A child belonging to a tender age of 11 years may be very confused with her present abusive situation, and she has probably not been able to confide in any one, which must be a key catalyst behind her running away. Such a child is also not in a position to weigh the consequences of running away from home. Their actions are mostly instinctual; according to them running way is probably the best way to end the present plight.

On the question of state of origin, it was found that most of the girls interviewed belonged to Delhi (31.4%) followed by Bihar and Uttar Pradesh (16.5%; Table 5.1). The high percentage of girls belonging to Delhi could be attributed to the fact that the study was

Figure 5.1

Age of Respondents

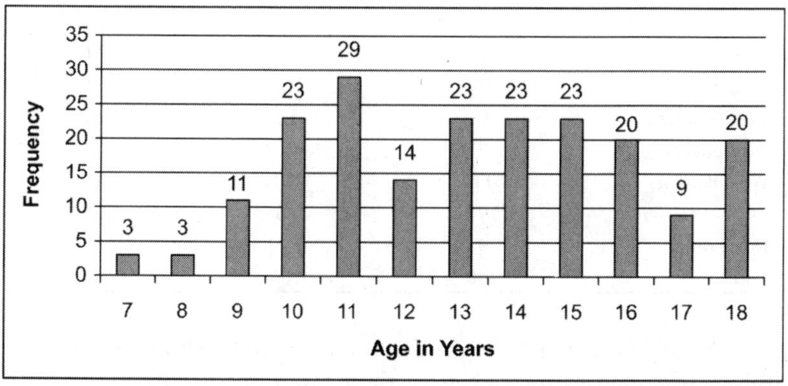

conducted in Delhi resulting in a high number of Delhi domiciles in the study sample. Another reason could be the effect of fast and continuing urbanization in Delhi. Continuing urbanization also poses a serious threat to the juvenile section of our society. The rapid urbanization may result in weakened family support systems and the burden of survival, protection, and development of the children, with both parents needing to go out for work, resulting in vagrancy, waywardness, and destitution of children. The basic features of the urban environment foster the development of new forms of social behaviour deriving mainly from the weakening of primary social relations and control, increasing reliance on the media at the expense of informal communication, and the tendency toward anonymity. These patterns are generated by the higher population density, degree of heterogeneity, and the rapid rate of increase in population in urban centres due to migration from villages. Rural grouping rely mainly on family and community control as a means of dealing with antisocial behaviour and thus exhibits lower crime rates.[10]

Table 5.1

State of Origin of Respondents

State	*Frequency*	*Percentage*	*Valid Percentage*
Andhra Pradesh	6	3	3.0
Assam	9	4	4.5
Bihar	31	16	16.5
Delhi	60	30	31.4
Goa	3	1	1.5
Gujarat	3	1	1.5
Jharkhand	11	6	6.0
Madhya Pradesh	6	3	3.0
Orissa	6	3	3.0
Punjab	11	6	6.0
Uttar Pradesh	31	16	16.5
Uttaranchal	3	1	1.5
West Bengal	11	6	6.0
Total	191	96	100.0
Don't Know	9	4	
Total	200	100	

Majority of migrants are those hailing from Uttar Pradesh and Bihar, who had to migrate with their families to Delhi in search of employment. A large number of families migrate from rural areas to urban hubs in search of occupation. The impediments these families face such as social deprivation and lack of level-playing field, specifically in relation to access to earning opportunities, lead to delinquency. The adults have to struggle harder to secure a place in the urban community. The families live in overcrowded localities, unhygienic surroundings, and an unhealthy environment. The children of these families suffer more than the adults in the whole process. Coming from rural areas, these children are suddenly forced to adjust and compete with urban children economically as well socially, which in turn leads to culture shock and maladjustment with such children both at school and in their neighbourhood.[11]

The fact that most of the respondents belonged to the above states suggests that urban areas have higher incidences of female delinquency compared to rural areas where exist strong social communities and control mechanisms.

Marital Status

A typical phenomenon in Indian families is the prevalence of child marriages. The practice of child marriage is rampant in many parts of the country and the incidence of such marriages is the highest in the states of Rajasthan, Bihar, Uttar Pradesh, Chhattisgarh, and Madhya Pradesh. According to Census 1991, the percentage of married females to the total number of females in the age group of 10–14

Figure 5.2

Marital Status

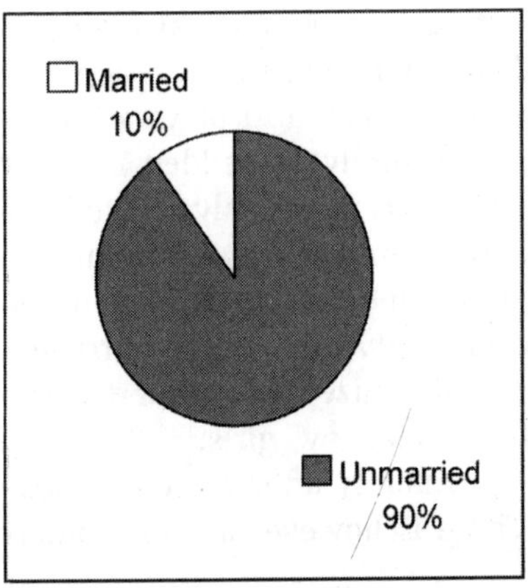

years was 13.2 in Rajasthan, the highest in the country. Girl child marriage undermines the "best interest of the child" as it leaves a negative impact on the health and overall well-being of the child. The total number of reported of child marriage in this study was 20 cases.

Marriage age of 40% of respondents was reported to be 15 years, and 30% claimed to have been married at the age of 12. The remaining 30% were married between the age of 17 and 18 years.

Table 5.2

Age at Marriage of Respondents

Marriage Age	*Frequency*	*Percentage*
7	0	0
8	0	0
9	0	0
10	0	0
11	0	0
12	6	30
13	0	0
14	0	0
15	8	40
16	0	0
17	3	15
18	3	15
Total	20	100

Despite the existence of the Child Marriage Restraint Act, 1929, that prohibits marriage below age 18 for girls and age 21 for boys, child marriage continues to be a social reality in India today. The family, caste, and community pressures are more effectual than any remote legislature. Patriarchy also plays an important role in child marriage. Through culturally embedded concepts of virginity and chastity, women's sexuality is not only controlled by men but is often held as a symbol of honour and status of a family, clan, caste, ethnic group, or race. Consequently, adherence to such values exerts pressure on the community to perform marriages for girls at a very early age in order to minimize the risks of dishonour associated with improper sexual conduct by girls.[12] Therefore, marriages are arranged either immediately after or sometimes even before a girl attains puberty. There is however a gross underreporting of cases.

The practice is very prevalent, particularly among the backward states and lower-income strata.

An analysis of data from a National Family Health Survey, which involved 22,807 Indian women who were aged between 20 and 24 at the time of the survey, was conducted for the period 2005–2006; the survey findings show that 22.6% of the women surveyed were married before they were 16 years old, 44.5% were married when they were aged between 16 and 17 years, and 2.6% were married before they turned 13 (see Table 5.3).

Table 5.3

National Family Health Survey, 2005–2006

Age at Marriage of Girls	*Percentage*
16–17 years	44.5
16 years	22.6
13 years	2.6

India introduced laws against child marriage in 1929 and set the legal age for marriage at 12 years. The legal age for marriage of girls was increased to 18 years in 1978. Survey findings showed that while the practice of child marriage has decreased slowly, its prevalence still remained unacceptably high, and rural, poor, less educated girls and those from central or eastern regions of the country are most vulnerable to the practice.

The survey's findings indicate that child marriage affects not only adolescents aged 16–17 years but also a large number of pubescent girls aged 14–years and that existing policies and gains made via economic development have failed to help rural and poor populations in this regard. Child marriage prevention programmes should be broadened to include interventions for women married as children and men who might pursue children for marriage, the researchers added.

Religion and Caste

It is believed that religion is instrumental in developing and maintaining morality. It has influenced, since times immemorial, the behaviour and the life of individuals. By and large, the religious patterns and beliefs may guide the behaviour pattern in the family, community, and society. Like religion, caste may also influence some

Figure 5.3

Religion of Respondents

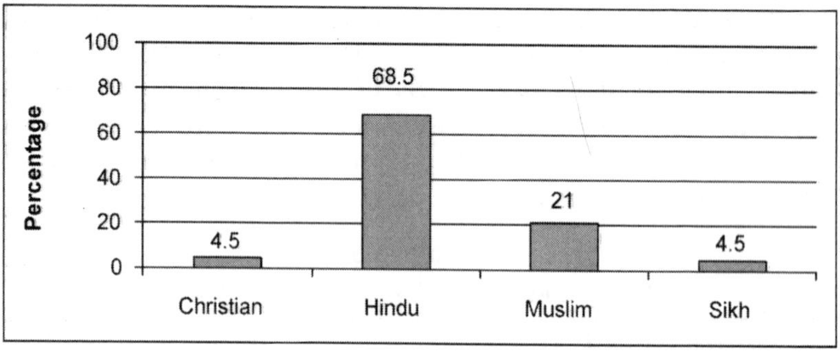

aspects of individual behaviour. In a country like ours, religious background and caste of a particular group or individual becomes vital to understanding the reasons for their interface with law. In other words, caste is an important construct in the Indian society. Although some sort of caste system is found to exist among all religious groups in India, it is palpably more prominent and rigid among Hindus. In the sample of respondents recruited for the present study, most children (responses from 197 girls) claimed they were Hindus (68.5%), followed by those who claimed to be Muslims (21%), Christians (4.5%), and Sikhs (4.5%), and 3 respondents (1.5%) stated they weren't aware of their religion.

As for religion, social restrictions on women and also general notions about women's private and public roles are derived from religious beliefs. Particularly in Hindu religion, numerous regulations and restrictions are imposed on women. Theses constrains continue to operate actively even today. Thus, religion as a system of belief constituting a set of rituals to be followed rigorously continues to legitimize and reinforce deferential treatment to girls. Over the years these operational constraints on women may have had an impact on their personality patterns. In view of these realities, women may have been finding it difficult to adjust with the changing patterns in a culturally plural society like India. Differences in regard to religion and caste may also develop strong, emotionally charged behaviour, such as rebellion or running away. It can thus be said that due to avoidance and discrimination, girls may start feeling alienated or even isolated. These sentiments of alienation and isolation may contribute to girls committing delinquent acts.

Figure 5.4

Caste of Respondents

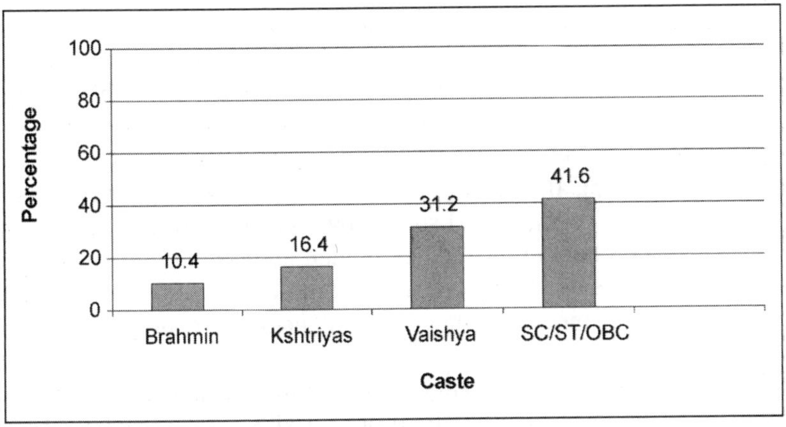

Our analysis of respondents' castes found that out of the total number of Hindu children who mentioned their caste ($N = 55$), 41.6% belonged to SC/ST/OBC groups, 31.2% belonged to Vaishya, 16.4% Kshatriyas and 10.4% were Brahmins.

As already mentioned in the opening chapter of this book, under caste hierarchies, elders in families and significant members in the caste groups disciplined both family and caste members. Also, the higher-caste elders disciplined members of lower castes. Children were reared to fit into the family, caste, and higher-caste expectations.[13] Failure to conform to these expectations not only involved social criticism and sanctions against perpetrators but also against their group to reinforce collective responsibility for the behaviour of group members. Consequently, every family taught children the norms and rules they should abide by and maintain separateness from other families and groups to keep family matters private and to avoid harmful outside influences.

Similarly, every caste group saw to it that its families and individual members behaved in a disciplined manner, as the reputation of the caste depended on their behaviour. The attachment of the children to family, caste, elders, and conventional groups and their impact on them help to explain the generally conforming and submissive nature of juveniles in India.

What is inferred from the foregoing discussion is that caste plays an important role in children resorting to delinquency. The number of upper-caste delinquents is almost negligible as compared to those of lower castes. One reason for this could be that economic status and social status go hand in hand, mutually inclusive and reinforcing one another. Thus, the upper-caste children do not become delinquent given the economic stability of their families. In contrast, a girl child of lower caste goes through double trouble of both patriarchic control and poverty; she is subjected to unimaginable oppression via gendered norms and controls and also acute poverty and, thus, the pain of suffering the lack of even basic necessities in household. Therefore, a lower-caste girl suffers by both restrictions imposed by caste elders on her family and her gender, and for her there is no way out unless she leaves the household. All these lead to some of the girls resorting to delinquent behaviour and negative coping with their suffering.

Even after so many years of India's independence and despite the excellent laws in place to protect Dalits, and especially Dalit women, they are still suffering atrocities and discrimination. It is believed that thousands of cases of atrocities have gone unreported and unpublicized because the poor Dalit girls have no control over their lives, given the wealth of upper castes and the power and influence they wield through the backdoor over the justice system, political bodies, police as well as the media.[14] Thus our findings showed that the respondents strongly believed that the only way to escape the vicious cycle of poverty, abuse, and oppression is to either run away or act out to defy routine gendered expectations.

The social disparities arising out of caste system have a direct bearing on the young minds of these girls. Despite the constitutional provisions and the emphasis on individual rights in today's scenario, the society at large still clings and conforms to social hierarchies created hundreds of years ago, which leaves the people of lower castes socially handicapped and emotionally disturbed. It follows that if a person is not socially secure his or her will and capacity to fulfil her social obligation is obviously impaired. These are some of the main reasons for higher incidences of social vices among the under-privileged people.

Schooling and Education

According to a recent amendment in the Indian Constitution, schooling and education among children has become free and compulsory for children aged 6–14 years (up to 6 years to be covered under early childcare projects). The government has started a comprehensive programme of education for all children up to the age of 14 years through the Sarva Shiksha Abhiyan, a programme launched in 2001–2002 and undergoing active implementation in all the states. Sarva Shiksha Abhiyan is an effort to universalize elementary education with a component of community ownership in the school system.

Although the programme has made major headway in most states, a high percentage of children, especially from poor families, are still out of the school and even those who go to school drop out eventually. In the present sample (*N* = 200), 114 children (57%) children were going to school and most of them were studying in Class 2 (21.1%) and Class 3 (21.9%). The remaining 86 girls (43%) were not going to school, and out of these 50% reported to have never attended school.

The other 50% of the respondents who had gone to school earlier reported dropping out because they had to do household chores (53.4%). Some have also mentioned they were asked to leave school because of a family member's view that education was not important for girls.

Why do children drop out and why do fewer girls complete the primary studies is a question that has worried administrators and commentators alike. Large surveys such as National Sample Surveys

Figure 5.5

Number of Respondents Who Were Going to School at the Time of This Study

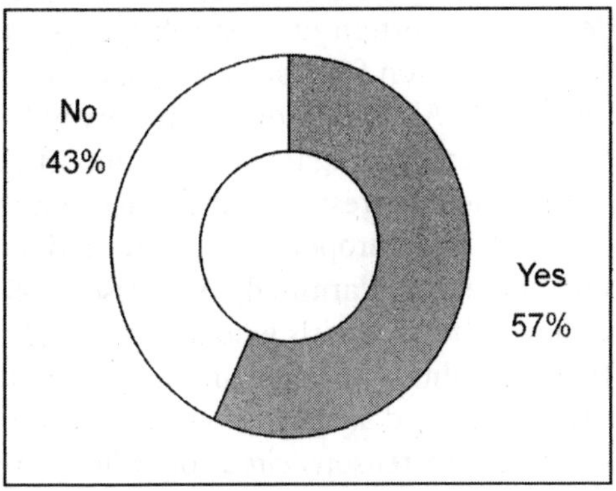

Figure 5.6

Reasons for Dropping Out of School

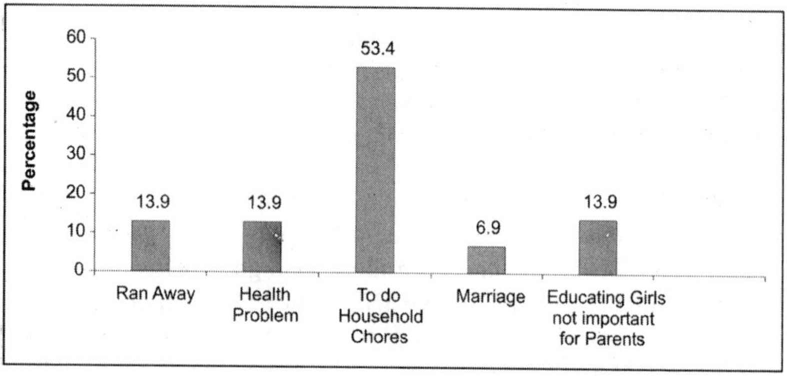

(NSS) and National Family Health Survey (NFHS-2)[15] have collected information on reasons for children's non-attendance at school. The reasons differ for boys and girls and between rural and urban children. According to NFHS-2, overall 15% of boys and 22% of girls were not attending school at the time of the survey. Children are simply never enrolled in school because, according to reports, the children themselves and/or their parents are "not interested".

A large percentage of children are unable to take advantage of nearby educational facilities because they are needed at home to participate in the basic tasks of household economy. Many children who are not in school are instead working eight hours or more every day; moreover, they are not earning any significant income, as they are relegated to doing tasks such as caring for their siblings or tending grazing cattle rather than taking up jobs that help them earn wages. A considerable proportion of urban dropouts cite "failure to pass examinations" as a reason for discontinuing education.

According to the 7th All India Education Survey,[16] high cost of private education, children needing to work to support their families, and, as a result, diminished interest in studies are some of the reasons given by three out of four dropouts covered under the survey. Dropout rates have increased alarmingly in Classes 3–5 (50% boys, 58% girls). More than half of the girls who had dropped out of school attributed it to their usefulness at home and helping with household work. Education was perceived as unnecessary for girls in nearly 14% of the responses. The major reasons cited for children who dropped out of school were lack of interest and the necessity for them to work—for cash or kind—at home or outside.[17]

Thus, we can see there are several reasons for low levels of literacy among girl children in India, not the least of which is the high level of poverty. According to the World Bank, over one-third of the population is estimated to be living below the poverty line. Although school attendance is free, the cost of books, uniforms, and transportation to school can be too much for poor families. Poor families are also more likely to keep girls at home to care for younger siblings or to work in family enterprises.

If a family has to choose between educating a son or a daughter because of financial restrictions, typically the son will be chosen. Negative parental attitudes toward educating daughters can also be a barrier to girls' education. Many parents view educating sons as an investment because the sons will be responsible for caring for the aging parents. As a result, such parents see the education of daughters as waste of money because their daughters will eventually leave the family after marriage and any income earned by the daughters will go to their husbands' families and thus they will not benefit directly from their education. Also, marriage of daughters with higher levels of education will likely attract higher dowry expenses as their families usually want a groom with equal or higher education, job position and income.

Higher educational qualifications achieved by a girl are commonly viewed as commodities necessary to attract a groom from a rich family rather than as intrinsically valuable. Her achievements become something that she confers on her husband rather than on herself.[18] Whatever else one may be or do, the central purpose of existence for most women in India is to be a good wife, daughter-in-law, mother, and homemaker. Most Indian girls expect marriage to be arranged for them by members of their family, with one minor benefit of this arrangement in the present times being the increased autonomy afforded to them in deciding who to marry from the potential list of grooms paraded before her in "arranged marriage" situations. And being "married off" is the ultimate (and desired) destiny of most Indian girls, usually to become the lowest-level servant in the home ruled by their mother-in-laws.

The vast majority of adolescents in India know with certainty that their marriage will be arranged. This has an enormous impact on their behaviour and relationships. Girls, for instance, are seldom required to make difficult decisions on their own, either in their own families or the families they married into, because typically in an Indian household important problems are dealt with taking into consideration the views of all members of the household after sufficient deliberations. Even for girls who have the opportunity to mix with boys, for example, at modern coeducation institutions, their relationships tend to remain shallow, frivolous, and titillating dalliances at best. Deeper attachments are still rare because their parents and the society frown upon such relationships and attract a greater element of societal stigma than is the case with the West where individual autonomy in matters of the heart is given due importance.[19]

Family Composition

India's heritage of stable family life and family structure can be spread over centuries. The spirit of family solidarity has remained a sustaining power, which has provided meaning to the daily lives of the Indian people (Beteille, 1964[20]). The son follows father's footsteps when choosing a profession or career or business; for example, he acquires confidence and skills in the family business through continuous association with other male relatives. Similarly, a young wife or a mother are required to learn from the experience and wisdom of other older women in the family.

The traditional Indian family also draws its values from religious prescriptions.[21] Here, an individual accepts an assigned role in the family hierarchy and fulfils his or her obligations at the cost of his or her own interest. Depending on their position in the sibling hierarchy, sons enjoy varying rights and responsibilities within the family where, of course, the father has the highest authority. The mother, however, wields a lot of influence over her children and enjoys supreme control over the daughter-in-laws. The head of the household, typically the father, is supposed to take into account the wishes, needs, and desires of all members in the family. However, the traditional family setup is not always a just and fair environment, where sometimes select family members enjoy more powers, freedom, and autonomy to the chagrin of other, not-so-privileged, members.

The joint family has its own norms and values compared to a nuclear family which has one couple and their offspring. For example, marriages were arranged through the consent of the head of the family, for example, the grandfather. Interpersonal relationships and affiliations within the family are so strong and the monitoring and controlling of family members is so effective that any deviation from social norms is virtually impossible. This is strongly relevant to premarital relationships (or romantic relationships between a girl and boy without the approval or blessings of the family) or other deviant behaviours. Married women are not expected to work outside their homes, exception being women hailing from poor labour classes where both partners need to work to make ends meet.

The joint family system, however, has a number of limitations.[22] Being tradition bound, the family protocol left little room for a gifted individual to take any leadership role. This system also provided little incentive for individual efforts and hard work, since no individual gains were associated with them. The joint family, by and large, left little scope for enterprise and initiative and perpetuated rigid customs and any little change seen as going against customs was met with severe resistance. It also tended to perpetuate abusive situations for children; the children were raised to simply do what they were told without any scope for dialogue and were taken for granted, which indicated little consideration is given to children's psychosocial needs. Such oppression could also result in delinquency.

There are however disadvantages of family breakups into nuclear units of a two-by-two or two-by-one matrix, that is, both parents and two children or a single child. Alienation among children is bound to occur when both parents tend to compete with each other on individualistic lines, for example, economic and social recognition. Thus, the protective roles of families in urban setting get badly disturbed. In affluent families where excessive competition and consumerism prevail, typically parents' major focus is on continuously creating measures to enhance wealth and career success, with the children at home getting neglected due to parents' lack of adequate interest in focussing on the emotional well-being and bonding of children within the family. This results in gross violation of children's rights and also makes the child extremely vulnerable to going out of control. Thus, adequate parental attention, love, care, and protection should be given to the child in order to ensure his or her positive development.

It is thus clear that with the advent of development, and socialization making inroads into the family structure, the protective role of the family is gradually declining. Children are being left to be taken care of by institutions like schools, government-run as well as private children's homes, and in the case of destitute or runway children, orphanages, foster care homes, and so on. These institutions can be at best like disaster management where the goal is to prevent loss of lives, and they cannot provide, or be a substitute for, the psychological support and emotional care that only parents can provide. While children in institutional care and in schools have to bear the brunt of abusive situations by caregivers, parents tend to ignore their protective meaningful roles in the formative years of children's lives by depending excessively on such institutions.

A look at the sample size shows that about 93% of respondents have a family. The remaining 7% either gave no response or did not have any member of their family that they knew of. As much as 20% children have a family of 5 members, 18.5% have 7 members, and 1.5% have as many as 12 members in the family. If we club them into two groups, that is, 2–6 members and 7–12 members or more, data will show that 58.5% have a family of 2–6 members and 34.5% have more than 6 members in the family. These 34.5% children live mostly in joint family settings.

This seems to suggest that joint families have lesser number of delinquents. This is due to the greater amount of control exercised on the child by the members in the joint family. In the joint family system, which was the traditional model of living, members were bound together by ties of common ancestry and property (Ross, 1961). The traditional joint family had certain advantages. Since all members lived together, it was very easy to take care of the aged and the infirm. They commanded respect and shared major family

Figure 5.7

Number of Members in the Respondents' Family

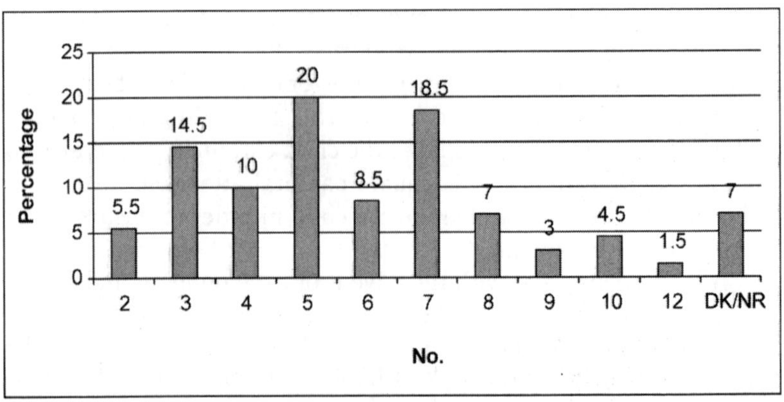

decisions. The child, on the other hand, grew up in an atmosphere of warmth and affection, which are prerequisites for the growth and development of its personality.

The high percentage of five-member families (21.5%) have a nuclear family setting, which proves that large family in a nuclear setting has a negative effect on delinquency. This could be due to less parental supervision leading to more strain and increased exposure to delinquent peers. There are also situations where children have been running away from homes because of the deprivation of adequate care, love, and affection and the high degree of exploitation they experienced. These children again fall in the vulnerability trap, as children on the street, children of the street, abandoned children, or children working as child labourers to eke out a living.

Parents' Occupation and Income

There is no doubt that a number of delinquent acts are committed because of family conditions arising out of economic deprivation. The economic condition of a family is dependent upon the occupation of the father and the mother.

Table 5.4

Occupation of Respondents' Father

Type of Occupation	*Frequency*	*Percentage*
Unemployed	8	4
Daily Wage Worker	29	14.5
Artisan (Electrician, etc.)	26	13
Shopkeeper/Shop Owner	29	14.5
Self-employed	9	4.5
Farmer	20	10
Domestic Worker	3	1.5
Vendor	10	5
Any Other	26	13
Total	160	80
Dead/No Response	40	20
	200	100

In the present study, the influence of economic conditions was significant. As shown in Table 5.4 regarding their fathers' occupation, 4% reported unemployed fathers, 14.5% daily wage earners, 14.5% shopkeepers or small shop owners, and 1.5% domestic workers.

As seen in Table 5.4 majority of mothers were unemployed and were housewives (35.7%). Of the remaining numbers, 14.3% worked as domestic help and 7.1% were daily wage earners.

Table 5.5

Occupation of Respondents' Mother

Type of Employment	*Frequency*	*Percentage*
Unemployed	71	35.7
Daily Wage Worker	14	7.1
Artisan (Electrician, etc.)	3	1.4
Shopkeeper/Shop Owner	14	7.1
Self-employed	3	1.4
Farmer	9	4.3
Domestic Worker	29	14.3
Vendor	17	8.6
Any Other	3	1.4
Total	163	81.4
Dead/No Response	37	18.6
	200	100

Regarding family income of respondents, 106 responses were received. The remaining 94 respondents either did not know their family income or did not respond to the question. Out of 106 respondents only 6 (5.7%) had a family income of more than ₹ 5,000 per month, and the remaining 94.3% had a monthly income below ₹ 4000. So one can see that poverty is also a crucial possible factor of social delinquency. Poverty creates a feeling of helplessness and forces the child to indulge in criminal activities. Obviously, if a child does not have means to ensure the survival of herself and her family she will resort to other illegitimate means of ensuring the same. Poverty also leads to broken homes and families, which results in the breakdown of joint family system and social values; this in turn leads to lack of control giving rise to delinquency.[23] Merton talks about the inadequate means of attaining social goals as a factor of delinquency. In India, most of the crimes committed by children are due to hunger and utter poverty.[24]

Table 5.6

Family's Monthly Income in Rupees

Income in ₹	*Frequency*	*Percentage*	*Valid Percentage*
Up to 1,000	17	8.6	16
1,000–2,000	23	11.4	21.7
2,000–3,000	14	7.1	13.2
3,000–4,000	20	10	18.9
4,000–5,000	26	12.9	24.5
5,000 onwards	6	2.9	5.7
Total	106	53	100
Don't Know/No Response	94	47	
Total	200	100	

Parental occupation and earnings have an important bearing on the way children are brought up. Parents struggling for sustenance are frustrated, which manifests in unkind or vicious behaviour toward children. Thus, parents with higher incomes are likely to provide a better standard of living for children. Child labour, a direct marker of child abuse, is generally prevalent in low-income families.

Parental Attitude toward the Delinquent Child

In most cases of delinquency, the common feature is the lack of communication between parents and the children, and parents remain clueless about child's delinquent behaviour up until the time is it is too late, such as children running away. Parents do not speak with their children to get them to open up and communicate their problems, whereas children may not say so explicitly but always expect their parents to support them and understand their needs, and when that doesn't happen it leads to children resorting to deviant behaviour.

Our findings show shows that 29% of the total sample respondents (N = 200) felt that their parents should understand why they indulged in delinquent acts, 4% said that their parents should allow them to study, and another 4% wanted their parents to forgive them. A large number, 21% said, that they do not expect their parents to understand why they had become delinquent.

Despite all that had happened 103 respondents out of the total sample (N = 200) expressed their desire to return home. The remaining 77 respondents said that they do not want to go back to

Figure 5.8

Reasons for Not Wanting to Go Back to Family

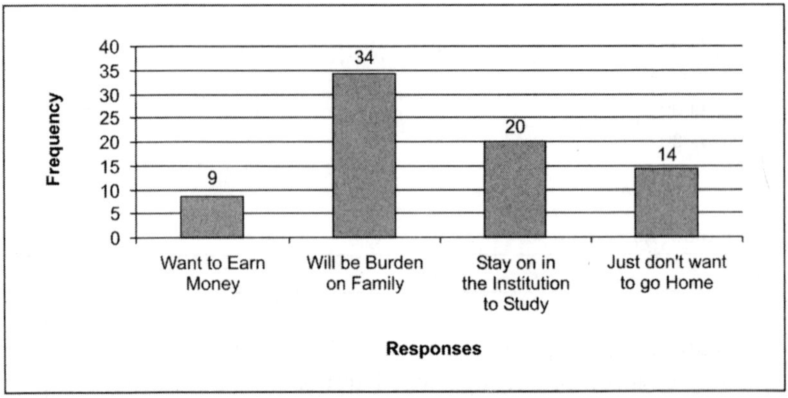

their home. The reasons given for such a decision ranged from desire for earning money to having a feeling that they would be a burden on their parents (Figure 5.8).

Table 5.7

Child's Expectations of Her Parents about What They Should Do about Her Delinquent Acts

	Expectations	*Frequency*	*Percentage*
Valid	Parents should understand	57	29
	Not understood by parents	43	21
	Parents should stop fighting with her	3	1
	Allow her to study	9	4
	Expected the family to support her	9	4
	They should forgive me now	9	4
	Can't say/don't know	71	36
		200	100

The respondents were also asked about their expectations from the parents in case the child returned to their respective homes. Responses received have been elicited in Figure 5.9. As seen in Figure 5.9, out of the total sample size (N = 200), 41% wished that they could be accepted back by the parents, 34% felt that the parents

Figure 5.9

Expectations from Parents in Case They Return

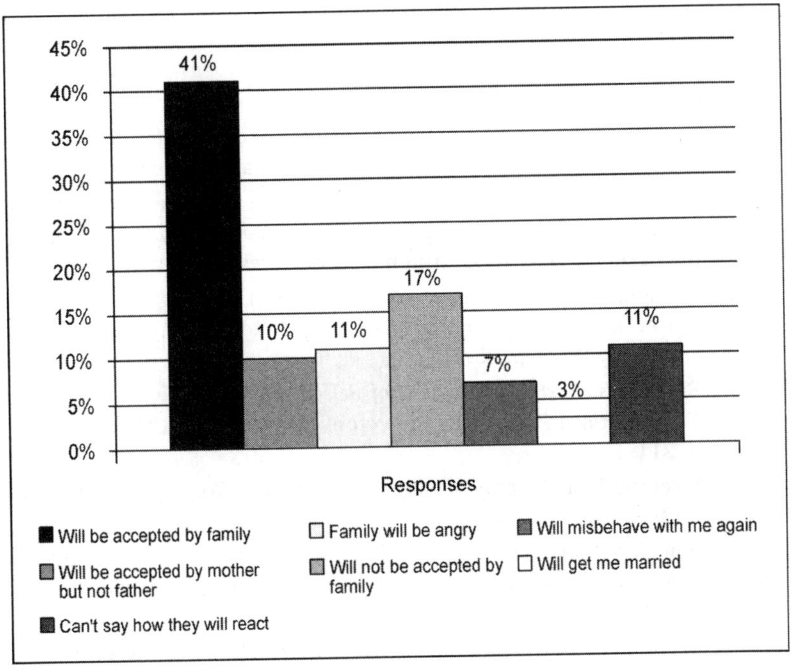

would never accept them now, 14% feared that their parents would misbehave with them, and 23% had no idea about what to expect from their parents.

The analysis of the above data shows that children want their parents to understand and accept them. Some of them however felt that it was better to stay in the institution than to return to their families. They did not want to go back to the same circumstances and also felt they will not be accepted back by the society. They were found to be very upset from the society's reaction and parental attitude and wished that the society would understand they even they may have aspirations and have the right to get what they wanted. Since the circumstances to fulfil these rights were not in their favour they had to act out to forcefully fulfil their aspirations.

The causes and conditions for girls to take up acts of delinquency are usually found at each level of the social structure, including society as a whole, social institution, social groups and organizations, and interpersonal relationships. The child's delinquent act is fostered by a wide range of factors, the most important of which are described in the next chapter.

Notes

1. Hartjen, C.A. and Kethineni, S. (1996), *Comparative Delinquency: India and the United States*, London, Taylor and Francis, p. 150.
2. Vicentnathan, S.G. (2006), Juvenile Justice in India. In *Delinquency and Juvenile Justice System in the Non-Western World* (ed. P.C. Friday and X. Ren), New York, Criminal Justice Press, p. 31.
3. Erikson, E. (1979), Report to Vikram: Further Perspectives on Life Cycle. In S. Kakar (ed.), *Identity and Adulthood*, Delhi, Oxford University Press, p. 25.
4. Roland, A. (1988), *In Search of Self in India and Japan: Towards a Cross-Cultural Psychology*, Princeton, NJ, Princeton University Press, p. 211.
5. Vicentnathan, Juvenile Justice in India, New York, Criminal Justice Press, p. 32.
6. Vincentnathan, S.G. (1992), The Social Construction of Order and Disorder in Two South Indian Communities, *Journal of Legal Pluralism*, 32, 86.
7. Singh, R. (1990), *The Womb of Mind: A Sociological Exploration of the Status-Experience of Women in Delhi*, New Delhi, Vikas Publishing, p. 50.
8. Ibid., p. 109.
9. Mines, M. (1988), Conceptualizing the Person: Hierarchical Society and Individual Autonomy in India, *American Anthropologist*, 90, 568–579.
10. United Nations Department of Economic and Social Affairs (2004), *Juvenile Delinquency, World Youth Report 2003: A Global Situation of Young People*, New York, United Nations Publication, p. 194.
11. Haberfeld, Y., Menaria, R.K., Sahoo, B.B., and Vyas, R.N. (1999), Seasonal Migration of Rural Labour in India, *Population Research and Policy Review*, 18(4), 73–89.
12. Sagade, J. (2005), *Child Marriage in India: Socio-legal and Human Rights Dimension*, New York, Oxford University Press, p. 257.
13. Dumont, L. (1970), *Homo Hierarchicus*, Chicago, University of Chicago Press, p. 9.

14. Zezulka-Mailloux, G. and Gifford, J. (2003), *Culture + The State*, Edmonton, AB, Canada, CRC, p. 153.
15. Ramachandran, V. (2004), *Gender and Social Equity in Primary Education: Hierarchies of Access*, New Delhi, Sage, pp. 44–48.
16. http://7thsurvey.ncert.nic.in/
17. Ramachandran, *Gender and Social Equity*, p. 44.
18. Hartjen and Kethineni, *Comparative Delinquency*, p. 149.
19. Ibid.
20. Beteille, A. (1964), Family and Social Change in India and South Asian Countries, *The Economic Weekly*, 16, p. 239.
21. Singh, *The Womb of Mind*, p.49.
22. Sharma, R.K. (1996), *Fundamentals of Sociology*, New Delhi, Atlantic, pp. 241–242.
23. Clough, P., Garner, P., Yuen, F., and Pardeck, J.T. (2005), *Handbook of Emotional and Behavioural Difficulties*, London, Sage, pp. 175–176.
24. Vincentnathan, S.G. (1985), *Caste, Class and Crime: India and the United States. Comparative Social Research, Vol. 3: Deviance*, Greenwich, CT, Jai Press, p. 114.

6

Determinants of Female Juvenile Delinquency

Juvenile delinquency among girls is an important social problem. The number of crimes has increased and the problem is being widely discussed. However, the discussions most often concentrate merely on the fact itself and its scale and tend to forget the factors that determine the situation. To better understand why young girls commit acts of delinquency it is essential to know the factors that determine juvenile delinquency.

This chapter discusses the main factors that influence the delinquent behaviour of young girls. Yet it does not mean that only these factors are important. It is also noteworthy to mention that the reasons analysed in this chapter cannot be construed as those that necessarily lead to delinquency. On one hand, all girls affected by these factors do not necessarily become delinquents; on the other, there are girls who become delinquents even though they haven't experienced such an influence. The presence of the factors determining delinquent behaviour only indicates the higher probability of delinquency.

Before discussing the factors, it is important to note that the sociocultural background of these girls is rather complicated and diverse. Respectively, the factors that lead to delinquent behaviour work in a complex way and they have to be linked to the sociodemographic background of the respondents which has been discussed in detail in the previous chapter.

We need to keep in mind that no single path leads to trouble; there are multiple, composite ways of reaching there even if one is not trying to. A combination of factors may collide just as a girl is hitting adolescence, leaving her at risk of delinquency.

Factors Prompting Female Juvenile Delinquency

A multitude of factors contribute to the understanding of what leads someone to engage in delinquent behaviour. The theories that attempt to explain or predict delinquency mention and examine many different *societal factors* or units within society that is applicable within the theories. Families, peers, schools, and socio-economic status are all social factors that are examined in many of the causal theories. socio-economic instability is often linked to persistent unemployment and low income among the youth, which can increase the likelihood of their involvement in criminal activity. Families are important to consider when trying explaining juvenile delinquency. The family unit is crucial to a child's development and healthy upbringing. In addition, much of what a child learns is through their family or guardians.

A criminal parent can *teach* their child adverse lessons about life when their child views or witnesses their parent's delinquent behaviour. Studies show that children who receive adequate parental supervision are less likely to engage in criminal activities. Dysfunctional family settings—characterized by conflict, inadequate parental control, weak internal linkages and integration, and premature autonomy—are closely associated with juvenile delinquency. Children in disadvantaged families that have few opportunities for legitimate employment and face a higher risk of social exclusion are overrepresented among offenders.

The plight of ethnic minorities and migrants, including displaced persons and refugees in certain parts of the world, is especially distressing. The countries in transition are facing particular challenges in this respect, with the associated insecurity and turmoil contributing to an increase in the number of children and juveniles neglected by their parents and suffering abuse and violence at home.

Peers can also teach an adolescent or child criminal behaviour just as the family member can. Family members and peers can also cause delinquent patterns of behaviour by labelling their child as *delinquent*. This is somewhat like "if the shoe fits, wear it" saying. If a child feels as though he or she is viewed as delinquent, then he or she will act as such and find a sense of self-esteem by doing so.

Youth policies seldom reflect an understanding of the role of the peer group as an institution of socialization. Membership in a delinquent gang, like membership in any other natural grouping, can be part of the process of becoming an adult. Through such primary associations, an individual acquires a sense of safety and security, develops knowledge of social interaction, and can demonstrate such qualities as loyalty or leadership. In "adult" society, factors such as social status, private welfare, race and ethnicity are of great value; however, all members of adolescent groups are essentially in an equal position and have similar opportunities for advancement in the hierarchical structure. In these groups well-being depends wholly on personal qualities such as strength, will, and discipline.

Quite often delinquent groups can counterbalance or compensate for the imperfections of family and school. A number of studies have shown that juvenile gang members consider their group a family. For adolescents constantly facing violence, belonging to a gang can provide protection within the neighbourhood. In some areas those who are not involved in gangs continually face the threat of assault, oppression, harassment, or extortion on the street or at school. If a juvenile has many *ties or bonds* to members in society, he or she is less likely to make the choice to commit a crime for fear of ridicule, embarrassment, or scorn from those they associate with.

The demographic characteristics of a person's living environment can also be a contributing factor to criminal patterns of behaviour. Adverse living conditions and a crime-prone neighbourhood can lead to criminal activity.

Cultural factors also exert a very real influence, probably greater than it is realized. The very definition of criminality is culturally determined, varying form one society to another. Murder in defence of family honour may be condoned or condemned; the taking of someone's life is not everywhere or always a crime; the same is true for alcoholism or suicide. Delinquency in any community will be influenced also by the patterns of behavioural characteristics of the police, the members of the Juvenile Justice Board, and all other officials with whom the young offenders come into contact. Both initial reactions and recidivism may vary considerably according to whether "they" are regarded as friends or foes.

The stress on cultural factors in the etiology of delinquency makes the assumption that this form of behaviour may be *learned.*[1] Imitation of others is rarely a blind process. We imitate because we think we can gain something, either materially or in terms of acceptance or prestige, or because imitation has been a rewarding experience in the past. All these factors may play a part in the learning of delinquency. The fact remains that such learning is usually limited to the patterns of behaviour already present in our social environment. Delinquent behaviour often occurs in social settings in which the norms for acceptable behaviour have broken down. Under such circumstances many of the common rules that deter people from committing socially unacceptable acts may lose their relevance for some members of society. They respond to the traumatizing and destructive changes in the social reality by engaging in rebellious, deviant, or even criminal activities.

The contradiction between idealized and socially approved goals and the sometimes limited real-life opportunities to achieve them legally creates a sense of frustration in many young people. A criminal career becomes one form of addressing this contradiction. One of the reasons for delinquent behaviour is therefore an excessive focus on proposed goals (achieving success) coupled with insufficient means to achieve them.

Another factor leading to delinquency is *neglect*. The neglected and the delinquent children cannot be regarded as two exclusive and separate entities, and, hence, they need to be considered together. This is why the Juvenile Justice Act/System cater to both of them with same priority. The analyses of the various causative situations indicate that the factors for neglect and delinquency are mostly common. In most of the crimes, neglected children turn delinquent on account of various socio-economic and psychological reasons. Poverty, broken homes, urbanization leading to migration, breakdown of social values and joint family system, atrocities by parents or guardians, faulty educational system, influence of media besides the specific reasons of slums, and a variety of other conditions explain the phenomena of juvenile delinquency.

The neglect of children by their parents, family, society, and the nation create a detrimental effect on their growth and personality. The unhealthy living conditions and abuse and exploitation of children, inevitably, result in delinquency. To that extent, delinquency must be considered a direct offshoot of neglect.

Media too plays a very crucial role in juvenile delinquency. Television and movies have popularized the "cult of heroes," which promotes justice through the physical elimination of enemies. Many researchers have concluded that young people who watch violence tend to behave more aggressively or violently, particularly when provoked. This is mainly characteristic of 8–12-year-old boys, who are more vulnerable to such influences.

Media brings an individual to violence in three ways.[2] First, movies that demonstrate violent acts excite spectators, and the aggressive energy can then be transferred to everyday life, pushing an individual to engage in physical activity on the streets. This type of influence is temporary, lasting from several hours to several days. Second, television can portray ordinary daily violence committed by parents or peers (the imposition of penalties for failing to study or for violations of certain rules or norms of conduct). It is impossible to find television shows that do not portray such patterns of violence, because viewer approval of this type of programming has ensured its perpetuation. As a result, children are continually exposed to the use of violence in different situations—and the number of violent acts on television appears to be increasing. Third, violence depicted in the media is unreal and has a surrealistic quality; wounds bleed less, and the real pain and agony resulting from violent actions are very rarely shown, so the consequences of violent behaviour often seem negligible. Over time, television causes a shift in the system of human values and indirectly leads children to view violence as a desirable and even courageous way of reestablishing justice. However, it seems that the effect of media is more on boys than on girls when it comes to taking up acts of juvenile delinquency.

Each year the Federal Bureau of Investigation (FBI) compiles crime data from over 10,000 law enforcement agencies in the United States and publishes these figures in *Crime in the United States: Uniform Crime Reports*. The report includes information on characteristics of persons under the age of 18 arrested for a variety of offences. From the 2003 arrest figures of delinquency derived from statistics maintained by law enforcement officers, the most obvious finding is that far fewer girls than boys are arrested for delinquent behaviour. Although 378,895 arrests of girls occurred in 2003, arrests of males outnumber arrests of female by more than a 2:1 ratio, meaning that more than two boys are arrested for every girl.

Table 6.1

Arrests of Persons under 18, by Sex, 2003

	Male		*Female*	
	Number	*Percent*	*Number*	*Percent*
Total	9,10,981	100	3,78,895	100
Index crimes				
Homicide	560	*	59	*
Forcible rape	2,366	*	49	*
Robbery	13,262	1.5	1,383	*
Aggravated assault	26,923	3.0	8,298	2.2
Burglary	44,700	5.0	6,203	1.6
Larceny-theft	1,19,520	13.1	78,703	20.8
Motor vehicle theft	20,114	2.2	4,257	1.1
Arson	4,089	0.4	544	*
Total violent	43,111	4.7	9,789	2.6
Total property	1,88,423	20.7	89,707	23.6
Total index	2,31,534	25.4	99,496	26.2
Part II Offences				
Other assaults	91,865	10.1	44,043	11.6
Forgery/counterfeiting	1,813	*	1,043	*
Fraud	2,817	*	1,519	*
Embezzlement	433	*	296	*
Stolen property	12,400	1.4	2,202	*
Vandalism	54,957	6.0	8,766	2.3
Weapons	20,230	2.2	2,343	*
Prostitution	232	*	656	*
Other sex offences	9,916	1.1	1,034	*
Drugs	87,805	9.6	18,488	4.9
Gambling	306	*	14	*
Offences against the family	2,330	*	1,438	*
DUI (driving under influence)	9,200	1.0	2,295	*
Liquor laws	51,646	5.7	28,348	7.5
Drunkenness	7,841	0.9	2,335	*
Disorderly conduct	73,573	8.1	33,301	8.8
Vagrancy	1,044	*	353	*
Curfew and loitering	60,165	6.6	26,084	6.9
Runaway	30,724	3.4	43,949	11.6
All other offences	1,60,165	17.6	60,983	16.1

*Less than 0.1%.

Source: Federal Bureau of Investigation, *Uniform Crime Reports*, 2003.

Arrest statistics also can provide a portrait of the character of both female and male official delinquency. The distribution of arrests within each sex cohort (Table 6.1) shows that most offences for which both boys and girls are arrested are relatively minor and that many do not have a clearly defined victim. For example, larceny-theft dominates both boys' (13.1%) and girls' (20.8%) delinquency.

Status offences play a more significant role in girls' arrests than in boys' arrests. The status offences of running away and curfew/loitering accounted for about 19% of all girls' arrests in 2003, but only 10% of boys' arrests. Arrests of girls for one status offence alone, *running away*, account for almost 12% of all girls arrests, compared with only less than 4% of boys' arrests. Both girls and boys are arrested in large numbers for alcohol-related offences, but burglary and vandalism (which account for about 11% of boys' offences) are relatively unimportant in the delinquency of girls (accounts for only 4% of their arrests).

Generally, official delinquency is dominated by less serious offences, and this is particularly true of female delinquency. A ranking of offences that account for the greatest number of girls and boys arrests over time (Table 6.2) clearly shows this. For the past two decades, boys were most likely to have been arrested for larceny-theft and "all other" offences. Larceny-theft ranks first among girls' arrests for both 1994 and 2003, accounting for a quarter of all girls' arrests in 1994 and just over one-fifth in 2003. *Running away* also dominates girls arrests, constituting just under one-fifth in 1994 and about one out of six in 2003.

In recent years, drug offences have jumped into the top five for boys arrests, accounting for just under 10% in 2003. Thus, running away and larceny-theft continue to dominate girls' delinquency-related arrests, as has been the case since 1970, and together these two offences have accounted for more than one-third (44% in 1994) of all women's arrests. Arrests for disorderly conduct emerged in the top five for boys for the first time in 2003, while for girls this offence was number five for both years.

As stated earlier, girls predominantly come in contact with the juvenile justice system for nonviolent crimes. These offences are activities like running away from home, being defiant, or being beyond parental control and are often called status offences.[7] Even in the present study the data collected from the 200 respondents who were interviewed from both the homes revealed broadly three

Table 6.2

Rank Order of Arrests for Juveniles, 1994 and 2003

Male		*Female*	
1994	*2003*	*1994*	*2003*
Larceny-theft (17.8)	All others (17.6)	Larceny-theft (24.8)	Larceny-theft (20.8)
All others[3] (14.9)	Larceny-theft (13.1)	Runaways (18.9)	All others (16.1)
Other assaults (7.7)	Other assaults (10.1)	All others (13.3)	Runaway (11.6)
Vandalism (7.3)	Drugs (9.6)	Other assaults (8.3)	Other assaults (11.6)
Drugs (6.7)	Disorderly conduct (8.1)	Disorderly conduct (5.8)	Disorderly conduct (8.8)

	Male		*Female*	
	1994	*2003*	*1994*	*2003*
Arrests for serious violent offences[4]	5.9	4.7	2.8	2.6
Arrests for all violent offences[5]	13.5	14.8	11.1	14.2
Arrests for status offences[6]	10.0	10.0	25.1	18.5

Source: Federal Bureau of Investigation, *Uniform Crime Reports*, 2003.

Figure 6.1

Reasons for Respondents' Entry into the Juvenile Justice System

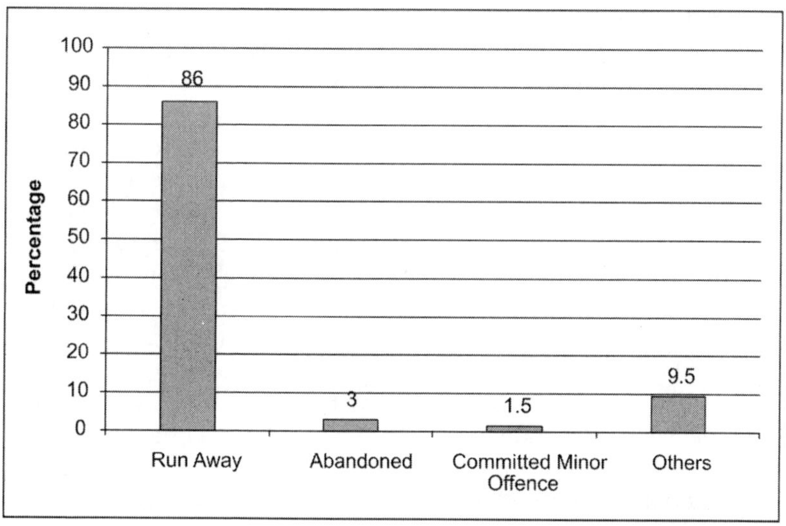

reasons—running away (172 respondents), minor thefts (3 respondents), or abandonment by family (6 respondents)—that have played a major role in bringing girls into the juvenile justice system. Keeping in mind the high percentage of girls running away from home this chapter will focus more on the reasons behind running away while briefly discussing minor thefts and abandonment.

Reasons for Respondents' Entry into the Juvenile System

Minor Thefts

Overall, girls' delinquency is a smaller problem than male delinquency in terms of numbers. They commit far fewer crimes than boys. In the year 2000, the ratio of girls apprehended to that of boys was 1:3 under IPC.[8] The number of girls apprehended in 2000 (4,128) declined by 6.1% when compared with figures for 1999. Girls who break the law may not be perceived as a danger to society because, traditionally, they have come into contact with the juvenile justice system for nonviolent offences, which include minor thefts. Even in the present study's sample of respondents, girls apprehended for minor crimes was merely 1.5% of the total sample.

Abandonment

There are more than 11 million abandoned children in India,[9] where a growing number of newborn babies are being dumped anonymously in cots placed outside orphanages in an initiative to deter infanticide. About 90% of those abandoned are girls whose poor young mothers cannot afford to keep them. They face a bleak future as beggars, prostitutes, or menial labourers if families cannot be found for them.

Although the Government in India has woken up to "a national crisis," the response has been to condone the abandonment of female babies. "If you don't want a girl, leave her to us," Renuka Chowdhury, India's Minister of State for Women and Child Development, said recently. The government "will bring up your children. Don't kill them." The announcement was a desperate response to stem India's dramatic deficit of women. In the West, women outnumber men by at least 3%. India has almost 8% more men than women.

A son, by contrast, is seen an asset to his family. Even leaving aside the wealth his bride will bring, a boy will retain the family and the caste name. He will also inherit the property, which is seen on the part of parents as a way to ensure they are cared in old age. Indians, therefore, have come to view the girl child as a burden, an investment without return. A favourite Hindi saying translates as "Having a girl is to plant a seed in someone else's garden." One of the results is that women themselves face immense family pressure to get rid of the girl in their womb. Feminists in India argue that criminalizing women who have got rid of the girl in their womb is to ignore how fiercely patriarchal the value system is. As some see it, a woman who participates in the killing of her own child is actually denying her own self-value and should not be punished but be treated with concern.

In developing countries, the birth of a girl causes great upheaval for poor families. When there is barely enough food to survive, any child puts a strain on a family's resources, but the monetary drain caused due to a daughter is realized even more severely, especially in regions where dowry is practiced. The dowry practice makes the prospect of having a girl even more distasteful to poor families. It also puts young women in danger: A new bride is at the mercy of her in-laws should they decide her dowry is too small. National Crime Records Bureau's Crime in India, 2005, estimates that there are 6,787 dowry deaths and 58,319 cases of torture reported in the year 2005.

In the sample, there were six girls who were deliberately lost by their parents or their guardians for the despicable yet very harsh Indian reality being that these girls would grow up to be a burden on them, a burden in many cases which their supposed caretakers could not, literally, afford. But why the girl child in almost every case when they might have over five sons? Because society has declared that the girl child is the burden to them. She will bring no monetary respite to family in its hard times; instead, the dowry issue will only take away from the hard-earned money of the family. Again, why? Because she will not be *allowed* to work or make something of herself; it's not even an option, so what if she might be the most talented among all her siblings? Being abandoned at a most vulnerable age of her childhood can be the most devastating and scarring experience that could take an entire lifetime to correct.

Run-away Phenomenon

The relationship between girl's problems and her attempts to escape victimization by running away are unique aspects of girls' interaction with the system. All of the girls from the present study's sample who ran away ($N = 172$) from home were reported to have taken such a step because of neglect ($N = 26$), family turbulence ($N = 60$), and physical and sexual abuse ($N = 86$) and considered their running

Figure 6.2

Reasons for Running Away from Home

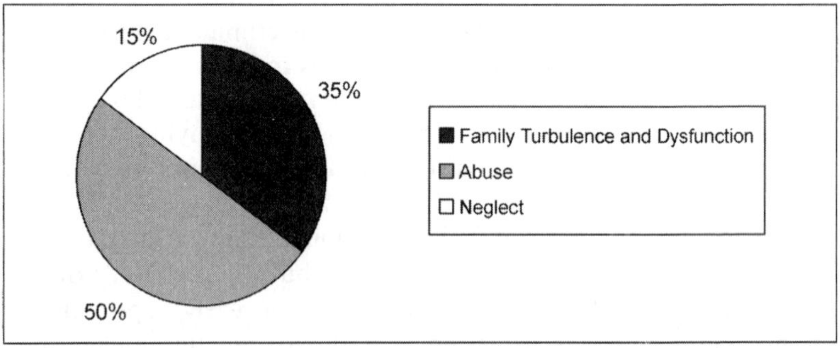

away as an act of rebellion against their situation at that point of time (Figure 6.2).

A multitude of factors exist that contribute to the understanding of what leads someone to engage in delinquent behaviour. Several specific factors put girls at a greater risk of coming in direct contact with the juvenile justice system by running away. Seldom do these factors occur in isolation. More typically, risk factors are interconnected like a web; with each risk potentially both cause and consequences of the other. Risk factors of special concern to girls in the present context include:

Family Turbulence and Dysfunction

The family unit is a crucial body for the child development and healthy upbringing. In addition, whatever a child learns is mainly through their family or guardians. The family and the surrounding of the children is the main cause of their delinquent behaviour.

Studies show that children who receive adequate parental supervision are less likely to engage in criminal activities. Dysfunctional family settings—characterized by conflict, inadequate parental control, weak internal linkages and integration, and premature autonomy—are closely associated with juvenile delinquency. Children in disadvantaged families that have few opportunities for legitimate employment and face a higher risk of social exclusion are overrepresented among offenders. The plight of ethnic minorities and migrants, including displaced persons and refugees in certain parts of the world, is especially distressing. The countries in transition are facing particular challenges in this respect, with the associated insecurity and turmoil contributing to an increase in the number of children and juveniles neglected by their parents and suffering abuse and violence at home.

The family as a social institution is currently undergoing substantial changes; its form is diversifying with, for example, the increase in one-parent families and non-marital unions. The absence of fathers in many low-income families can lead boys to seek patterns of masculinity in delinquent groups of peers. These groups in many respects substitute for the family, define male roles, and contribute to the acquisition of such attributes as cruelty, strength, excitability, and anxiety.

The importance of family well-being is becoming increasingly recognized. Success in school depends greatly on whether parents have the capacity to provide their children with "starting" opportunities (including the resources to buy books and manuals and pay for studies). Adolescents from low-income families often feel excluded. To raise their self-esteem and improve their status they may choose to join a juvenile delinquent group. These groups provide equal opportunities to everyone, favourably distinguishing themselves from school and family, where positions of authority are occupied by adults.

A notable observation from the sample of the present study was that family fragmentation and dysfunction was one of the factors that

Figure 6.3

Family Turbulence and Dysfunction

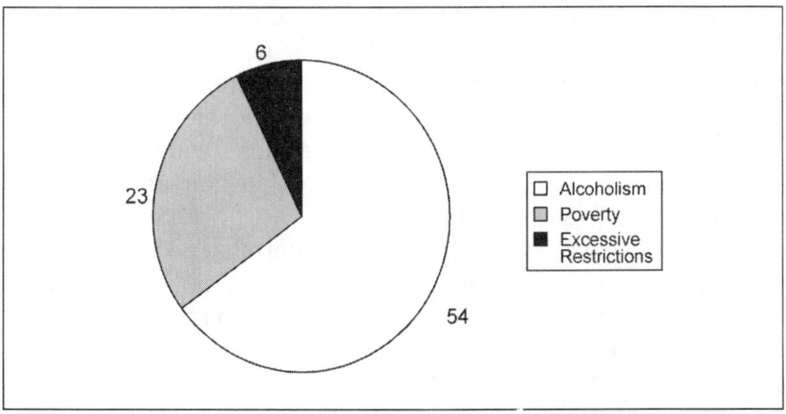

provoked these young minds to take up such drastic steps in their life. A total of 54 respondents said that family fragmentation and dysfunction was the reason behind them leaving their homes.

The common family problems were alcoholism of parents (N = 54), lack of freedom to girls (N = 6), and poverty and socio-economic instability resulting in financial crisis (N = 23).

Poverty in family of origin was found to have major influence on their decision of running away. The reasons could be that overly stressed parents experiencing financial stain (possibly working multiple jobs) may be unable to provide adequate nurturance of monitoring of the child's behaviour. Most of the official statistics indicate that delinquency rates are higher in inner-city, high-crime, and poverty-stricken areas than in suburban and wealthier areas. According to Janice Joseph (1995),[10] number of sociologists postulated that socio-economic status was a major factor contributing to delinquency.

However, later researchers suggested that socio-economic status was a determining factor in whether a juvenile becomes part of the official statistics rather than in whether a particular juvenile will become delinquent. Police may devote more resources and time to lower socio-economic areas, and, consequently, the apprehension and arrest rates may be higher in these areas. This relationship may also be explained by police discrimination whereby police may be more likely to arrest and apprehend lower-class juveniles more often than those from middle and upper classes. However, the class–delinquency relationship remains one of the most controversial phenomena in criminology.

Another common family problem found in the present study was *alcoholism or substance abuse by parents*. A number of researches show that children of substance-abusing parents are more likely to experience abuse—physical, sexual, or emotional—or neglect than children in non–substance-abusing households.[11] Parents who abuse substances are less likely to be able to function effectively in a parental role. This can be due to:

1. Impairments (both physical and mental) that occur while under the influence of alcohol or other drugs.
2. Expenditure of often limited household resources on purchasing alcohol or other drugs.
3. Time spent seeking out drugs.
4. Time spent using alcohol or other drugs.

The basic needs of children, including nutrition, supervision, and nurturing, often go unmet due to parental substance abuse, resulting in neglect. In addition, families in which one or both parents abuse substances, and particularly families with an addicted parent, often experience a number of other problems including mental illness, unemployment, high levels of stress, and impaired family functioning, all of which can put children at risk for abuse. According to the U.S. Department of Health and Human Services, 1999, maltreated children of substance-abusing parents are more likely to have poorer physical, intellectual, social, and emotional capacities and are at a greater risk of developing substance abuse problems themselves.

Substance-abusing parents may divert money that is needed for basic necessities, in order to buy drugs and alcohol. Parent's substance abuse may interfere with their ability to maintain employment, further limiting the family's resources. Substance-abusing behaviours may expose children to criminal behaviours and dangerous people. Substance-abusing parents may be emotionally or physically unavailable and not able to properly supervise their children, risking accidental injuries. Children living with substance-abusing parents are more likely to become intoxicated themselves, either deliberately, by passive inhalation, or by accidental ingestion. Parent's severe drug use can interfere with their ability to provide the consistent nurturing and caregiving that promotes children's development and self-esteem.[12]

Neglect

The neglected children and the delinquent children cannot be regarded as two exclusive and separate entities, and, hence, they need to be considered together. This is why the Juvenile Justice Act/System cater to both categories of children with the same level of priority. The analyses of the various causative situations indicate that the factors for neglect and delinquency are mostly common. Unfortunately, the rejection of the girl child happens even before her birth: prenatal sex determination tests followed by quick abortions eliminate thousands of female fetuses before they can become daughters. This can be attributed to the preference for male children and the presumed burden of having to pay high dowries at marriages for daughters. Many female children are killed in the womb or at birth or through neglect of physical and medical needs during childhood.

A midwife in Bihar, for instance, regularly killed female infants upon request of parents, which made it easier than killing them later. She charged ₹ 40 for delivering a baby, and it if were a girl, an additional ₹ 40 to snap the spinal cord and declare the infant stillborn.[13] In 1997, there were on an average 105 female infants killed every month in Dharmapuri District of Tamil Nadu.[14] Death of females due to murder and neglect has created a gross imbalance in India's sex ratio. According to the 2001 Census, there were 933 females in India to every 1,000 males, and for the youngest age group, birth to age 6; there were only 927 females to every 1000 males, indicating a worsening trend.

Those girls who manage to survive till birth and beyond find that the dice is heavily loaded against them in a world that denies them equal access to food, health, care, education, employment, and simple human dignity.

According to widely accepted criteria on status assessment, there has been a deterioration of the relative status of women in post independent India. Indian women, though not a minority numerically, are acquiring the features of a minority in terms of enjoying lower class, status and political power.[15] In spite of the constitutional provisions to ensure equal rights to life for women in India, the alarming drop in their numbers vis-à-vis the growth rate of male population is clearly a cause of the debilitating disadvantages that women experience on several fronts—life expectancy, literacy rate, internal migration rates, and economic participation—which leads to a tremendous sense of insecurity and helplessness on the part of women. Girl's enrollment in schools is much lower than that of boys. Although women theoretically have access to all avenues of learning and public appointments in India, the ground reality proves otherwise—only a small percentage of women are either highly qualified or hold a top position in a public or private organization. Members of a girl's family, both men and women, socialize her in such a way as to ensure her transformation into a docile, submissive, and subordinate being. Amniocentises in the urban areas whose sole purpose is to determine foetus's sex, female infanticide among poor agricultural labour families, widespread harassment of brides, and an increasing number of dowry deaths among the middle and upper classes speak all too clearly of women's predicament.

The report of the Committee on the Status of Women in India contains statistical data on important social and economic variables affecting the personal development and patterns of social behaviours of women in India.[16] Nevertheless, it couldn't succeed in touching upon the subjective dimension of the status of women, which to a considerable extent determines their perceptions. This report documents a decline over the years in the actual position of women relative to men: a rising life expectancy versus a persisting and widening gap between male and female life expectancy; a decline in dowry practice versus the persistent notion that a woman's place is in the home; absolute decline in women's participation in the labour force and in agriculture versus a rising percentage of farm labourers. Since independence, fewer women have become political leaders though voting participation of women has risen. Similarly, there is an absolute rise in the number of illiterate women although the rate of growth in women's education since independence has been described as phenomenal. All of this goes to show that nothing has changed for women; regardless of the positive changes, at times only notional or tokenistic, ushered in by government's initiatives and programmes implemented to empower them, they suffer one way or the other, good times or bad times.

Born into indifference and reared on neglect, the girl child is caught in a web of cultural practices and prejudices that divest her of her individuality and mould her into a submissive, self-sacrificing daughter and wife. Her labour ensures the survival and well-being of her family but robs her not only of her childhood but also of her right to be free of hunger, ignorance, disease, and poverty. In developing countries, the birth of a girl causes great upheaval for poor families. When there is barely enough food to survive, any child puts a strain on family's resources, but the monetary drain caused due to a daughter is viewed an even more severe problem, especially in regions where dowry is practiced. For the same reason, women, particularly the girl child, are considered more of a burden than a boon for the family. The birth of a boy upgrades the social status of the family as boys are considered to be breadwinners.

The dowry practice makes the prospect of having a girl even more terrible to poor families. It also puts young women in danger: A new bride is at the mercy of her in-laws should they decide her dowry is too small. National Crime Records Bureau's Crime in India, 2005, estimates that there were 6,787 dowry deaths and 58,319 cases of torture reported in the year 2005. Sex-selective abortions are even more common than infanticides in India. They are growing ever more frequent as technology makes it simple and cheap to determine a fetus's gender. Either girls are killed in the womb itself or if born are subjected to various forms of discrimination and deprived of their rights to health, nutrition, education, and overall development. An integrated and holistic approach to the girl child's development is essential for the creation of a new environment in which she can be valued and nurtured.

According to P. Kapoor (1995),[17] the human rights of female children in India and elsewhere are guaranteed only on paper and are violated systematically in practice. An equitable and egalitarian world order must be established. A comprehensive campaign is needed that combats gender-based inequalities, discrimination, exploitation, oppression, abuse, violence, inhuman values, and violations of human rights, particularly against the girl child. People must radically change their attitudes and actions toward the girl child. A woman is not a commodity or sex-object but "an equally worthy human being to be loved, respected, and cared for." Strategies that accomplish these ends include the promotion of human and spiritual values of love, compassion, and nonviolence, and discouragement of consumerism and materialism that tie individual perception of self-worth to mere material possession and wealth and not to traits such as altruism and respect for collective goodness and fellow humans that perhaps every individual possesses innately but loses along the way.

Effective education and mass media should counter corruption, dishonesty, selfishness, and inhuman actions. Family structures need to be strengthened and enriched. The abuse of girl child occurs because of the following interrelated factors: entrenched patriarchal value systems, perpetuation of traditions and practices that identify girls as inferior to boys, gender-biased and discriminatory attitude that identifies girl children as a burden or liability and as a sex-object or commodity, and prevalent illiteracy, poverty, and negative parenting lifestyle patterns. Other factors include low status of women, reduction in human and spiritual values, and rise of consumerism and corruption. The issues are many for girls: female infanticide, feticide, lack of social and economic development, burdensome domestic work, early marriage and childbearing, neglect and denial of healthy living conditions, sexual abuse and exploitation, prostitution, rape, and a denial of their right to protection.

The neglect of children by their parents, family, society, and the nation creates a detrimental effect on their growth and personality.

Figure 6.4

Neglect by Family Members

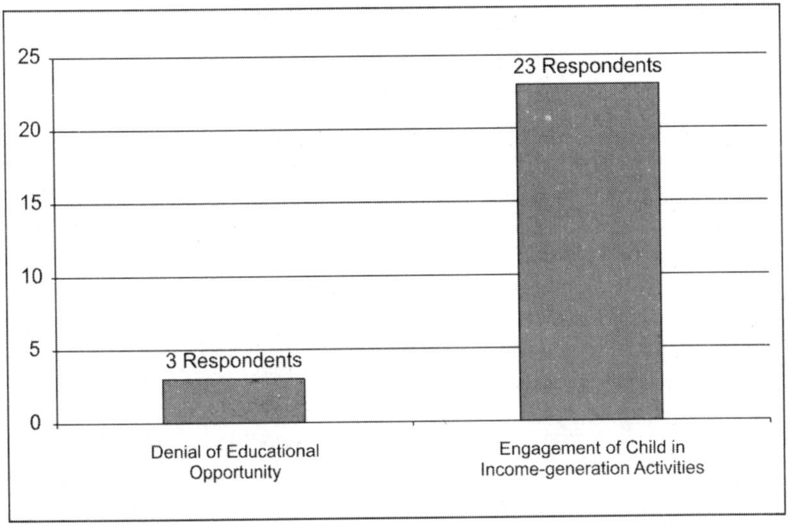

Even in the present study 32.5% (65 girls) of the sample claimed to have felt neglected in some form or the other. The indicators of neglect for the purpose of this study were less attention and less food given to the girl child, asked to leave good food for siblings, more faultfinding, and denial of opportunity.

However, despite being neglected only 26 girls reported to have run away because of neglect from their family members. The indicators of neglect in such cases were lack of education opportunity and engagement of children in income generation activities. Despite the ongoing efforts of the government toward free and compulsory education, children are still not being enrolled in schools and are encouraged by the parents in income generation activities. It is this denial of the "Rights of the Child" as envisaged in the UNCRC that constitutes to the neglect of children.

Abuse and Exploitation

Numerous national studies have found that juvenile girls are much more likely to have been a victim of sexual and/or physical abuse or exploitation than juvenile boys. Most often abuse is perpetrated by family members or close family friends who are perceived as trusted adults; such sexual abuse can have a profound impact on a girl during adolescence, resulting in lessened self-esteem, inability to trust, and other serious concerns. Researches have argued that victimization triggers girls' entry into delinquency as they try to escape abusive environment.[18] Table 6.3 reflects data on crime against girls.

Table 6.3

Crime against Girls in India between 1994 and 1996

Crime classification	*1994*	*1995*	*1996*	*Punishable under Indian Penal Code*
Child rape (up to 16 years)	3986	4067	4083	Section 379 to 379
Kidnapping and abduction	864	726	571	Section 360, 361, 366, 367
Procurement of minor girls	206	107	94	Section 366 A
Selling of girls for prostitution	34	17	6	Section 372
Buying of girls for prostitution	4	19	22	Section 373
Exposure and abandonment	491	570	554	Section 317
Infanticide	131	139	113	Section 315
Foeticide	45	38	39	Section 315 and 316
Child Marriage Restraint Act	53	57	89	

Source: Crime in India, 1996, National Crime Records Bureau, Ministry of Home Affairs.

Adolescent females who are unable to end abuse and crime against them through legal channels often run away and end up on the streets with few legitimate survival options. A similar trend was seen in the present study sample; 69 girls reported to have faced physical abuse and 17 said that were raped by one of the family members and thus they ran away from home (see Figure 6.5).

For example, one of the respondents from the study sample was repeatedly raped by her father for a period of two years and further was subjected to torture and physical abuse by her stepmother. This was the main cause for her rebellion and running away from home. When asked whether she wanted to go back, she said that this act of running away has put a stigma on her and the people around will call her a delinquent, but she does not consider herself to be a delinquent. This life history throws light on the fact that the society tends to castigate girls as delinquents while they actually may not be so. Most of the children were victims of physical abuse. Here it is noteworthy to mention that the extent of physical abuse was so grave that the condition of children in their own family settings was deplorable.

Figure 6.5

Abuse of Respondents by Family Members

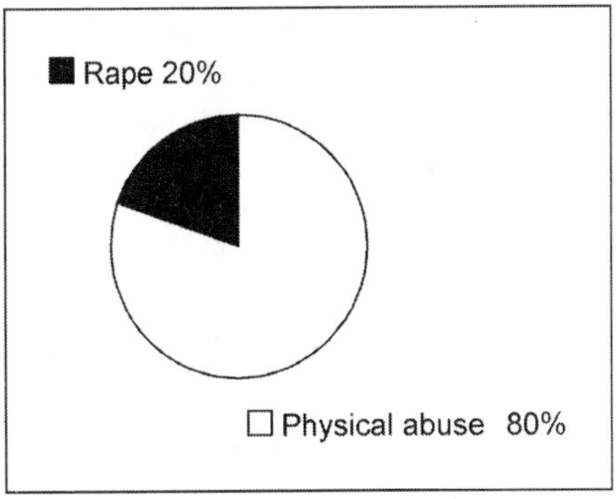

They also felt that due to the financial constraints and lack of support from the parents they will never be able to achieve what they want. The educational status of parents was very poor and also their financial status was not satisfactory. This may be one of the reasons why the parents were behaving in such a non-cooperative manner as a result of which the girls act out from what is expected from them by the society and family.

After interacting with the girls it was found that one of the main reasons for them to adopt delinquent behaviour is physical and sexual abuse and neglect. Most of them run away because of sexual abuse at home. It could be by a family member or a friend, but the punishment for not quietly accepting it as "fate," and choosing instead to escape the torment, society terms these children as *delinquents*, while the real perpetrator and the guilty person goes scot free, leading a guilt-free life. Is that fair? No. But it certainly is reality for these children.

The process of juvenile justice can thus be defined as a dynamic process. It is not just a legal phenomenon with purely legal consequences but is rather a much more complex sociological phenomenon. What we need to understand is that no child actively wants to disobey or violate the law. He or she is forced to do the same. This external force acts upon the child and governs his or her behaviour. The various delinquency theories by and large support the above inference. The researcher too feels after interacting with the delinquents that indeed the social environment in which the offence was committed is very important if we want to ensure that the child is back in the mainstream of society.

It is very simple to send the child to prison and treat him or her like an ordinary criminal. However, the implications of such measures have to be kept in mind; after all, it is the child's future that we would be playing with. There is no denying that a separate juvenile system is essential if our long-term aims are to be achieved. However, what is equally important is to understand how the system works in our daily lives. Is it in accordance to the ideals and substance of the substantive law or does it make it useless and ineffective? What in essence is being said is that the procedural law should ensure that the substantive law is being implemented properly. So there would be no use of acts like Juvenile Justice Act if such acts are not implemented properly.

There is much more to be done for a healthy revival of the delinquent and restoring his or her life to normalcy. The family and cultural support systems have to take up the challenge and fight alongside children to bring justice and peace for the affected children. The problem should be looked from a wider perspective. Issues related to religion, caste, poverty, and deprivation are all interconnected and thus to juvenile delinquency as well. Policies should be made with the active awareness of all these issues. It is a long road to the goal of bringing down the juvenile crime to a minimum in our country, but it is not unachievable. With right approach and attitude it can be achieved. No doubt the juvenile crime rate in our country has declined over the years,[19] but it is still substantial and it must be brought down further.

Case Studies

The following stories are true-life experiences of the girls whom I have interviewed during the data collection for my PhD work. The narrations given by the girls were further corroborated with the official records of the institutions.

Case Number 1

For as long as I can remember my mother and I never got along. We were always fighting and she would beat me up on some pretext or the other. She was very conservative and didn't allow me or my sisters to go out to play, let alone attend school. While she was nice to the other children she was always mean to me. She would tell my siblings to stay away from me and wouldn't allow me to mingle saying I would influence them.

One day while I was washing clothes, my mother and I got into a huge fight. She took the washing bat and beat me with it. I couldn't take it anymore and ran away from home. I went to my maternal uncle's home where I fell in love with a boy. As everyone was opposed to our relationship, we eloped and went to Madras. There too things were no better. My husband's family convinced him to leave me. Deserted I went back home but they too disowned me.

Left with no choice I came to Delhi and found a job. The person I was living with was into sex trade and she tried to get me involved in the same profession despite my resistance. I became friendly with a girl who stayed there too. Soon she eloped with her boyfriend. It came as a shock to me as well, but her family blamed me for it and filed a case against me. That is how I got dragged into this Juvenile Justice System. My family hasn't come to visit me ever. I also never want to go back home. There's nothing worse that can happen to me now, and I know I can survive without anything or anybody.

Case Number 2

I am around 16 years old, with a sister and a brother and belong to a very poor family. My father passed away when I was very young, and my mother brought us up with great difficulty. My earliest recollection of childhood is, me being raped by a boy. Though at the time I didn't know what was happening except for the fact that I didn't like it. I realized much later that it was rape and that my life had changed forever.

After that incident, my mother withdrew me from school since she thought my life is ruined and education is not necessary. At the age of 12, I was married off to a man who was more than twice my age. It seemed as if my mother was getting rid of me and I had suddenly become a burden on her. I resigned to my fate. Later I also realized that my husband was promiscuous and had illegitimate relations with a lot of women. He came drunk every night and would brutally beat me on any small pretext (and at times even without it). My in-laws too treated me very badly and taunted me for not bringing enough dowry. When I was around 8 months pregnant, my drunken husband got into a fit of rage and tried to burn me.

Fortunately (or unfortunately) I escaped from his wrath. That night, I ran away. A stranger gave me the number of an institution. I reached there, and from there I was brought to this current institution. I was heavily pregnant, and had to be admitted into the local hospital. I delivered my baby. He brought a hope in my life and I saw purpose to my existence. I loved him dearly. After 28 days the authorities at the institution told me he had died. None of my questions met with any answers. I'm quite sure that he has been given away for adoption. I hate this institution, I want my baby back and I want to get out of here. I have even tried committing suicide twice. Everything would be fine if I could just have my baby back, my hope back. I love him.

Case Number 3

I am 17 years old and I have studied till 10th standard. Till few years back life was quite normal for me. I still hadn't fallen in love. 4-5 years ago I became friendly with this boy and soon we realized that we were in love with each other. My parents never approved of our friendship and did their best to stop me from meeting him. Finally, I eloped with him and got married. My parents were furious when they found out and sent me away to stay with one of our relatives in Rohtak, where I was locked up in a room for days.

For two years, I was kept under a strict watch and was tortured, physically and emotionally. I was treated worse than an animal. My parents put a false charge of "kidnapping" against my husband and wanted me to give a testimony for the same. They also threatened to kill him, and I knew they had the means of doing so. I succumbed to their pressures (since it was a choice between having him dead and having him convicted). I soon came to know that my husband had been arrested on the false charges.

I had to save my husband and managed to escape from the room. The police found me on the streets and brought me to this institution. My parents still came to see me; they conspired with the authorities and produced evidence that I am a minor, when I am sure that I am over 18 years of age now. They want to keep me here, in this prison-like accommodation, so that I cannot save my husband. I just want to go back to him, rescue him and live peacefully. I don't want to go back home; my parents will never forgive me and would want to kill me. I wish I get rid of the guilt for testifying against my husband, and I wish he forgives me.

Case Number 4

I was very young when in an unfortunate accident both my parents passed away. I was thus orphaned and sent to live with my uncle and his family. My uncle and his family never really accepted me. I felt like a burden on them and was treated very badly. I was kept like one would keep a dog. They never let me study or do anything I wanted, and I was to live in this tiny corner of the house. They were forcing me to get married and would continuously beat me. Around this time my uncle raped me. I ran away from home at age 12. I was found by the police and sent to the institution. I now have an untenable temper and the only way I can control my anger is by physically hurting me. I do things like cut myself or burn myself. Sometimes when I think of how my life has been I think that someday I will end up killing myself. I want to go back home to my uncles, only to teach him a lesson.

Case Number 5

My life was as normal and good as it could be, but after both my parents passed away within one month of each other, life took on an unbearable turn. I have a sister and an elder brother who I was living with after my parents passed away. I was taken out of school as my brother could not afford to continue sending us and my extended family didn't want to keep us either. I couldn't take it any longer; there were constant fights at home with my brother. My sister and I decided to run away. On the train we met this kind couple who befriended us and took us home with them as they realized we were runaways. There she contacted our brother. My brother came and took us back home. Things continued to be bad, and we ran away again.

This time in we met this girl who was very kind and who took us to her home in Rohini. We stayed with her for a few months despite the fact that the girl's parents weren't too keen to have them there. We were however treated nicely. We did odd jobs around the house. Then one day, their neighbour in Rohini, on the pretense of getting them registered in court, brought us to this institution. Since then we have been here. Life is very unhappy at the institution. The children are very unfriendly, and a lot of fighting goes on. The matron in-charge of us is very unkind and rude. She does not look after us properly. The reason why I am staying on in the institution is because of the educational opportunities, which we are getting here. The only thing I want to do in life is study hard and become something so I am not dependent on others and can stand on my own feet.

Case Number 6

When I was young I was orphaned as both my parents were killed in an accident. I lived with my paternal uncle and his family, but they never really accepted me. I was being denied not only educational opportunities but also the love and affection of family members. I could not take it anymore and I ran away from home at the age of 11. I was out on the roads when some boys raped me. They left me on the roads after which I was taken to the hospital and then sent to this institution. I do not like to live here. There are many restrictions and I want to go out. I will never be happy till I am not out on my own.

I also had a boyfriend who convinced me of his love for me. One day when I was returning from school, I ran away to meet my boyfriend. Though I have tried running from school at least two to three times, I was successful only once.

As I was outside the school, a man promised to help me reach my boyfriend's house but instead took me to a deserted route and raped me. I was again sent back to the institution. I am now 18 years old. I am waiting to be released from here so that I can marry my boyfriend. I am uncertain about my future. My boyfriend drinks a lot and that scares me. However, I am sure that I do not wish to return to my family as they have never loved me and don't care for me. I only pray to God that no one goes through the same trauma of rape and not being loved by family just the way I have been through.

Case Number 7

I remember mother and father use to fight a lot. Father would often come home drunk and hit both me and mother. I think my mother had an affair with this uncle who would often come home when father was not there. I was too young to understand the complexities behind such things. It was in my innocence that one day I told father about the man who came to visit mother at very odd time in the night. I was only ten years of age when one morning police came and took my father away. He was charged for killing my mother. Life changed completely for me. I was sent to a shelter home for girls in Delhi. I now share my room with 15–20 girls. I don't like living in Delhi or in the shelter home. I miss my mother and father very much though I am very upset with him. Why did he have to kill her? Maybe if I hadn't told father about the mother's affair she would be alive, father would not be in jail.

Case Number 8

I thought I was old enough to look after myself and moved out of home to live in a hostel. I was not happy living at home with my stepfather and mother. My stepfather would humiliate me for minor mistakes and for spending time with a boy whom I liked. I hated these restrictions and missed talking to someone about how I felt.

Soon after settling at the hostel, an older girl offered to help me to make my life economically better. But it was too late before I would understand the intentions of this girl. All her promises and stories were a lie. But I found it out much too late. She took me to a hotel room one day under the pretext of arranging an interview for me. But the reality was something else. She locked me in the hotel room with a strange boy who drugged me and took me to Pune.

In Pune life was a hell for me. I was regularly beaten and molested over and over again for many days before I agreed to be sold into prostitution. I was asked to have sex with my clients and was raped by every customer. This misery continued for an entire year.

Finally, with the help of the police, I escaped to Delhi. I now live in a home run by an NGO. I have started going to school and have a clean, spacious place to sleep every night. There is breakfast every morning, a visit to the doctor if it is needed, people are friendly to me, and I am happy to be living here.

Case Number 9

Everyone says that I am not mentally sound. Though I am not mentally retarded I am slow in almost everything I do and it takes me time to understand certain instructions. Probably this is the reason why my parents left me in a shelter home for girls because they were incapable of taking care of me. Even in the village people would have pity on me and would sympathize with my parents about my condition. Children of my age made fun of me and did not like playing with me because I was slow in almost everything that I did. Though I like living in this institution, I wish to go out and make friends. The shelter home authorities had got me admitted in a school by the name of Tamanna. But I am not allowed to go there anymore.

This all happened after the incidence of my running away from the school. It so happened that a boy would wait for me every day after school and would want to talk to me. I could not talk to him because we were supposed to be in a line and get into our bus after school; we even had a caretaker who would ensure that none of us went haywire. One day he managed to ask me to bunk school the next day. So I decided to run out of school once the caretaker had showed us in. It worked, he was waiting for me. I did not realize his intentions. He took me to his friend's room and there he forced me to have sex with him. I could do nothing except to succumb to the pressure. Later he dropped me back to the institution. It was then that I told them about what had happened to me.

These composite case studies illustrate a combination of factors that may collide just as a girl is hitting adolescence, leaving her at risk of delinquency. These young girls suffering from a degraded opinion of their value as people are more likely to engage in damaging and disempowering and self-defeating behaviours.[20] The stories told by the girls prove this point.

It is very simple to send the child to a prison and treat him or her like an ordinary criminal. However, the implications of the above have to be kept in mind, after all it is the child's future that we would be playing with. Institutional care for delinquents has been the answer for the above problem. This system tends to be better than prisons, but the fact remains that it is not an adequate solution. What we need to do is substitute such institutionalization to an approach which would promote community-based family-focussed services. However, as of now the only solution we have is the institutions for delinquent children and care must be taken to ensure that the best interests of children are kept in mind.

The next chapter throws light on the institutional treatment of the girls and the condition of these institutions.

Notes

1. Gibbens, T.C.N. and Ahrenfeldt, R.H. (1966), *Cultural Factors in Delinquency*, London, Tavistock, p. 170.
2. United Nations Department of Economic and Social Affairs. (2004), *Juvenile Delinquency, World Youth Report 2003: A Global Situation of Young People*, New York, United Nations Publication, p. 196.
3. "All other" refers to a variety of offences, usually state and local ordinances. Among the most common include public nuisance, trespassing, failure to appear on warrants, contempt of court, and, for

juveniles especially, violation of various court orders (e.g. probation, parole) and certain status offences. This category does not include traffic offences.

4. Arrests for murder, robbery, rape, and aggravated assault.
5. Also includes arrests for other assaults, a Part II crime.
6. Arrests for curfew and runaway.
7. Sharp, C. and Simon, J. (2004), *Girls in the Juvenile Justice System*, Washington, DC, Child Welfare League of America Publications, p. 4.
8. India, Ministry of Home Affairs, National Crime Records bureau (2002), *Crime in India 2000*, New Delhi.
9. India Pleads: Adopt Our Orphan Girls: British Couples Urged to Aid 'Lost' 11 Million. Dean Nelson, Delhi, *The Sunday Times*, April 8, 2007.
10. Janice, J. (1995), *Black Youths, Delinquency, and Juvenile Justice*, Westport, CT, Greenwood Publishing, pp. 12–13.
11. Dube, S.R., Anda, R.F., Felitti, V.J., Croft, J.B., Edwards, V.J., and Giles, W.H. (2001), Growing up with Parental Alcohol Abuse: Exposure to Childhood Abuse, Neglect and Household Dysfunction, *Child Abuse and Neglect*, 25(12), 1627–1640.
12. Chaffin, M., Kelleher, K., and Hollenberg, J. (1996). Onset of Physical Abuse and Neglect: Psychiatric, Substance Abuse, and Social Risk Factors from Prospective Community Data, *Child Abuse and Neglect*, 20(3), 191–203.
13. Carmichael, M. (2004), No Girls Please, *Newsweek*, January 26, p. 50.
14. *The Hindu* (1998), Female Infanticide Alarming in Dharmapuri, August 2, p. 1.
15. Singh, R. (1990), *The Womb of Mind: A Sociological Exploration of the Status-Experience of Women in Delhi*, New Delhi, Vikas Publishing, p. 45.
16. Singh, *The Womb of Mind*, p. 47.
17. Kapur, P. (1995), Girl Child Abuse: Violation of Her Human Rights, *Social Change*, 25, 2–18.
18. Chesney-Lind, M. (1995), Girls, Delinquency and Juvenile Justice: Toward a Feminist Theory of Young Women's Crime. In *The Criminal Justice System and Women* (ed. B.R. Price and N.J. Sokoloff), New York, McGraw-Hill, pp. 71–88.
19. *Crime in India*, NCRB, Ministry of Home Affairs, Government of India, 2006.
20. Richie, B.E., Tsenin, K., and Widom, C.S. (1999), *Research on Women and Girls in the Justice System: Plenary Papers*. Conference on Criminal Justice Research and Evaluation-Enhancing Policy and Practice through Research, Vol. 3, p. 29.

7

Institutional Treatment of Female Juvenile Delinquents

Indian Juvenile Justice System Distinct from Criminal Justice System

To understand the system of juvenile protection and welfare, one needs to clearly understand juvenile justice system as distinct from criminal justice system. The differential treatment given to the child, which has been in the process of evolution over hundreds of years, creates a separate juvenile justice system, other than the criminal justice system which is, obviously, meant for the adults, that is, those over 18 years of age. This system of separate legal and administrative treatment operates beyond the realm of law alone and drifts into the complex dynamics of socio-economic, psychoemotional, and the family- and community-based institutional and non-institutional interventions and organizations.

Under British rule in India the Common Law practice of "parens patriae" (*Parens patriae* is Latin for "father of the people"; in law, it refers to the public policy power of the state to intervene against an abusive or negligent natural parent, legal guardian, or informal caretaker and to act as the parent of any child or individual who is in need of protection) marked the practice of differentiating juveniles from adult cases.[1] However, the British law had meager effect as most communities had few crimes, and most interpersonal problems were settled in *panchayats*, that is, informal village courts. Children's law violations and disciplinary problems were handled by parents and caste elders and panchayat leaders. These practices continue to some extent even today. Nation-building activities after India's independence established centralized regulatory and legal institutions. Population growth, economic development, democratization, modernization, urbanization, and inter-caste and communal strife have also stimulated expansion of these institutions.

The Indian legal system, which was founded on Common Law practices, was introduced during the British occupation of India. The impact of Common Law on juveniles in India began with the Apprentices Act of 1850, which provided power to magistrates to commit destitute, vagrant, and delinquent children to parents, guardian, or specified institutions as apprentices to learn trades for employment. This act related to juveniles between the ages 10 and 18, who could be held in these types of programmes until they become 21 years old. The Reformatory Act of 1897 reduced the severity of punishment to juveniles who had committed serious offences.

It also required juvenile offenders to be separated from adult prisoners and placed in reform schools.[2] The Code of Criminal Procedures of 1898 elaborated the methods of accomplishing these aims. The Madras Children's Act of 1920, which was the first comprehensive act to be introduced in India, provided for juveniles courts, juvenile institutions, and juvenile treatments. These courts were established with broad powers. They could be either separate or part of adult courts with "parens patriae" focus.[3] Juvenile hearings were conducted separately, privately, informally, and practically without the right to appellate review.

In the name of providing treatment, education, and occupational training and rehabilitation for juveniles, and stressing that children need only these, officials often sacrifice legal rights and procedures. Felony cases for which juveniles mighty be given death sentence were not handled in the juvenile or magistrate courts but were sent to higher courts with jurisdictions over adults. The Madras Borstal School Act of 1925 created industrial schools for occupational training, moral development, and rehabilitation of delinquents.[4] Enactments and changes were eventually introduced to modify the system. The Constitution of India, created in 1949 after independence, recognizes the rights of the accused the right against self-discrimination, right to an attorney, and right to freedom (Article 20, 21, and 22 of the Indian Constitution). Many of these rights are yet to be realized through enactments, practices, and case decisions. Even though the Children's Act of 1960 was in essence largely a reflection of earlier acts and practices, it recognized the importance of legal rights and later led to their development. For example, the act recognized that a defence attorney can be present in juvenile hearings.

The Juvenile Justice Act of 1986 conferred greater power to juvenile courts even to hear capital cases involving juveniles. The Juvenile Justice Act of 2000 made more significant strides in providing for legal safeguards, procedures and rights, in addition to rehabilitation services. It saved children from being subject to death penalty. This act was heavily influenced by the 1985 United Nations Standard Minimum Rules for Administration of Justice, the 1989 United Nations Conventions for the Rights of the Child, and the 1990 United Nations Rules for Protection of Juveniles Deprived of Their Liberty.[5]

Even though juvenile delinquency rates are currently lower in India than in many other countries, they are bound to increase in future. At present, however, cruel treatment, punishment, and victimization of children are a more serious problem. Since Independence, several acts have been introduced to improve the juvenile justice system. More than any other act before, the Juvenile Justice (Care and Protection of Children) Act, 2000, provides legal rights, protection, and rehabilitation for juveniles in conflict with law and for children in need of care and protection. If its rationale and suggested practices are followed the juvenile justice system will significantly improve.

It is quite possible to handle the problem of neglected child through the informal system of social control through family and community. It is possible for social workers and NGOs to look after neglected children on their own with help and support from government agencies within the existing infrastructure.

Institutional care has been the response to delinquency. This system is definitely better than prisons, but the fact remains that it is not an adequate solution. This system tends to substitute family care, which is not possible in reality and the result is that it deprives the child of emotional and social support. Such systems also exclude the child from community care and consciousness where children are brought together in a group of unrelated children and adults. It is estimated that government spends approximately 7.5 crore annually on institutional care, which is extremely inadequate, almost peanuts, considering the fact that there are estimated 35 million children in situations of neglect in the country and couple of lakhs of juveniles are in conflict with the law. The institutional care system for all these children/juveniles put together do not handle more than 35,000 to 40,000 juvenile children, a figure that is infinitely smaller than the real number of juveniles getting into trouble every day and go undetected.

The procedures to deal with children and juveniles in the institutions have to be ultimately modelled after the informal and natural institutions such as family and society or some such institutions that allows for active participation of the juveniles' families in their initiatives. In fact, the ideal conditions in any informal system of formal institution for both the neglected and the delinquent child may be achieved if the attributes of the informal institutions are brought into the formal systems. Only the love and care within the family or within the time-tested social institutions, which are being developed by a number of voluntary organizations in the country, can create the ideal situation conducive to the reformation of juveniles. Most of the formal institutions created by the law do not serve the basic purpose due to the absence of these natural attributes, lack of personalized care, and love and empathy that breathes life into any programme pertaining to children. As such, in formal institutions, certain regimentation and discipline, organized activities, and programmes may be extremely useful for delinquent children and children with special needs, and the absence of genuine love and care often renders the system soulless.

Treatment of Offenders

The juvenile justice system tries to treat and rehabilitate youngsters who get involved in delinquency. The methods are many, including community treatment, residential treatment, nonresidential community treatment, and institutionalization.[6] In most instances, community treatment involves placing the child on probation. When the child is not believed to be harmful to others, he or she is placed under the supervision of an officer of the juvenile court and must abide by the specific rules that are worked out between the officer and the child. In some instances, community treatment also takes the form of restitution, in which case the child reimburses the victim either through direct payment or through some form of work or community service.

Residential treatment generally takes place in a group home where the juvenile is provided with psychological and vocational counselling. Other forms of residential treatment include rural programmes such as forestry camps and work farms. Youngsters placed in nonresidential community-based treatment programmes live at home and receive treatment from mental health clinics or similar services.

Institutionalization is the most severe form of treatment for juvenile offenders. Goffman's (1961) *Asylums Essays on the Condition of the Social Situation of Mental Patients and Other Inmates* discussed in detail the concept of institutionalization and total institutions. Based on his participant observation field work the book details Goffman's theory of "total institution" and the process by which it tries to maintain predictable and regular behaviour on the part of both the "guard" and the "captor," suggesting that many features of such institutions exist only to ensure that the victim–captor status quo remains unchanged; the victim is a problem to the society and the captor's function is to remind the juveniles of their "victimhood"; in other words, institutions merely "institutionalize" the victims, leaving no scope for victims to regain their personhood and eventually go out believing they can be full-fledged participants in the mainstream society. In the Indian context, the effect of adverse situations and the feeling of frustration and gloom that drove children to become juvenile in the first place never go away despite the protective, rehabilitative role the institutions and care homes are supposed to play; rather, if anything the children feel worse staying inside, living through what is a constant remainder of their sorry plight.

In *Asylums*, Goffman used his research in a mental hospital to develop a theory of the world of "total institutions," a category that includes not only mental hospitals but also prisons, armed services, and so on. Goffman defines total institutions as a place of residence and work where a number of individuals in similar situations are cut off from the wider society and lead an enclosed, formally administered life. The key fact of total institution is that many human needs of whole blocs of people are under bureaucratic control. In the total institutions there is a basic cleavage between the small, managing group and the large, managed group. The staff is concerned with surveillance, and the inmates with conformity. Each group sees the other through the prism of narrow, hostile stereotypes. Their association is marked by misunderstanding and mistrust.[7]

Goffman concludes that adjusting the inmates to their role has at least as much importance as "curing" them. A total institution, also referred to as a voracious institution, as defined in his work Asylums, is an institution where all parts of life of individuals under the institution are subordinated to and dependent upon the authorities of the organization.

The institution is responsible for child's counselling, education, recreation, room and board, and other daily activities. The child is incarcerated in a secure facility and denied freedom to step out and mingle in the community. Institutionalized children are considered as a highly deprived class of population. These children are left helpless, abandoned, neglected due to social, economic, and personal reasons by the parents/caregivers. They are almost always deprived of one or more necessities of life. Early separation from parents, deprivation of parental care, love, affection, warmth, security, acceptance, and lack of discipline during childhood disrupt their normal socio-emotional development. So it becomes necessary to know whether institutionalized children who are robbed of family life and its emotional warmth grow up normally and how well they are able to rationalize and cope with their personality traits and the demands of the environment/society around them. Therefore, one of the goals of the present study was to know the level of adjustment of institutionalized children to both internal and external environments.

Whatever be the noble reasons for institutionalizing a child, a child perceives the loss of freedom as punishment in itself. Juveniles, most of whom have been on their own and making their choices since a very young age, do not welcome the protection advanced by the juvenile justice system and look upon it as an intrusion. The traditional reason for sentencing juveniles to institutions was rehabilitation; it was believed that academic and vocational training will lead to them becoming less delinquent while they go out.[8]

The Beijing Rules reflect this philosophy when it deals with the objectives of institutional treatment. "The objective of training and treatment of juveniles placed in institutions is to provide care, protection, education and vocational skills, with a view to assisting them to assume socially constructive and productive roles in society.[9]" And the Beijing Rules further state, "Juveniles in institutions shall receive care, protection and all necessary assistance—social, educational, vocational, psychological, medical and physical—that they may require because of their age, sex, and personality and in the interest of their wholesome development."

Lundman observes that the reason for institutionalization of juvenile offenders has since changed; the focus now is on revenge, incapacitating the juvenile from continuing a life of crime and deterrence. Institutionalization is being advocated not for reformation or rehabilitation of juveniles; when "Doing time in a juvenile correctional facility is painful and it almost certainly is the pain, rather than the treatment all institutions provide, that makes the lasting impression."

By institutionalizing juveniles the state sends a strong message into society that it intends to deal strictly with juveniles, especially those who have committed serious offences, such as murder and rape. There is also the element of public fear toward crime committed by the juveniles. Therefore, incarceration is used to placate the fearful public that strong action is being taken against juvenile offenders and what treatment or disciplinary measures they go through in the correctional facilities is to ensure their future welfare. The preamble to the 2000 Act spoke of "ultimate rehabilitation through various institutions established under this enactment." This preamble has been altered by the 2006 amendment to convey that even though rehabilitation of juveniles is the ultimate goal, it shouldn't be left exclusively for institutions to achieve that goal but that different mechanisms must be developed and used to ensure the well-being and development of juvenile children.

It is documented that institutions rarely provide conditions favourable for rehabilitation. Maintenance of discipline is inherent in an institutional setting and could result in use of force or threats; such an environment is in no way conducive for a child's rehabilitation. Therefore, to ensure that a juvenile does not undergo prolonged institutionalization, bail is to be granted at the earliest in most juvenile cases, and there is a wide range of orders, other than institutionalization, that a Juvenile Justice Board can pass at the time of final disposal. Furthermore, juveniles perceive institutionalization as punishment; hence, there have been cases of juveniles escaping from the confines of an Observation Home or Special Home or from the care of a fit person. In such case, under Section 22 of JJA 2000, the juvenile has to be sent back to the custody of the Observation Home or Special Home or fit person.

Child psychologists believe that the period between 10 and 18 years of age is the formative stage of an individual. The inputs and exposure during these years will instruct the child's personality development. Therefore, it is necessary to examine the techniques and means employed by institutions in their treatment programmes. The test of these programmes is whether the intervention will assist children to overcome the forces that push them into a life of crime, and check recidivism. Institutions with distinct roles are to be established for the treatment of juveniles during their journey through the juvenile justice system.

No specific treatment has been proven to be the most effective thus far. Effectiveness is typically measured by recidivism rates, that is, by the percentage of children treated who subsequently commit additional criminal acts. The recidivism rates for all forms of treatment, however, are about the same. A large percentage of delinquent acts are never discovered, which further complicates this measurement. Thus, the mere absence of subsequently reported delinquent acts committed by a treated child may mean nothing more than that the child was not caught.

Role of Police in the Treatment of Offenders

Mostly police arrest juveniles and produce them before the Juvenile Justice Board (JJB). Very rarely, if at all, a juvenile is produced before JJB by a private party or voluntary organization. Hence, a juvenile's first contact with the Juvenile Justice System is through police. A private party or voluntary organization producing a juvenile before JJB should simultaneously keep the police informed. Mostly, the police investigates a juvenile case and submits the charge-sheet before the competent authority.

The dispensing of distinct treatment to juveniles as obligated under juvenile legislation is defeated if the police treat juveniles in the same manner as they treat hardened criminals. So the Statement of Objects and Reasons of JJA 2000 includes to create special juvenile police units with a humane approach through sensitization and training of police personnel. Accordingly, JJA 2000 envisages the setting up of the Special Juvenile Police Unit (SJPU) in every district and city, and the designation of at least one police officer attached to a police station as "the juvenile or the child welfare officer."

Section 63 (1) of the Juvenile Justice (Care and Protection of Children) Act, 2000, states the following points: (1) In order to enable the police officers who frequently or exclusively deal with juveniles or are primarily engaged in the prevention juvenile crime or handling of the juveniles or children under this Act to perform their functions more effectively, they shall be specially instructed and trained. (2) In every police station at least one officer with aptitude and appropriate training and orientation may be designated as the "juvenile or the child welfare officer" who will handle the juvenile or the child in coordination with the police. (3) Special juvenile police unit, of which all the police officers designated as above, to handle juveniles or children will be members, may be created in every district and city to coordinate and to upgrade the police treatment of the juveniles and the children.

The Model Rules of the Juvenile Justice (Care and Protection of Children) Act, (2000)[10] visualize the SJPU at the district level to function under a juvenile or child welfare officer (of the rank of Inspector of Police and two paid social workers, of whom one shall be a woman, having experience of working in the field of child welfare). This ensures social intervention in a juvenile case from the time of arrest. It would be of optimum effect if the social workers appointed to assist SJPUs are trained in child psychology. In 1952, the Juvenile Aid Police Unit (JAPU) was created in Greater Mumbai and continues as a special cell within the force to mainly handle destitute and neglected children.

Different methods have been innovated for the establishment of SJPUs. In the state of Karnataka, the SJPUs are to be assisted by recognized voluntary organizations.[11] In Bangalore, SJPUs are established in two zones. Each SJPU is assisted by an organization working with children. The SJPUs are situated at police stations, headed by a senior-level police officer, and its members are the Child Welfare Officers (also called "Designated Police Officers") attached to different police stations within that zone. As soon as a juvenile offender is arrested the relevant voluntary organization will be informed. The voluntary organization ensures that the provisions of juvenile legislation are adhered to and that the child enjoys the rights guaranteed to him or her within the juvenile justice system. In case of minor offence, the endeavour is to "divert" the juvenile with the permission of JJB.[12] Diversion is a process by which a juvenile offender, in appropriate cases, does not enter the juvenile justice system, and hence, is not compulsorily made to face an inquiry before JJB.

It is necessary to examine the role of the police under juvenile legislation:

1. It is the police who apprehends the juvenile suspected of having committed an offence.

2. Immediately upon apprehension, the juvenile is to be placed under the charge of SJPU or juvenile welfare officer.[13]
3. Within 24 hours of apprehension, the SJPU or the Juvenile Welfare Officer, as the case may be, is to produce the juvenile before JJB.[14]
4. Pending production before JJB, the juvenile is to be kept in the Observation Home. Under no circumstances should a juvenile be kept in the police lock-up or jail.[15]
5. The SJPU or juvenile welfare officer must inform the parent or guardian[16] or any other person of the juvenile's choice about juvenile's apprehension.
6. The SJPU or juvenile welfare officer must inform the Probation Officer[17] about the juvenile's arrest so that information may be obtained "regarding the antecedents and family background of the juvenile and other material circumstances likely to be of assistance to the Board for making the inquiry."
7. Section 12(2) of JJA 2000 gives the police the authority to immediately on apprehension release a juvenile on bail. The same provision contained in JJA 1986[18] and Bombay Children Act (BCA) 1948.[19] But the police, however insignificant the crime alleged to have been committed, do not release a juvenile on bail as they would an adult alleged to have committed a bailable offence. This is the correct practice. In the case of the juvenile it is not the offence that determines whether or not he or she should be released on bail, but the juvenile's situation, and that can only be determined by a body having the requisite expertise and assistance. Moreover, the police decision to grant bail may be based on extraneous reasons and result in arbitrariness.
8. The JJB while considering a bail application will seek the police's response to the same. Sadly, the police almost always files its report opposing the grant of bail on some pretext or the other in absolute contravention of the spirit of juvenile legislation. It has been observed that most police responses habitually oppose the grant of bail on grounds other than those prescribed under Juvenile Justice (Care and Protection of Children) Act 2000. Gravity of offence or likelihood of tampering with prosecution witnesses or difficulty to obtain juvenile's presence during inquiry are the reasons generally plead by the police to deny bail to a juvenile. It must be noted

that the three conditions set out in juvenile legislation are in existence only in rare cases, but the police lack the magnanimity to accept the actuality.

9. In the absence of documentary proof of age, and juvenile not being able to till his/her age, the JJB directs the police to take the person produced for medical examination to ascertain his or her age. It is imperative that the PO or any other functionary of the Observation Home also accompanies the juvenile.
10. The SJPU or juvenile welfare officer investigates the matter and files a charge-sheet before JJB. At this stage, it is essential to recall that every police station will be embodied in the SJPU through its juvenile welfare officer, and hence, assistance of the relevant police station will be taken to carry out the investigation.
11. Under juvenile legislation, the juvenile in conflict with law will always be under the charge of JJB, and there is nothing like police custody. Once a juvenile is produced before JJB, the police loses control over the juvenile. If the police requires interrogating the juvenile, they will need prior permission from JJB to do so. Granting of such permission is at the discretion of JJB, and if it does give permission, it will ensure that the interrogation is done in the presence of the Probation Officer or any other functionary attached to the Observation Home.
12. During inquiry, it is the police who is directed to produce the prosecution witnesses before JJB.
13. On completion of inquiry, it is the police who escorts the juvenile to the Special Home or to his or her place of residence if he or she is aged below 18 years.
14. The police while dealing with a juvenile case should be in plain clothes and not in uniform.[20]
15. A juvenile should never be handcuffed[21] when brought to the Observation Home or otherwise.

It is imperative for state governments to ensure that issues pertaining to juvenile justice forms part of the police's training curriculum. That the law treats the juveniles not in the same manner as an adult criminal, and the reasons for such distinct treatment should be engraved in the mind of every police personnel. This will be a step toward assuring a juvenile his or her rights. It will also curtail the police's prevailing practice of treating juveniles and adults with a heavy hand.

Only time will tell whether training changes the perspective of police officers who are trained to believe that those who commit crimes deserve to be treated stringently and punished. It is not only the public, it is also policemen who believe that juvenile legislation deals leniently those from whom society requires protection. The model rules provide, "Any police officer found guilty, after due inquiry, of torturing the child, mentally or physically, shall be liable to be removed from service besides being prosecuted for the offence."[22] It is hoped that the above rule will deter the physical abuse of children at the hands of the police.

Role of Probation Officers in the Treatment of Offenders

As repeatedly mentioned, reformation and rehabilitation of the juvenile is the end hoped to be attained by the juvenile's contact with the juvenile justice system. It calls for balancing the juvenile's care with the control of his future behaviour. There is a fine, yet sharp line of demarcation between reformation and rehabilitation. Reformation is founded on the belief that a juvenile is capable of changing his or her attitudes and recognizing that what he or she did was wrong. Rehabilitation is founded on the belief that circumstances resulted in the juvenile committing the crime. Therefore, the concentration is on setting right these circumstances. The focus is entirely on the juvenile and his or her particular life circumstances. This calls for concerted attention toward a juvenile and his or her existing familial and social environment. That is the reason JJB uses the "principle of proportionality" as the base for its decisions and the demand for a socio-legal approach: "reaction to any case of delinquent act and to the offender should be dictated not only by the gravity of the offence but also by the circumstances of the offender and those in which the offence was committed by him."[23] The circumstances could relate to the juvenile's family situation, social status, and so on.

A Probation Officer (PO) is appointed by the state government or recognized as such by state government, or in any exceptional case, any other person, who, in the opinion of the court, is fit to act as a PO in the special circumstances of the case.[24] The Model Rules[25] authorize the competent authority to co-opt as POs, voluntary organizations, and social workers found fit to render probation services. The Probation Offenders Act 1958 enumerates the "Duties of Probation Officers"[26] as follows:

"1. Inquire, in accordance with any directions of a court, into the circumstances or home surroundings of any person accused of an offence with a view to assist the court in determining the most suitable method of dealing with him and submit reports to the court;
2. Supervise probationers and other persons placed under his supervision and, where necessary, endeavour to find them suitable employment;
3. Advise and assist offenders in the payment of compensation or costs ordered by the court;
4. Advise and assist, in such cases and in such manner as may be prescribed, persons who have been released under Section 4; and
5. Perform such other duties as may be prescribed."

The role of a PO is two-fold within the juvenile justice system:

1. To assist the JJB while making decisions or passing orders with regards to the juvenile, and
2. To be a friend to the juvenile, and to assist and advise him during the probation period so that he fulfils his promise not to re-offend during this period, and, hopefully, ever again.

POs provide JJB with information about the child and also supervise the juveniles whom the JJB has returned to the community. The PO's report is sought by the JJB whilst entertaining a bail application and also at the time of final disposal of the case. The main purpose of this report is to examine the juvenile's background so as to identify the reasons for commission of the offence. The order of JJB should treat the reasons as a doctor treats an illness. This report is a social worker's evaluation of juvenile in his familial or social environment and whether such environment is conducive for his reformation and rehabilitation. Section 87 of the Model Rules deals with the "Duties of a Probation Officer or Child Welfare Officer or Case Worker," and states that "the probation officer shall inquire into the antecedents and family history of the juvenile or the child and such other material circumstances, as may be necessary and submit a social investigation report as early as possible."

Furthermore, the PO is to do "follow-up of juveniles after their release and extending help and guidance to them" and to visit "regularly the residence of the juvenile or child under their supervision and also places of employment or school attended by such juvenile or child" and submit fortnightly reports. Depending on the

PO's suggestions, recommendations, and reports, JJB will decide what treatment plan should be prepared for the juvenile's comprehensive rehabilitation.

Hence, the PO's Report is an important document that will determine the future treatment of a juvenile who is found to have committed an offence. Although the PO's Report has only recommendatory value, it is imperative for JJB to peruse the same prior to taking any decision in respect of the juvenile and to decide upon its action accordingly. If the juvenile does not hail from within the jurisdiction of JJB, the PO may take the assistance of (i) the PO having territorial jurisdiction over the place where the family resides or (ii) an NGO working in that area. Generally, the PO interacts with the juvenile and his parent, guardian, or relative while preparing the report.

The Beijing Rules have also stressed the importance of Social Inquiry Reports in Section 16.1, stating that in all cases except those involving minor offences, before the competent authority renders a final disposition prior to sentencing, the background and circumstances in which the juvenile is living or the conditions under which the offence has been committed shall be properly investigated so as to facilitate judicious adjudication of the case by the competent authority.

Section 15 of JJA 2000 deals with orders that the JJB can pass on reaching a finding that a juvenile has committed an offence, and Subsection (2) of Section 15 states that the "The Board shall obtain the social investigation report on juvenile either through a probation officer or a recognized voluntary organization or otherwise, and shall take into consideration the findings of such report before passing an order."

The PO has always played a pivotal role under juvenile legislation. When BCA 1948 was in force, the youthful offender was not permitted legal representation, and it was the Juvenile Court and the PO who decided the fate of the child. The Report of the Child Welfare Officer (Probation) had to be considered by the Juvenile Court when passing orders.[27] The JJA 1986 also included "the reports made by the probation officer" to be one of the circumstances to be considered while passing an order in respect of a juvenile.[28]

Section 57(2) of JJA 1986 enumerated the duties of a PO as under:

1. to inquire, in accordance with the direction of a competent authority, into the antecedents and family history of any

juvenile accused of an offence, with a view to assist the authority in making the inquiry;

2. To visit neglected and delinquent at such intervals as the probation officer may think fit;
3. To report to competent authority as to the behaviour of any neglected or delinquent juvenile;
4. To advise and assist neglected or delinquent juveniles and, if necessary, endeavour to find them suitable employment;
5. Where a neglected or delinquent juvenile is placed under the care of any person or institution on certain conditions, to see whether such conditions are being complied with; and
6. To perform such other duties as may be prescribed."

Moreover, the PO was also empowered to visit institutions established under JJA 1986 and submit inspection reports to the State government.[29] It is felt by some that the 2000 Act has tokenized the role of a PO in favour of due process and legal procedures and that this shift in focus could in future result in an increase in recidivism, caused due to minimal contact with POs.

Probation is non-institutional social treatment of the adjudged juvenile or youthful or adult offender.[30] The social treatment will be prescribed by the adjudicating authority. Probation is an alternative to institutionalization and is the most-often-utilized sentencing option for juveniles. The juvenile makes a promise before JJB that he will not reoffend. His word is accepted by JJB, and he is released on the assumption that he will fulfil his promise and not reoffend during a stipulated period of time. Section 15(1) (e) and (f) of JJA 2000 provides for release of the juvenile on probation for a period not exceeding three years.

The promise is made by the juvenile's parent or guardian or the fit person in whose care the juvenile is being released, by such person executing a written bond. During the period contained in the order, the juvenile who is released on probation is coerced into good behaviour as otherwise he could face institutionalization in a Special Home. There is no specific provision under juvenile legislation for the juvenile to be released on his personal bond, the argument being that the juvenile has not attained the age of majority, and hence cannot contract. Although not specifically provided in the act, a juvenile who has ceased to be a juvenile at the time of final disposal of the case, can be released on his personal bond, that is, on his own assurance of good behaviour.

The JJB while passing any order may direct that the juvenile shall remain under the supervision of the PO. A supervision order may be passed by JJB at the time of granting bail[31] or at the time of final disposal of the juvenile case.[32] If during the period of supervision the PO reports that the juvenile has not been of good behaviour, the JJB may, after making inquiry, order the juvenile's placement in a Special Home. Similar provisions for release of a youthful offender under the supervision of a Child Welfare Officer (Probation) existed under BCA 1948.[33]

It is not only a juvenile who can be released on probation of good conduct; adults too can be so released. Section 360 CRPC deals with releasing an accused on probation of good conduct or after admonition instead of sentencing him to imprisonment, and the Probation Offenders Act 1958 also deals with the same issue. Both of them lay down the circumstances under which an accused may be released by the court on probation. Under these laws, probation cannot be claimed as a right by the accused; it is a discretionary power of the court to decide whether or not to release an accused on probation for good conduct.

Contact with a PO is essential for the well-being of a juvenile. It is submitted that even if a juvenile is released on bail, pending inquiry his contact with the PO should continue. It is the PO who will be the juvenile's guide and lead to juvenile's self-realization of his wrongdoings and the will not to repeat the same on release after completion of inquiry. The test of a proficient PO is that the juveniles with whom he has worked continue to remain in touch and seek his guidance, especially when faced with a difficult situation.

Role of Social Workers and NGOs in Juvenile Justice System

Social workers play a crucial role in the treatment of juvenile offenders. As earlier mentioned, JJB consists of a metropolitan magistrate or a judicial magistrate of the first class and two social workers. The social workers should have "been actively involved in health, education, or welfare activities pertaining to children for at least seven years."[34] The Model Rules have prescribed the criteria necessary for appointment as a social worker on the Juvenile Justice Board. The social worker to be appointed as a member of the Board shall be a person not less than 35 years of age; who has a postgraduate degree in social work, health, education, psychology, child development, or any other social science discipline; and has been actively involved and engaged in the planning, implementation, and administering of measures relating to child welfare for at least seven years.[35] The two social workers are to "be appointed by the State Government on the recommendation of the Selection Committee."[36]

The Selection Committee has as its members, among others, "two representatives of reputed non-governmental organizations working in the area of child welfare."[37] The social worker members on JJB must be assertive and not get overwhelmed by the magistrate, as they have an important role to play in the rehabilitation of the juvenile. Under Section 5(4) of JJA, 2000, the social worker members can overrule the magistrate. They should familiarize themselves with the provisions of juvenile legislation, as also with the papers and proceedings of each case pending before JJB to ensure that justice is done to juvenile.

It is for the social worker members to gain the confidence of the juvenile and yet portray to him that though his best interest is on their minds he is to be dealt with sternly. It is under the orders of JJB that the juvenile is placed in an institution. Hence, it is imperative that JJB, especially social worker members, regularly visit Observation Homes, Special Homes, and other institutions where juveniles are sheltered, to ensure that the objective of reformation and rehabilitation is satisfied.

The 1986 Act also recognized the importance of social workers whilst dispensing justice to juveniles. The Juvenile Court was to "be assisted by a panel of two honorary social workers possessing such qualifications as may be prescribed, of whom at least one shall be a woman, and such panel shall be appointed by the State Government.[38]" The 2000 Act elevated the social worker to being part of the Bench that constitutes the JJB, instead of merely assisting the magistrate. Even though social work intervention plays an important role, the same is always described with words such as "honorary," "voluntary," and "charitable," making it sound like a rather toothless well-meaning cosmetic activity that doesn't have any power or effect, legal or otherwise.

Not only the 1986 Act mandated the inclusion of "two *honorary* social workers" (emphasis added) assisting juvenile court, a similar trend also continued under the 2000 Act. The social worker members on JJB are to be paid "travel and sitting allowance"[39] as may be fixed by the state government. It is high time that governments recognize that social workers are professionals, are playing a crucial role, and the importance of their work requires due recognition and appreciation.

POs are qualified social workers. The superintendents of childcare institutions are also academically trained social workers, as also are the other senior staff employed in the homes. POs and the staff attached to institutions have several critical parts to play in the lives of juveniles. First is that of a friend so that the child feels comfortable to speak freely with them; second, that of an advisor and guide so that the child has confidence to approach them when in need; third, that of a reformer so that the child understands that what he did was wrong; and fourth, that of a healer who helps the child accomplish his full-potential and directs him toward his future. Setting up child guidance mechanisms in an institution is vital as repeated sessions with the juvenile are crucial to bring about a change in his attitude. It is a qualified and trained child psychologist or psychotherapist in a child guidance clinic who can bring about a positive change in the juvenile's future.

NGOs too play a pivotal role. Under the provisions of JJA 2000 they can seek to take charge of juveniles pending or on completion of inquiry in the capacity of a "fit person" or "fit institution." The 2000 Act has empowered voluntary organizations under agreement with state governments to establish and maintain observation homes and special homes. Moreover, voluntary organizations need to provide services within institutions established and maintained by the state government, such as counselling, imparting education and vocational training, and so on, to secure the juvenile his comprehensive rehabilitation.

Role of Media

Media is a double-edged tool. On one hand it plays an important role in moulding public opinion, and on the other, its character is to sensationalize issues to attract readers. In furtherance of its objective to reform a juvenile and not penalize him, Section 19 has been incorporated in JJA 2000. This section ensures that "a juvenile who has committed an offence and has been dealt with under the provisions of this Act shall not suffer disqualification, if any, attaching to a conviction of an offence under such law." An identical provision was also provided in JJA 1986.[40]

Furthermore, Subsection (2) of Section 19 states, "The Board shall make an order directing that the relevant records of such conviction shall be removed after the expiry of the period of appeal or a reasonable period as prescribed under the rules, as the case may be." The Model Rules provide for the records or documents relating to a juvenile to be preserved for seven years and thereafter to be destroyed by JJB.[41] The law, thus, sends a clear message that the future of a child is not to be adversely impacted due to his past conduct.

Despite the inclusion of Section 19 in the statute, juveniles in conflict with law find it difficult to rejoin the mainstream society. Schools have been known to expel juveniles in conflict with law claiming that they would be a bad influence upon other students. Their employment opportunities dwindle as the stigma follows them into the job market, and they are compelled to depend on underpaid, unorganized sectors for earning a livelihood. To curtail this victimization, juvenile legislation protects the juvenile's right to privacy by restricting media reportage.

Section 21 states that prohibition of publication of name, and so on of juvenile in conflict with law or child in need of care and protection involved proceeding under the JJ Act, it states that: (1) No report in any newspaper, magazine, news-sheet, or visual media of any regarding a juvenile in conflict with law or a child in need of care and protection under this Act shall disclose the name, address, or school or any other particulars calculated to lead to the identification of the juvenile child nor shall any picture of any such juvenile or child be published: Provided that for reasons to be recorded in writing, the authority holding the inquiry may permit such disclosure, if in its opinion such disclosure is in the interest of the juvenile or the child. (2) Any person who contravenes the provisions of Subsection (1), shall be liable to a penalty which may extend to twenty-thousand rupees.

Similar provision constraining the media is also contained in the Beijing Rules:

"8.1 The juvenile's right to privacy shall be respected at all stages in order to avoid harm being caused to her or him by undue publicity or by the process of labelling.

8.2 In principle, no information that may lead to the identification of juvenile offender shall be published."

Moreover, records of juvenile offenders are to "be kept strictly confidential and closed to third parties"[42] and "not be used in adult proceedings in subsequent cases involving the same offender."[43] These provisions are inserted to avoid stigma and to enable a juvenile offender to enjoy opportunities offered to other children his age. Nor should an unlawful act committed due to immaturity of judgement be treated as his antecedents.

Nevertheless, repeatedly photographs of the juveniles are splashed in newspapers with detailed description of the juvenile offender and the crime he is alleged to have committed. The juvenile and his support system, if any, is most concerned with the case pending before JJB, and take no action against the errant media. So the media continues to exploit the situation to the detriment of the juvenile. To deter unmindful media reporting, JJB and the high court should take suo moto action under Section 21(2) of JJA 2000.

The Maharashtra Juvenile Justice (Care Protection of Children) Rules 2002 prescribes, "The Board shall initiate action against any media for publishing any matters relating to the children in conflict with law which would lead to the identification of the Juvenile."[44] Moreover, those working in the field of child rights should bring such publications to the notice of the judiciary, as well as dialogue with the media, and apprise them of the law and the effect their reporting could have on a young life.

Section 21 in no manner fetters reporters and journalists from bringing to the attention of readers conditions prevailing in childcare institutions, apathy of the government toward children, illegal detention of juveniles in prisons, backlog of cases before JJB, and other such topics. On the contrary, such reports or articles should be encouraged as media coverage could improve the situation for children. Proactive journalism has played a positive role in changing the appalling position of children. It is also not correct to hold that the media should blank out crimes committed by juveniles, but currently only gory crimes committed by juveniles are highlighted, which has resulted in the public believing that all juvenile crimes are violent crimes. It is imperative that the media portrays the true picture in respect of juvenile crime.

Reasons for Placing Children in Residential Care

According to the World Report on Violence Against Children,[45] the most common reasons for placing children in residential care are disability, family disintegration, violence in the home, lack of social support systems, and poor social and economic conditions, including poverty. In some countries, natural disasters, armed conflict, or effects of HIV/AIDS pandemic may leave parents unable to care for their children. Illness, accidents, and incarceration may also separate children from their parents.

Poverty. This is a significant factor in the decision of many parents to place children in residential care. When parents feel unable to provide for their children and believe that children can receive better access to education, healthcare, and adequate nutrition in residential facilities, they may choose to place their child in care, believing he or she will be better off than at home.

Violence within families. Many children end up in care because of violence in their family, including neglect, and psychological, physical, and sexual violence. A similar scenario was seen in the present study where 172 respondents had run away from home and landed in the shelter homes for girls. Out of 172 responded 26 reported to have taken such a step because of Neglect, 60 because of family turbulence and 86 because of sexual and physical abuse subjected to them at home. Domestic violence in Latin America is also a leading cause for the loss of parental care. SOS Children's Villages, an NGO working for children, found that 73% of children in their villages in Venezuela had prior experiences of physical or psychological violence, including sexual violence. The organization found that 88% of children in SOS Children's Villages in Croatia, 75% of children in Belarus, and 55% of children in Lithuania had suffered physical or sexual violence within the biological family. Also, many children are removed from families because of substance abuse by their parents and caregivers. The Nithari incidence is an excellent example of such violence where skeletons of a number of apparently murdered women and children were unearthed in the village.

Disability. Because of the widespread stigmatization of children with disabilities as well as the lack of support provided to parents, these children are institutionalized at significantly higher rates than other children. In Jamaica, for example, 65% of children with developmental or physical disabilities live in homes run exclusively for children with disabilities. Country reports prepared by CEE/CIS for the 2002 UN Special Session on Children found that the overriding reason why families placed their children with disabilities in institutions was due to lack of caregiving capacity. Misdiagnosis, overdiagnosis, and an exclusive focus on the medical model of disability are also problems leading to the overuse of institutionalization in these countries. In some cases, lack of stimulation or lack of access to high-quality health and education can delay development, adding to children's disability.

Family catastrophes, including HIV/AIDS. Armed conflicts, natural disasters on a massive scale, HIV/AIDS pandemic, or other diseases naturally incline some humanitarian organizations to propose the establishment of care institutions and orphanages as a suitable response to the large number of children in need of care. In Russia, for example, babies born with HIV who have been abandoned are placed in special orphanages just for HIV-positive children, or isolated indefinitely in hospital wards, where they are deprived of any opportunities for social, physical, and mental development.

In some conflict-torn countries where a high proportion of children have lost one or both parents, levels of institutionalization may be unusually high. In Somalia, for example, although it is contrary to Islamic standards and traditional norms, use of children's homes or orphanages is strongly advocated by parents and careers, especially in urban areas. Children's homes, all of which subsist on external, mostly charitable support, provide children with food, shelter, and education, which are often not available elsewhere. Among the approximately 8,000 Somali children resident in children's homes, a high proportion of them have relatives.

Lack of alternatives. In many environments, alternatives to institutionalization, including support for vulnerable families and family-based care, have not been developed. This can lead to unnecessary overuse of residential placements. For example, the director of a psychiatric hospital in Turkey estimated that of 500 patients (including adults and children) at his facility, only 10% would need to be confined as in-patients if community-based services were available. In Romania, the population of children in orphanages has been reduced, but many children with disabilities have simply been moved from larger institutions to smaller ones. The extensive funding needed for these new institutions has drained scarce resources from developing foster care and services that would support community integration.

Children who are victims of sexual or economic exploitation are frequently detained as if they were criminals, including girls fleeing forced marriages, trafficked children, and children in commercial sex industry. For example, under "safe custody" laws in Bangladesh, boys and girls can be detained in jails or homes for vagrants in cases where they have been the victims of rape or sexual assaults, rescued from brothels or from traffickers, or, in the case of girls and women, where they have married someone from another religion or without the consent of their guardians. Similarly, in India and Nepal, trafficking survivors and girls found in brothels are often forced by the police and NGOs into "protective custody" in secure institutions.

The use of so-called protective custody disproportionately affects girls who are most often victims of sexual abuse and exploitation. Detention for the protection of girls who have been sexually abused is particularly acute in countries where "honour crimes" are practiced. For example, in Syria, girls who have been sexually assaulted are often put into an institution for juvenile delinquents rather than handed over to their parents, due to fears that the girls may be killed to preserve the family honour, or forced to marry their rapist.

Since girls are usually detained in much smaller numbers than boys, governments may have even fewer facilities to ensure their segregation from adults. A 2002 paper on juveniles and the law commented that "The numbers of juvenile girls within the system are small, and as a result they are simply tacked onto the rest of the system with little recognition that their needs are different and separate from older women. It also means that they attract fewer resources. Girls in detention facilities are at particular risk of physical and sexual abuse, particularly when detained in mixed-sex facilities, or where a general lack of facilities for girls results in placement in adult facilities. An additional concern is the lack of female staff in facilities detaining girls. Male staff often engages in 'sanctioned sexual harassment', including improper touching during searches or watching girls while they dress, shower, or use the toilet. Male staffs also use their positions of authority to demand sexual favours, and are responsible for sexual assault and rape."

Reformation and rehabilitation, instead of penalizing the child, is the essence of juvenile jurisprudence. Toward this end, it is necessary to place the juvenile in a specialized setting where his or her development is of paramount importance. If adult offender and juvenile are kept together there is a danger of the juvenile being corrupted by hardened criminals or being abused by them. The harsh treatment meted to inmates in police lockups and jails is not commensurate with the juvenile's age and is likely to scar him.

Under no circumstances is a juvenile to be kept in a police lockup or jail. This has been the sentiment of juvenile legislation since the enactment of the Children Acts. Separate detection facilities were established for placement of youthful offenders under BCA 1948; pending enquiry they were to be detained in Approved Centres and those found to have committed an offence were to be kept in Classifying Centres. Distinct institutions for the placement of juveniles continued under JJA 1986 and Juvenile Justice (Care and Protection of Children) Act, 2000.

Institutions under Juvenile Justice (Care and Protection of Children) Act, 2000

Juvenile Justice (Care and Protection of Children) Act, 2000, is a big leap forward in terms of being a progressive and proactive legislation for care, protection, treatment, and rehabilitation of child in need of care and protection and juvenile in conflict with law. It is a comprehensive legislation for justice to the children in the situation of abuse, exploitation, and social maladjustment. The act provides for safety and security from abandonment and for development of character and personality of the juveniles to become useful citizens of the country.

It enjoins on states to make provisions for proper care, treatment, development, and rehabilitation of children/juveniles. It also calls upon the state to develop networks with voluntary organizations working in various fields of child welfare to come forward and shoulder the responsibility along with the state to further the care of child in need of care and protection and juvenile in conflict with law.

The institutions under the new JJ Act, 2000, are supposed to act as places of safety that are conducive to positive character and personality development of children. The institutions therefore have to develop suitable programmes to achieve this. The institutions now provided under the new JJ Act, 2000, are observation homes, special homes, children's homes, shelter homes, and after-care organizations. These are either government-run institutions or bonafide institutions run by NGOs that are expected to provide a congenial atmosphere for the holistic growth and development of children/juveniles.

The preamble of the Juvenile Justice (Care and Protection of Children) Act, 2000, is very comprehensive and enumerates needs for proper care, protection, and treatment of juveniles/children supporting catering to their rehabilitative and developmental needs while adopting a child-family approach. The final disposal/dispositions/rehabilitation processes established through various institutions under this act have to be in the best interest of the juvenile/child.

The homes under the Juvenile Justice Act, 1986, now Juvenile Justice (Care and Protection of Children) Act, 2000, are mostly under the direct charge of the government. The act, however, stipulates the involvement of voluntary sector in the management of these homes, but very little initiative has so far been taken. On a very small scale in Delhi, voluntary organizations like Prayas and Samarth have been associated with government-run homes. Maharashtra, however, has many more examples of government–NGO partnership, the major one being the Children Aid Society, which has been running most of the government institutions for a long time, and, in Mumbai, perhaps Don Bosco has access to a few government homes.

The new act stipulates establishment of various kinds of institutions for the residential care of the children/juveniles and prescribes therein for the observance and enforcement of minimum standards for the care of juveniles/children. The various types of homes run for children/juveniles are detailed as follows:

1. *Observation homes.* An observation home is an institution established for the temporary reception of juveniles in conflict with law during the pendency of their inquiry before JJB.[46] The law provides for an observation home to be set up in each district or a group of districts by the state government or by a voluntary organization under an agreement with the state government.

   Maintenance of these institutions is an integral part of law and order and is the responsibility of the state. Voluntary organizations should be encouraged to provide their expert services to benefit the juveniles housed therein. It is preferable for JJB to hold its sittings at the observation home. This prevents delay in disposal of juvenile cases because the presence of the juvenile not released on bail is guaranteed on each JJB date; he is not at the mercy of police escort for production before JJB.

   Juveniles are to be segregated in an observation home according to their age, that is, 7–12 years, 12–16 years, and 16–18 years. This separation is essential to curtail bullying of the younger juveniles at the hands of older ones and to protect young juveniles from the influence of older juvenile offenders, who may have committed violent offences or have been consistently engaging in criminal activities. This segregation takes place pursuant to preliminary inquiries that are conducted in the reception unit of the observation home where the juvenile is initially kept for classification according to age and physical and mental status. Separate observation homes are to be maintained for boys and girls.

It is hoped that very few juveniles would remain in the observation home pending their inquiry as most would have been released on bail. It is also hoped that the period of stay in the observation home would be short as the inquiry is to be expeditiously completed. Unfortunately, the reality at these homes is very different. Observation homes are filled to the brim, as many juveniles are unable to avail of bail provisions, mainly because they are migrants having no family or monetary support and therefore unable to access legal representation or provide surety to the satisfaction of JJB. Furthermore, JJBs rarely dispose of juvenile cases within the period contemplated by law and juveniles continue to languish in the observation home for long periods. Hence, it is imperative to provide the juvenile with educational and vocational training in the observation home so that his stay there is not wasted.

State governments in their respective rules framed under juvenile legislation are to prescribe the standard to be maintained in observation homes and the measures to be taken for the rehabilitation and social integration of the juvenile. It is necessary to recollect the affirmations made in the Beijing Rules under Rule No. 13.1: "Detention pending trial shall be used only as a measure of last resort and for the shortest possible period of time," and Rule No. 13.2: "Whenever possible, detention pending trial shall be replaced by alternative measures, such as close supervision, intensive care or placement with a family or in an educational setting or home." Under Clause 13.5, it is set out that "While in custody, juveniles shall receive care, protection and all necessary individual assistance such as social, educational, vocational, psychological, medical and physical they may require in view of their age, sex and personality."

2. *Special homes.* These are set up for reception and rehabilitation of juveniles in conflict with law under the act. A special home is to be established "for reception and rehabilitation of juvenile in conflict with law under this Act."[47] On completion of inquiry, if JJB is of the opinion that a juvenile should be institutionalized, he is required to be placed in a special home for his treatment.

The state government is required to set up special homes in a district or group of districts by itself or under agreement with a voluntary organization. Under the 1986 Act, only the state government could establish special homes and observation homes.[48] The entry of voluntary organizations in the establishment or management of these detention facilities is vociferously opposed because the potential for abuse in a close institution is very high and the levels of accountability of private entities would be very low.

Placement of a juvenile in a special home is under the law restricted to a period of years. During their stay in the special home a juvenile should be able to avail of education or vocational courses depending upon his aptitude as well as facilities for sports and co-curricular activities such as music, painting, reading, drama, yoga, and so on. An incarcerated juvenile must benefit from his stay in a special home as otherwise his detention will amount to punishment and the object of juvenile legislation will be defeated. Moreover, the stay in the special home, as also the observation home, should lead to realization in the child that what he had done was wrong. It is not only education or vocational training that can bring about this change. While in the institution he should be under the guidance of a PO, and in certain cases intensive counselling, and at the same time undergo life-skill training to help him face the challenges he will face in the big bad world.

3. *Children homes.* These are established for the reception of children in need of care and protection during the pendency of any enquiry and, subsequently, for their care, treatment, education, training, development, and rehabilitation.
4. *Shelter homes.* The state government may identify reputed and capable voluntary organizations and provide them assistance to set up and administer as many shelter homes for the juveniles or children as may be required. These shelter homes shall function as drop-in-centre for children in need of urgent support.
5. *After-care organization.* The government may by rule made under this act provide for the establishment or recognition of after-care organizations for taking care of juveniles or children, after they leave special homes or children's homes for the purpose of enabling them to lead honest, industrious, and useful

life. After-care organizations are for the care, guidance, and protection of juveniles in conflict with law or children in need of care and protection who have completed their term in the special homes or children's homes, and their rehabilitation process is not completed. After-care is the means and rehabilitation is the end.[49] "The objective of these organizations shall be to enable such children to adapt to the society and during their stay in these transitional homes and these children will be encouraged to move away from an institution-based life to a normal one."[50]

It is the PO who will refer a juvenile to the after-care home and monitor his progress in such facility. As a juvenile's stay in an after-care home is to advocate independence and prepare him to face the world without institutional support, the law envisages that such stay should not exceed three years.[51] A juvenile cannot against his wish be admitted to an after-care programme.

Management of Institutions

The management of shelter homes is the true indicator of the spirit of Juvenile Justice Act being followed. It is the shelter home where the purpose of the act is either achieved or defeated. True to the expression, there should be family-like environment in the care homes and juveniles should be treated with humane approach and love and affection. The approach of treating the juveniles must be distinctly child-friendly. The home must have opportunities for the growth and development of character and personality of the juveniles. The treatment of juveniles should lead to reform them of their mistakes and inculcate in them some values which can help them become good citizens and social beings. For effective management, the home must have certain set of rules, procedures, and daily routine and have sufficient facilities. The following responses were received from the respondents regarding the infrastructure facilities in the institutions.

The available studies, however, show that there are very few homes in the country that cater to even the fringe of the problem. The official records point to the fact the living conditions in the homes are pathetic and inhuman. So much so that several Public Interest Litigations (PILs) were filed in the Supreme Court, Delhi High Court, and Patna High Court, and so on, against the prevailing conditions of the homes. These PILs have brought in some improvements, but they are not significant.

The entire situation seems to be paradoxical. On one hand, there is a need for more residential institutions for children, and on the other, the existing institutions are not providing a congenial environment as per the objectives of the JJ Act, 2000. The homes continue to be like prisons for both the children in need of care and protection and for juveniles in conflict with law. Despite the best of intentions, lack of coordination between various juvenile justice agencies causes the whole system to be dysfunctional. A report released by the National Commission for Protection of Child Rights (NCPCR) on February 6, 2008, throws light on the pitiful condition of juvenile delinquents languishing in reform homes in India. About 5,000 cases against juveniles are pending in courts. Apart from delayed justice, these children are victims of improper care by reform homes. Over 50% of juvenile homes do not provide any counselling services to juvenile delinquents; in addition, more than 80% of caretakers of these homes are not trained.

In 70% of juvenile care centres, physical punishment is a dominant method to discipline children. They are locked up for 24 hours or even more and not allowed to go out, and if they even try to peep outside, they are beaten up. The report has suggested that reforms should be undertaken by juvenile homes. Not only this, the caretakers of juvenile homes should be so trained and equipped to deal with juveniles under them with tenderness and care, as would be required for dealing with such children of tender age.

The juvenile homes are generally considered by all children as jails. This impression has to be erased from the mind of one and all. The fact is that in some ways, they are worse than adults' jails. Regular prisons have enough space for prisoners, but in most juvenile homes there is not even enough space for the juveniles to stay in proper humane conditions. For girls, the situation is even worse. At places, a hundred girls are made to spend their entire day inside one small room in the name of protection.

Institution for Girls in Delhi

There are three observation homes for girls, three juvenile homes for girls, and three juvenile-cum-special homes for girls in Delhi. All the nine institutions are located in the Nirmal Chhaya Complex in the form of nine buildings. These homes are located within the premise of Nirmal Chhaya, which is owned by the Government of Delhi and comes under the direct control of the Department of Social Welfare.

Let us first understand the nature of these three types of institutions.

1. *Juvenile-cum-special homes for girls.* This home was established in the year 1960 and has a sanctioned capacity of keeping 75 children (girls) at a time. It is a home where the destitute/neglected/delinquent juveniles are admitted under the state protection under the orders of Juvenile Welfare Board/Court till they cease to be juveniles. The board can extend the period of their stay, but in no case beyond 20 years of age. The girls falling between 12 and 18 years of age are admitted in juvenile home and between 7 and 18 years of age are admitted in special home. The inmates are provided with free boarding, lodging, medical care, school education, and vocational training facilities. It has also been designated as special home for girls where emphasis is given to the development of character and abilities and to training for reformation of delinquent girls.[52]
2. *Juvenile homes for girls.* This home was established in the year 1975 and has a sanctioned capacity of keeping 100 children at a time. The destitute/neglected juveniles (girls) are admitted under the state protection under the orders of Juvenile Welfare Board (age group 0–12 years for juvenile girls and 0–5 years for boys). The inmates are provided with free boarding, lodging, medical care, school education, and vocational training facilities.[53]
3. *Observation homes for girls.* It is a remand home/observation home established in the year 1960. It has a sanctioned capacity of keeping 50 children at a time. Destitute/neglected girls below the age of 18 years and boys below the age of 6 years who are found begging/or without ostensible means of subsistence/or whose parents/guardians are unfit to exercise control over them/or who are likely to be abused or exploited for immoral or illegal purposes/or are taken charge of by the police/or any other person/or organization authorized by the Government of India are kept here under the orders of the Juvenile Welfare Board/Court till their restoration or commitment by the board/court to the juvenile home. Free boarding and lodging, medical care, school education, and vocational training are provided to the children.[54]

Institutional Structure of Homes as Understood by the Present Study

Observation Home for Girls: Nirmal Chhaya Complex, Jail Road, New Delhi

Physical facilities. The above-mentioned observation home from where the respondents were selected is one of the homes for socially delinquent girl child. While it has a capacity of only 50 girls the website of the Delhi Social Welfare Department shows that the total number of girls in the institution in the year 2001 was 183. Even at the time when information was being gathered from the respondents for this present study the strength of the home was 200 girls.

Staff position. The home is composed of the following staff: superintendent, welfare officer/probation officer, care taker, educator, vocational instructor, peon, and a cook.

Food. In the breakfast, children are given bread, eggs, and so on. In the evening they get tea and biscuits. In the lunch, rice, dal, and vegetables are served. In dinner, chapatti, dal, and vegetables are given to the children. The quality of food was found to be good.

Education and vocational programme. Non-Formal Education and Vocational Training Skills are given to the girls.

Health. The home has a health centre. Children undergo health checkups at the time of admission. A doctor comes every day to the health centre. Children get the medicine and special diet as prescribed by the doctor Any complicated cases of illness are referred to the district hospital or private nursing home for treatment, and expenses are borne by the home.

Shelter Homes for Girls: Prayas, Tughlakabad Institutional Area

Physical facilities. This shelter home for girls was established in the year 1999 for those in need of care and protection. It has a capacity of 50 girls and at the time of data collection there were 50 girls. The Child Welfare Committee refers these girls to Prayas Shelter Home for rehabilitation and repatriation. It is an NGO-run institution under the authorization and permission of the government. Prayas has been declared a fit institution to run homes.

Staff position. The home is run by a shelter home manager, social worker, two house mothers, cook, and two officc attendants.

Food. For breakfast, children are given porridge, milk, fruits, bread, eggs, and so on. In the evening, they get tea and snacks. For lunch and dinner, chapatti, rice, dal, and vegetables are served. The quality of food was found to be very good.

Education and vocational programme. The girls are given non-formal education and vocational training skills according to the need and demand.

Health. The home has a medical room. Children undergo regular health checkups. A doctor comes every alternate day and gives medicines as and when required.

The responses received from the girls on the conditions present in the institutions where they were staying are as follows.

The above data show that 75% of the respondents from both homes felt they were getting adequate food. As much as 12% of the girls felt that there was a need for more number of toilets, 88% had no complaints in this regard however. It was felt that the overall medical facilities made available for girls were adequate. However, 10% of the girls reported facing problems in medical aid during emergencies.

The residential care has always been under severe criticism because it isolates children from the wider society. The poor physical conditions and prevalence of inhuman, unfriendly, atmosphere are two primary reasons for such criticism. So much so that in spite of its necessity, in principle, they have agreed to the principle of institution as a last resort. More important, there is a complete lack of understanding about the meaning and significance of the term "home" as discussed earlier among the functionaries.

Figure 7.1

Adequate Food in Institutions

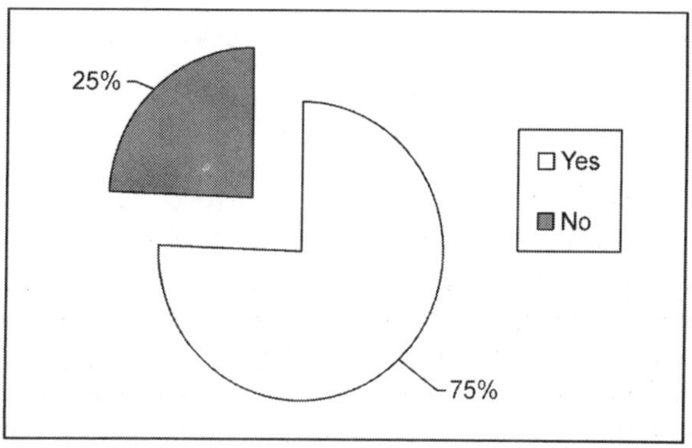

Figure 7.2

Access to Toilet in Institutions

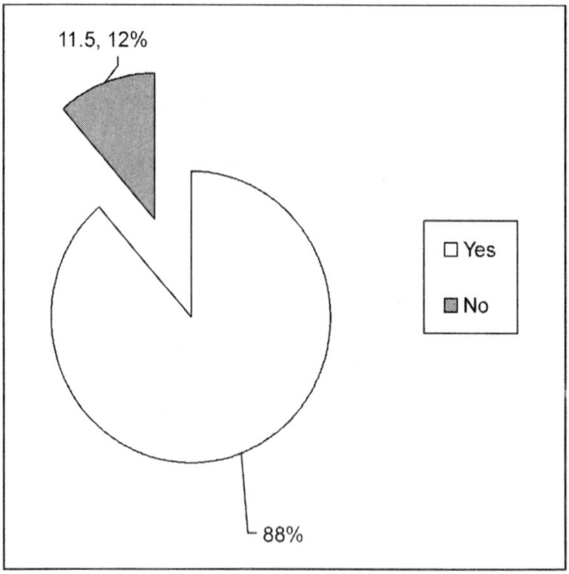

Figure 7.3

Adequate Medical Facility in Institutions

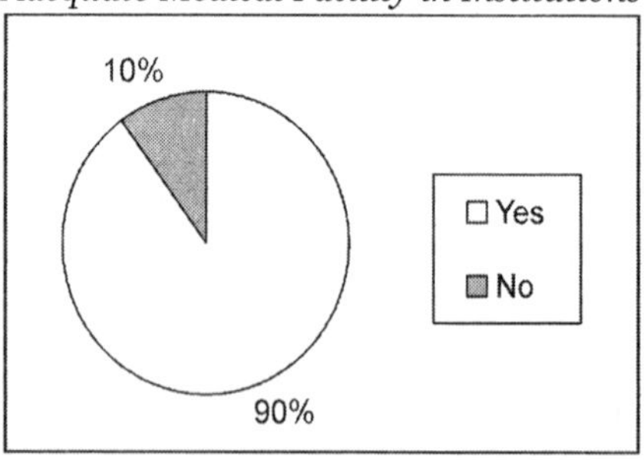

The meaning of residential care/institutional care must be understood in running a care home, both in terms of concept and management. The management (system) should be informal and interpersonal relationships between the children and the staff should be cordial. Only when the children have a say and rights of participation in the management (system) of the home can we have a good residential care system or a child-friendly care home.

Most of the times, it is seen that there are a number of undesirable practices prevalent in these institutions, which are often contrary to the provisions of the act and the rules laid down for handling juveniles. Perhaps this is a major reason for the deplorable living conditions at the institutions for children in India, and thus the inmates are not happy staying at these institutions. The present study's data show that almost 60% of the respondents expressed that they were not happy about living in the institutions. The reasons given for their unhappiness included misbehaviour by the staff (see figure below).

Figure 7.4

Reasons for Not being Happy in the Institution

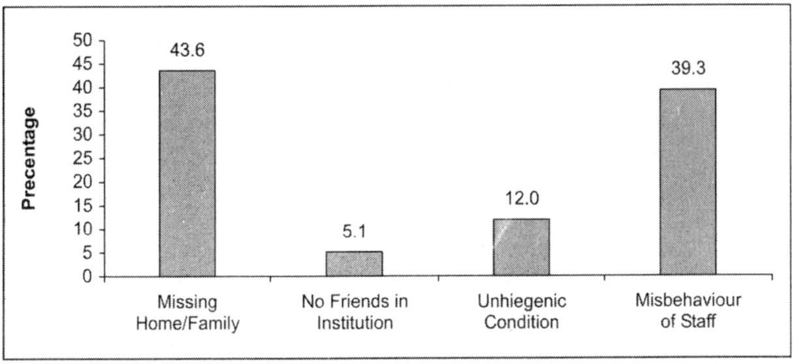

Respondents' Perspective on Girl Child Delinquency and Future Aspirations

Even though these children have gone through the worst in life, they still dream of being independent, having a career, and living on their own. As shown in the table above maximum number of respondents wanted to become doctors (24%) followed by teachers (18.5%), and 13% said their only ambition in life was to earn lots of money. Questions relating to how they saw their future revealed that out of the total sample of 200 girls, 40 of them wanted to do a job, 31 wanted to go back home, and 29 wanted to stay back and study more.

Most of the respondents were very unhappy (60%) with their present status, but a notable observation was that they wanted the society to make efforts to improve their present status and condition.

They felt that the best way to do it was to provide them with better educational opportunities. Others felt that the mechanisms should be worked out where their pending cases are decided at the earliest so that they can lead a free life. Some felt that best way to improve their present situation was to get a job, and for this they wanted to acquire various market-driven vocational skills.

Figure 7.5

Ambitions

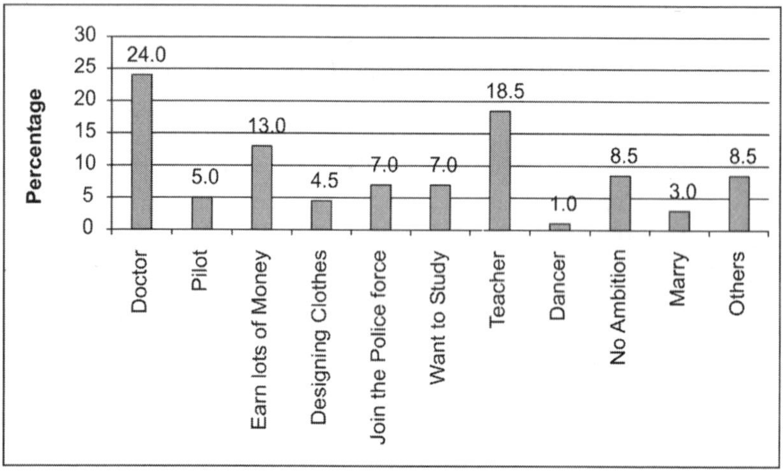

Figure 7.6

Immediate Wish of Respondents

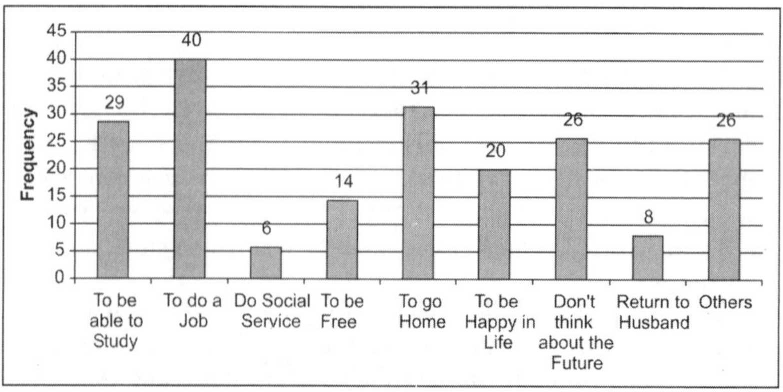

Figure 7.7

How to Improve Their Present Condition

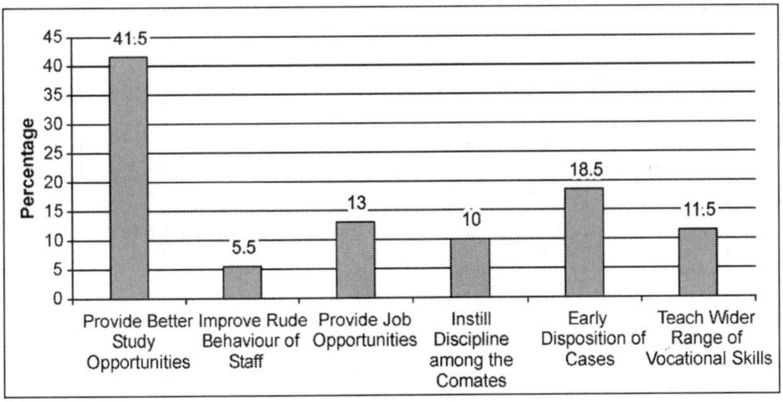

Table 7.1

Respondents' Expectation from Society

Child's Expectation from Society	*Frequency*	*Percentage*
People should know the problems of children	54	43.9
People should know the facts about the case before making their judgement	29	23.5
Abusers should be punished severely	9	7.4
People should not misbehave with children	20	16.3
Family should not differentiate between a girl and a boy	11	8.9
Total	123	100.0

Leaving aside 3% of the cases where the child came in contact with the juvenile justice system because of being abandoned by the family, the remaining 97% very affirmatively feel that what they did was due to their unfavourable conditions.

They were very upset with the society's reaction and parental attitude and wished that society would change their attitude toward girl child delinquency (66%) and understand that even they may have aspirations and have the right to get what they wanted. The kind of changes in the society's perspective included the following.

More than half of them felt that what they did was not antisocial and was only a means of running away from their plight and abusive circumstances. Since the circumstances to fulfil these rights were not

Figure 7.8

Does the Child Consider her Act as Antisocial

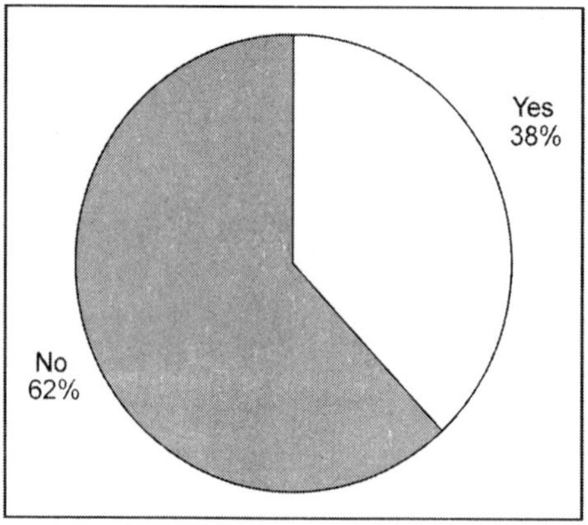

favourable they had to act out to forcefully fulfil their aspirations. The above analysis shows that no child actively wants to disobey or violate the law. She or he is forced to do so because of debilitating, stifling circumstances. This external force acts upon the child and govern his or her behaviour. After interacting with girls it was felt that the social environment in which the offence was committed is very important if we want to understand their delinquent behaviour and the reasons behind it.

Precisely for these reasons the Juvenile Justice (Care and Protection of Children) Act, 2000, prescribes for child-friendly approach and adjudication and disposition of matters in the best interest of the children in the preamble itself. Furthermore, the provision of involvement of social workers and voluntary organizations in running the institutions, protection of children, functioning of competent authorities and advisory boards have been made to make the institutions more homely and child-friendly. Only when the provisions of the Juvenile Justice Act are properly implemented will children feel happy to stay in these homes and will their proper growth and development happen. The child welfare and protection programmes should be more to help with rehabilitating the children and their reentry into the mainstream society as equal citizens. Provisions like adoption, foster care, and sponsorship aimed at rehabilitation can also be fine-tuned to become the means to deinstitutionalize children.

Notes

1. Vicentnathan, S.G. (2006), Juvenile Justice in India. In *Delinquency and Juvenile Justice System in the Non-Western World* (ed. P.C. Friday and X. Ren), New York, Criminal Justice Press, p. 25.
2. Siddique, A. (1978), *Criminology Problems and Perspectives*, Lucknow, UP, India, Eastern Book Company, pp. 129–130.
3. Vicentnathan, Juvenile Justice in India, p. 28
4. Arulselvam, M. (2002), *Law Relating to Juveniles and Probation*, Chennai, Marathi Publications, pp. 226–246.
5. Vicentnathan, Juvenile Justice in India, p. 29.
6. Pinheiro, P.S. (2005), *World Report on Violence against Children*, New York, United Nations Publication, pp. 195–196.
7. Wallace, S.E. (1971), *Total Institutions*, Piscataway, NJ, Transaction Publishers, p. 11.
8. Lundman, R.J. (2001), *Prevention and Control of Juvenile Delinquency* (3rd ed.), New York, Oxford University Press, p. 29.
9. Rule 26 of the Beijing Rules.
10. Rule 84 (1) of the Model Rules of Juvenile Justice Act (JJA), 2000.
11. Rule 12(1)(b) of the Karnataka (Juvenile Justice Care and Protection of Children) Rules, 2002.
12. Rule 11(2) and (3) of the Karnataka (Juvenile Justice Care and Protection of Children) Rules, 2002.
13. Section 10(1) of JJA, 2000.
14. Ibid.
15. Ibid.
16. Section 13(a) of JJA, 2000.
17. Section 13(b) of JJA, 2000.
18. Section 18(1) of JJA, 1986.
19. Section 64 of BCA, 1948
20. Rule 75 of the Model Rules of JJA, 2000.
21. Rule 76 of the Model Rules of JJA, 2000.
22. Rule 84 (11) of the Model Rules of JJA, 2000.
23. Sabnis, M.S. (1996), *Juvenile Justice and Juvenile Correction: Pride and Prudence*, Somaiya Publications, New Delhi, p. 86.
24. Section 13 of the Probation of Offenders Act, 1958.
25. Rule 85 of the Model Rules.
26. Section 14 of the Probation of Offenders Act, 1958.
27. Section 21 of the Bombay Children Act, 1948.
28. Section 33 (d) of JJA, 1986.

29. Section 57 (3) of JJA, 1986.
30. Sabnis, *Juvenile Justice and Juvenile Correction*, p. 251.
31. Section 12 (1) of JJA, 2000.
32. Section 15 (3) of JJA, 2000.
33. Section 75 of BCA, 1948.
34. Section 4(3) of JJA, 2000.
35. Rule 7(1) of the Model Rules of JJA, 2000.
36. Rule 5(4) of the Model Rules of JJA, 2000.
37. Rule 91(c) of the Model Rules of JJA, 2000.
38. Section 5(3) of JJA, 1986.
39. Rule 8 of the Model Rules.
40. Section 25 of JJA, 1986.
41. Rule 99 of the Model Rules.
42. Rule 21.1 of the Beijing Rules.
43. Rule 21.2 of the Beijing Rules.
44. Rule 6(20) of the Maharashtra Juvenile Justice (Care and Protection of Children) Rules, 2002.
45. Pinheiro, *World Report on Violence against Children*, pp. 185–186.
46. Section 8 of JJA, 2000.
47. Section 9 of JJA, 2000.
48. Section 10 and 11 of JJA, 1986.
49. Sabnis, *Juvenile Justice and Juvenile Correction*, p. 344.
50. Rule 38 (5)of the Model Rules.
51. Section 44 of JJA, 2000.
52. Information taken from the website of Social Welfare Department, Government of NCT Delhi; http://socialwelfare.delhigovt.nic.in/Asp/dspInstitute.asp?opt=SI&cat=C001
53. Ibid.
54. Ibid.

8

Coping Mechanism by the State

Acts for Girl Child Protection

In India children have been subjected to excessive and brutal punishments for their misbehaviour by parents, teachers, guardians, the police, and custodians of institutions. This is because most of the adults hold the negative view that children are not "persons" and therefore should not have a say in life choices but should submit to what adults wish. This attitude is gradually changing, especially because of the active efforts of many governmental and non-governmental organizations and child and legal advocacy groups. Increasingly, children are recognized as "persons" who deserve to be treated with care, protection, right, decency, and fairness.

Legal provisions toward this change began to evolve with the growing democratization of the country and new interpretations of the Constitution of India and the rights therein. The Juvenile Justice Act of 2000 is a great improvement as it includes not only the practices under the Common Law and Indian traditions but also incorporates United Nations recommendations, especially the UN Convention on the Rights of the Child (UNCRC) of 1989. The importance of the UNCRC for India is that, in addition to stressing the importance of "Participation right" and "Survival and development rights," it also stresses "Participation rights of children." This does not mean that adults have to consult small children on every matter but that "the child should grow to recognize its own voice and to respect those of others."

UN Convention on the Rights of Child (UNCRC) 1989

The UNCRC adopted by the General Assembly of the United Nations in 1989 to protect the rights of children is the most important instrument in the history of child rights at the international level. The convention has been ratified by most of the developed as well as developing countries, including India, which ratified the convention in 1992. The major articles in the convention leading to abusive situations among children are as follows:

Article 2(2). Protection against all forms of discrimination or punishment

Article 3. Protect the best interests of children

Article 19. Protect children from all forms of physical or mental violence, injury or abuse, neglect or negligent treatment, maltreatment or exploitation, including sexual abuse while in the care of parents, legal guardians, or any other person in whose care they are

Article 25. Protection of the physical and mental health of the child

Article 33. Protection from illicit use of narcotic drugs and psychotropic substances

Article 34. Undertake to protect children from all forms of sexual exploitation and sexual abuse

Article 35. Take all appropriate national, bilateral, and multi-lateral measures to prevent the abduction, sale, or traffic of children for any purpose or in any form

Article 36. Protection from all forms of exploitation prejudicial to any aspect of child's welfare.

The UNCRC has identified four core rights of children, namely, rights to: survival, development, participation, and protection. All children being deprived of these basic rights fall in the category of child abuse and neglect.

Constitutional (Indian) Provisions Related to Girl Child

The Constitution of India contains several provisions dealing directly or indirectly with children including the girl child:

Article 14. The state shall not deny to any person equality before the law or the equal protection of the laws within the territory of India.

Article 15. The state shall not discriminate against any citizen on grounds only of religion, race, caste, sex, and place of birth or any of them.

Article 15(3). Nothing in this article shall prevent the state from making any special provision for women and children.

Article 19(1)(a). All citizens shall have the right (a) to freedom of speech and expression.

Article 21. No person shall be deprived of his or her life or personal liberty except according to procedure established by law.

Article 23. Traffic in human beings and beggary and other forms of forced labour are prohibited and any contravention of this provision shall be an offence punishable in accordance with the law.

Article 24. No child below the age of 14 years shall be employed to work in any factory or mine or engaged in any other hazardous employment.

Article 38. The state shall strive to promote the welfare of the people by securing and protecting as effectively as it may a social order in which justice—social, economic, and political—shall inform all the institutions of the national life.

Article 39. The state shall, in particular, direct its policy toward securing (e) that the health and strength of workers, men and women, and the tender-aged children are not abused and that citizens are not forced by economic necessity to enter avocations unsuited to their age or strength and (f) That children are given opportunities and facilities to develop in a healthy manner and in conditions of freedom and dignity and that childhood and youth are protected against exploitation and against moral and material abandonment.

Article 45. The state shall endeavour to provide, within a period of ten years from the commencement of this Constitution, for free and compulsory education for all children until they complete the age of 14 years.

The Indian Penal Code

Crimes against children punishable under the Indian Penal Code (IPC) include:

(a) Foeticides (crime against children being born), Section 315 and 316
(b) Infanticides (crime against unborn children), Section 315
(c) Abetment of suicide (abetment to commit suicide to minor), Section 305

(d) Exposure and abandonment (crime against children by parents or others to expose or to leave them with the intention of abandonment), Section 317

(e) Kidnapping and abduction:
   - (i) Kidnapping for extortion (Section 360)
   - (ii) Kidnapping from lawful guardianship (Section 361)
   - (iii) Kidnapping for ransom (Section 363, read with Section 384)
   - (iv) Kidnapping for camel racing, etc. (Section 363)
   - (v) Kidnapping for begging (Section 363-A)
   - (vi) Kidnapping to compel for marriage (Section 366)
   - (vii) Kidnapping for slavery, etc. (Section 367)
   - (viii) Kidnapping for Stealing from Person (under 10 years of age only; Section 369)

(f) Procurement of minor girls (by inducement or by force to seduce or have illicit intercourse; Section 366-A)

(g) Selling of girls for prostitution (Section 372)

(h) Buying of girls for prostitution (Section 373)

(i) Rape (Section 376)

(j) Unnatural sex (Section 377)

The Juvenile Justice (Care and Protection of Children) Act, 2000

The Juvenile Justice (Care and Protection of Children) Act, 2000, which is considered a "Blueprint of Child Welfare," appears to be the most comprehensive law for the children in the country. It provides for the improved treatment of the child, with dignity, concern, and care. It is required under the act that those who work with juveniles in the roles of law enforcement or providing care and services, such as judges, police officers, and probation officers, should have special training in child psychology and treat children with care and dignity. The act brings juveniles under juvenile court jurisdictions for two main reasons: for being in conflict with the law, or for being in need of care and protection.

1. Children in need of care and protection include a child:
   - (i) found without any home or settled place or abode and without any ostensible means of subsistence.
   - (ii) found begging or is either a street child or a working child.
   - (iii) residing with a person (whether a guardian of the child or not) and such person (a) has threatened to kill or injure

the child and there is a reasonable likelihood of the threat being carried out or (b) has killed, abused, or neglected some other child or children and there is a reasonable likelihood of the child in question being killed, abused, or neglected by that person.

(iv) mentally or physically challenged or ill or suffering from terminal diseases or incurable disease and having one to support or look after.

(v) having a parent or guardian and such parent or guardian is unfit or incapacitated to exercise control over the child.

(vi) who does not have parents and no one is willing to take care of or whose parents cannot be found after reasonable inquiry.

(vii) being or is likely to be grossly abused, tortured, or exploited for the purpose of sexual abuse or illegal acts.

(viii) found vulnerable and is likely to be inducted into drug abuse or trafficking.

(ix) being or is likely to be abused for unconscionable gains.

(x) being a victim of any armed conflict, civil commotion, or natural calamity.

Under the subject matter of children in need of care and protection, many services are provided. Services are provided for abandoned, neglected, dependent, abused, begging, mentally ill, and physically ill children. Children, who are in danger from others, and those who are forcefully subjected to dangerous work, also come under this jurisdiction, as do matters relating to the adoption of children.

2. Children in conflict with law (also referred to as juveniles) include a child who is alleged to have contravened a provision of a criminal/penal legislation and is below the age of 18 when such offence is committed by him or her.

The Juvenile Justice Act outlines the rules and procedures that juvenile justice officials and organizations should follow for juveniles in conflict with the law. When a juvenile is accused of committing an offence it becomes the responsibility of the police officers to ascertain whether the offence has occurred, and if so register the case with the cooperation of the juvenile police unit or officer. The officer is also required to explain to the juvenile the charges against him or her in an understandable manner. The juvenile police officer then has to refer the matter to Juvenile

Justice Board (JJB) and inform the parents or guardians of the child and the probation officer as soon as possible and let them know where the juvenile will appear before the Board.

If the juvenile is not released to the parents of guardians, the juvenile police officer is required to place the juvenile in an appropriate facility or custody to make the child appear before the Juvenile Justice Board. The police cannot compel or threaten juveniles to gain incriminating information (Arulselvam, 2002: 131). The custodians in charge of the facility are required to provide the care, control, and protection that parents would normally provide. Temporary custody may be in observation homes or special homes (custodial or holding institution) either started by the state government or by a state-certified private agency. Juveniles placed there are studied and classified.

It is then decided whether they should stay with parents or guardians or be placed in observation homes or special homes, pending the inquiry by JJB. Juveniles are classified on the basis of gender, age, seriousness of the offence, and special psychological chrematistics. These observation or special homes are located in specified places in every district or a group of districts. There are not very many such institutions because juveniles needing official attention are very low in number.

The Juvenile Justice Act of 2000 states that juveniles who are accused of bailable offences can be released with or without surety. Such juveniles may not be released to their parents or guardians if their exposure could cause moral corruption, physical or psychological endangerment or if the purpose of justice cannot be met or the child may be taken away. Juveniles who should be detained are kept separately from adult detention facilities and are often placed in observation homes or a place of safety (detention institution).

The JJB consists of a qualified metropolitan magistrate (in cities) or a qualified judicial magistrate (in other areas), and two social workers, one of them female. The magistrate is required to have education and training in child psychology or child welfare. The social warders are required to have a minimum of seven years of experience handing children, in health, education, or welfare services. A juvenile can be brought before a member of the board for temporary action, pending a decision by the board. In the hearing of the case, rules of procedure should be followed and a record of proceedings should be maintained.

In the final disposition of the case, the principal magistrate should be present with at least one other member of the board. The decision of the majority of the board is final, but when majority support for a decision is absent, the decision of the principal magistrate is sustained. In addition, the Juvenile Justice Act specifies that juvenile and adult cannot be concurrently tried for an offence; it is specified in the act that a juvenile case should be completed within four months, unless special circumstances dictate otherwise. The state High Court and the Court of Sessions are courts of appeal for review of Juvenile Justice Board decisions.

Children in conflict with the law have procedural rights in the processing of their cases. Parents and children have the right to the use of an attorney (which in practice may have to be approved by the court), and when they do not have means to hire an attorney, one could be appointed with state support or support of legal aid organizations. According to be Constitution of India, Articles 20, 21, and 22, children also have the right to a speedy trial, right to remain silent, right to be adjudicated only with sufficient evidence, and right to life and liberty in accordance with set principles and provisions. Although these rights are talked about, they are not often adequately provided. It seems the justice dispensed in courts incorporates elements of both the accusatorial and the inquisitorial systems of inquiry, more of the latter than the former, again blended with informal, paternalistic, and rehabilitation thrusts.

The act specifies that the board should use the services of probation officers employed by the state. Volunteer probation officers who are selected to help regular probation officers may also provide services; probation officers collect information, which the board uses to inquire into juvenile cases, adjudicate them, and dispose them off with appropriate sanctions and placements. This contrasts with the American juvenile justice system, in which probation officers are mainly entrusted with doing persistence reports, but usually not inquiry reports to be used for adjudicating cases.

Many choices in the disposal of the cases exist. In some cases the board sends the child home to his or her parents or guardians and consults parents and guardians as well, without imposing any serious sanctions. It may order consoling, community service, or placing a juvenile on probation, not exceeding a period of three years. For good conduct observed from the reports of the probation officers, the probation period can be reduced. Sometimes fines are collected from parents, or from the juvenile, if the juvenile is over 14 years of age and his income. Juveniles who are stubborn, older, and unreceptive to treatment can be sent to special homes through appropriate changes made to their earlier placements. A 17-year-old juvenile, for instance, can be sent to a special home (custodial institution). Such decisions made for the protection of the juvenile and the public are required to be explained to the parents, guardians, or the institution responsible for the juveniles. Juveniles who have committed serious offences or are repeat offenders can be placed in reform schools or Borstal Schools for training, education, and discipline.

No juvenile can be subjected to death penalty or life sentence, as per the act. A juvenile cannot be held in custody for inability to pay a fine or a surety. A juvenile who has committed a serious offence, and is 16 years of age, if noted to possess characteristics that would be dangerous to other juveniles in special homes, can be placed, as noted above, in a place of safety for protective custody. This custody should not be above the maximum period of confinement already specified. Provisions exist for the aftercare of children released from custodial institutions.

After due evaluation of juveniles they are recommended for aftercare. The appropriate conditions that the children should follow and the services they should receive from persons and organizations to which they are entrusted are outlined. The records of juvenile convocations are made null and void after the expiry of the date of appeal to the case or a specified time as per the rules. Juveniles are also protected from publicity of their name and identities, but under specific circumstances when it is to the advantage of the juvenile, these may be revealed.

If parents, guardians, custodians, and other adults who are held responsible for the protection and care of children fail in their roles, and neglect, abandon, or cruelly handle children, they are subject to punitive sanction. Adults contributing to the delinquency of juveniles, who induct them into begging or prostitution, place children in bondage, exploit their labour for personal purposes, involve them in illegal and immoral activities, or place them in dangerous occupations are subject to server penalties. Similarly those who provide alcohol or drugs to juveniles are punished.

The Juvenile Justice Act contends that children are not responsible for their actions and requires the juvenile court, as a state agency, to fulfil its role ingrained in the notion of *parens patriae*, so that the best interests of children can be served. From the thrusts of the act and the kinds of agencies called for, one could say that the model of juvenile justice created is tilted more toward the welfare model than the legal model.

In the processing of delinquency case, procedural formalities and rights are recognized, and the parents or guardians can utilize the services of attorneys, but providing care, protection, services, and rehabilitation are given a higher priority. This act is very ambitious and requires the court to find out the causes of the delinquent behaviour and rehabilitate the offender. It remains to be seen how this act is going to be implemented. There are many legal and administrative issues and problems confronting the states that need to be resolved.

The scheme of law distinguishes and comprehensively covers these two categories of children and creates competent authorities such as Child Welfare Committee for children in need of care and protection (Section 29) and Juvenile Justice Board (JJB) for juveniles in conflict with law.

The Child Welfare Committee (CWC)

The Juvenile Justice Act of 2000, sensitive to issues regarding harm done to children, mandates, apart from the Juvenile Justice Board, a parallel organization known as Child Welfare Committee. They process and dispose cases of children "in need of care and protection." One or more CWCs are present in each district or group of districts within a state to receive, examine, and dispose of these types of cases. The committee includes five members: a chairperson and four other members chosen by the state government. One of these persons should be a woman, and another, a professional in the area of child welfare.

When the committee is convened it functions as a bench with the power of a magistrate court. The committee can order needed services for the care, protection, treatment, development, and rehabilitation of children. The committee is also given the role of helping to fulfil the basic needs of children and protection of their rights. The members of the committee are expected to be persons of honourable character and committed to the cause of children. Children needing help and services can be referred to this committee by police, public, public servants, welfare agencies, and citizens. Juveniles themselves can seek care and protection. A child in need of protection services may be temporarily produced before a member of a committee for safe custody, until the committee meets and decides a course of action by a majority decision, or if lacking such a majority, then by the decision of the chairperson of the committee.

A police officer of the committee may as a preliminary step inquire into the juvenile in question and refer the juvenile later for study and entrusting the juvenile to the care of a children's home maintained by the state or certified by it. The inquiry and the disposition should occur within four months. If the juvenile is not supported and protected by the family or guardians, he or she can be kept in children's homes or shelters until an appropriate placement is made. As there are many runaway, needy, abused, and begging children who are found to be away from their district of residence, provisions are made for their transfer to CWCs in their own districts, where inquiries are made and appropriate services are rendered to them for their "restoration" with parents and guardians.

The committee has the sole authority to deal with matters concerning children in need of care and protection. The committee should be constituted for each district or group of districts and consist of a chairperson and four other persons, one of whom at least should be a woman. The committee has the final authority to dispose of cases for the care, protection, treatment, development, and rehabilitation of the children as well as to provide for their basic needs and human rights. A child rescued from hazardous occupation, brothel, abusive family, or other such exploitative situations must be produced before the CWC, which will conduct an inquiry to ensure optimum rehabilitation with minimal damage to the child. Children in need of care and protection are sent directly to children's home by the CWC that passes necessary orders for their rehabilitation, restoration, and social reintegration.

The Juvenile Justice Board (JJB)

It has sole authority to deal with matters concerning children in conflict with law. The Juvenile Justice Board is constituted for each district or group of districts and consists of two social workers and a judicial magistrate. This is an attempt to bring change in the nature of the inquiry and decriminalize the administration of juvenile justice through the presence of two social workers. Once the crime is committed and the child is apprehended, the case comes before JJB. Pending enquiry, the child is kept in an observation home, unless otherwise released as per the law. On conviction, the child is sent to the special home or place of safety.

Under this law, every juvenile in conflict with law has a right to bail as granting bail is mandatory, except when it can pose a threat to the life or well-being of the juvenile. Instead of being sent to a jail, the law takes a reformatory approach and provides for release on probation after advice and admonition or places them in custody of special homes.

Even if the child is accused of doing an offence with an adult, the child must be tried separately in the Juvenile Court (Section 4) called the Juvenile Justice Board. The Juvenile Justice Board and Child Welfare Committees are constituted to ensure child protection through child-friendly administrative infrastructure, with provisions for proceedings, enquiry, and disposal.

It provides for custodial and protective care consisting of different types of homes for such children, namely children's home, shelter home, observation home, and aftercare home. Provisions for services such as drop-in-centre are also given in the act, wherein a child may seek assistance in the form of care, protection, and other support services, including a temporary abode, where he or she feels protected from an exploitative environment. In such a centre, a child may walk in to avail of humane services and walk out at his or her will. There are hundreds of such centres now being run by the Railway Police and Railway Protection Force besides many public servants who are not able to create Government- or NGO-run homes and shelters under the Juvenile Justice (Care and Protection of Children) Act, 2000. In the absence of such shelters and drop-in-centres the entire child protection system is likely to collapse.

The act has created a central advisory board at the central government level and state-level advisory boards to guide central and state governments on planning, implementation, and resource development activities connected with education and rehabilitation of juveniles needing care and protection, and those who have violated the law. In the cities, especially, many services are needed for juveniles. In this regard the Government of India's Ministry of Social Justice and Empowerment is given the role of promoting state government initiatives.

In the cities particularly with a larger juvenile population, city advisory boards have been created as appendices of the Directorate of Social Defence, an organization that coordinates with the central agency and facilitates many of the juvenile service activities (Department of Social Defence, n.d.). At the state level, within the districts, exist committees to monitor and facilitate the objectives of the act and coordinate with activities of state agencies and advisory boards.

The Juvenile Justice Act of 2000 has created a bifurcated system of services at the district-level advisory boards to guide central and state governments in planning, implementation, and resource development activities connected with education and rehabilitation of juveniles needing care and protection and those who have violated of the law (Ministry of Law, justice and Company Affairs, 2000: 31).

In Tamil Nadu, the state organization that coordinates with the central agency and facilitates many of the juvenile service activities is the Directorate of Social Defence (Department of Social Defence, n.d.).

The Juvenile Justice Act (Care and Protection of Children) Act, 2000 replaced the Juvenile Justice Act, 1986, and came into force in April 2001. Prior to enactment of the Juvenile Justice Act 1986, each state had a separate juvenile legislation with distinct provisions. The said act was amended in 2006.

The recent amendments (2006) to the act are given below:

Section Amendments to the earlier Act of 2000

1. 2(a)(a): Inclusion of *definition of adoption*: "Adoption" means the process through which the adopted child is permanently separated from his or her biological parents and becomes the legitimate child of his or her adoptive parents with all the rights, privileges, and responsibilities that are attached to the relationship.
2. 2(d)(i): "Child beggars" included in the definition of children need of care and protection.
3. 10(1): In no case a juvenile in conflict with law shall be placed in a police lockup or lodged in jail.
4. 14(2): Since the provision for enquiry to be completed within four months lacks proper implementation, as inquiries are pending before the boards for a long period of time, it is proposed that the *Chief Judicial Magistrate/Chief Metropolitan Magistrate shall review the pendency of cases of the board every six months*, and shall direct the board to increase the frequency of its sittings or may cause Constitution of additional boards.

5. 15(1)(g): The Juvenile Justice Board can make an order directing *the juvenile to be sent to a special home for a maximum period of three years only.*
6. 16(1): No juvenile in conflict with law can be put under imprisonment for any term which may extend to imprisonment for life.
7. 21: Contravention of provisions dealing with prohibition of publication of name, etc. of child shall be punishable with fine extending to 25,000 rupees as against existing 1,000 rupees.
8. 4 and 29: The state governments to constitute Juvenile Justice Board and Child Welfare Committee for each district within one year of the Amendment Act coming into force.
9. 33(3): The state governments may review cases pending before the Child Welfare Committee to ensure speedy completion of enquiry process.
10. 34(3): All state government/voluntary organizations running institutions for a child/juvenile shall be registered under this act within a period of six months from the date of commencement of the Amendment Act, 2006.
11. 41(4): State government shall recognize one or more of its institutions or voluntary organizations in each district as specialized adoption agencies for the placement of orphans and abandoned or surrendered children for adoption. Children's homes and the institutions run by the state government or voluntary organizations for children who are orphans, abandoned, or surrendered shall ensure that these children are declared free for adoption by the Child Welfare Committee and all such cases shall be referred to the adoption agency in that district for placement of such children in adoption in accordance with guidelines.
12. 62(A): Every state government shall constitute a child protection unit for the state and such units for every district, consisting of such officers and other employees as may be appointed by that government, are to take up matters relating to children/juveniles with a view to ensure the implementation of this act.

This law also creates a legal and rehabilitation/social reintegration package for adoption, foster care, sponsorship, and aftercare services. It is a big step forward in terms of being a progressive and proactive legislation providing for the care, protection, treatment, and rehabilitation of children in need of care and protection and juveniles in conflict with law. This act contributes to the building of a uniform juvenile justice system throughout the country and reaffirms the child's right to survival, protection, family development, and participation.

It also considers institutional and non-institutional services for children. The act has laid special emphasis on rehabilitation and social integration of the children and has provided for institutional and non-institutional measures for care and protection of children. The non-institutional alternatives include adoption, foster care, sponsorship, and aftercare. The act also envisages a system of partnerships with local communities and local governments to implement the legislation.

This act conforms to the UNCRC and seeks to promote a child-friendly juvenile justice system in India. The first example of this lies in the use of different and child-sensitive terminology used in legislation:

1. A child alleged to have committed an offence is known as a "child in conflict with law" not a criminal/accused or juvenile delinquent.
2. A juvenile can be "apprehended" not arrested.
3. A child in conflict with law is not subjected to a "trial" but to an "inquiry."
4. A child in conflict with law apprehended by police is supposed to be produced before the "Juvenile Justice Board" not before any other regular Court of Magistrate.

Goa Children's Act, 2003

The Goa Children's Act, 2003, is intended to take a holistic view of a child. It also attempts to blend the legislative, administrative, and children-related schemes to serve the best interests of the "child in need," that is, the expanded definition of "child in need of care and protection" and the "juveniles in conflict with law," as defined under the Juvenile Justice (Care and Protection of Children) Act, 2000. This act refers to the Directive Principles, 93rd Amendment to the Constitution making Elementary Education a Fundamental Right and United Nations Convention on the Rights of Child (UNCRC). This acts aims to protect the children from child abuse, sexual offences, child trafficking, child prostitution and violation of their rights and that they are given opportunity and facilities to develop in a healthy manner and in conditions of freedom and dignity.

However, at least on paper, this is the only act that addresses the issue of child abuse in the following sections:

1. *Section 2 (m)*: Child abuse
2. *Section 3*: Rights of the child (Sections 5 and 8)
3. *Section 7*: Child labour
4. *Section 8*: Child abuse
5. *Section 9*: Child sexual trafficking
6. *Section 10*: Children in difficult circumstances
7. *Section 11*: Girl child
8. *Section 14*: Violations and penalties

To understand the act better, one has to take an in-depth look at its provisions.

Rights of the child. The act adopts the rights enshrined in the UNCRC. This is a positive step as for the first time international law on the rights of a child has been recognized as part of the law of the land. UNCRC recognizes the doctrine of the "best interest of the child" as a primary consideration. The act toes the UNCRC line and adopts the "best interest of child" as the primary consideration. But "the best interest of the child" has not been defined by the act and is therefore open to interpretation. If the rights of the child are clearly laid out by the act, then those rights are guaranteed to the child and are legally enforceable.

Education. It is common knowledge that education does not reach every nook and corner of India. Child illiteracy is rampant in India. There are many villages where a school is still unheard of. The Goa Children's Act takes into account school curriculum, medical facilities in schools, holistic education, proper infrastructure, counselling facilities, adequate teaching aids, and banning of corporal punishment in schools. The act has declared that the government shall work toward the eradication of child illiteracy within a period of three years from the commencement of the act. A comprehensive plan of action is to be made by the state in order to achieve total eradication of child illiteracy, but by the time the plan of action comes into effect, the three years may be up. Implementation has always been one of the biggest problems of the state. The state should come up with a realistic plan of action to tackle the problem of child illiteracy by taking into account the social and economic conditions in the state. The state has also accepted the concept of "zero rejection" for children. No child can be denied admission to schools on grounds of absence of documentation, diseases, or if the child is differently-abled. However, punitive action for failure to implement this provision is not mentioned.

Health and nutrition. This issue has been covered quite thoroughly with mandatory immunization; maternity leave for natural, adoptive, and single mothers; crèches and day care centres; health cards; drug and alcohol abuse; and HIV/AIDS and leprosy-infected children.

Children's homes. Children's homes, governmental and nongovernmental, have often neglected to take into account the best interest of the child. Bogus institutions have also come up in many parts of the country and abused or neglected the children under their care. Under this act, all children's homes are to be registered and district inspection teams are to be constituted for the regulation and supervision of these homes.

Child labour. There has been a lot of debate over the central government's decision to divide child labour into hazardous and nonhazardous occupations. The Goa Children's Act, 2003, has however taken a bold step in the right direction. It has chosen to ignore the distinction between hazardous and nonhazardous occupations and has declared all kinds of child labour as prohibited by the state of Goa. There has been a drastic rise in the physical and sexual exploitation of children in nonhazardous occupations like domestic labour and the hotel industry. Children in nonhazardous occupations also work long hours and are paid less than the minimum wage. This is the first act to recognize that nonhazardous occupations are also hazardous to the well-being of a child.

This act has gone a step further by declaring that trafficking of children for the purpose of labour is also prohibited. This is the first time in India that trafficking of children other than for commercial sexual exploitation has also been recognized as a crime. Punitive measures will also be taken against employers of children under the age of 14 years. The state is to formulate a plan of action to eradicate all forms of child labour within two years from the commencement of this act and also include schemes for the identification, release, and rehabilitation of child labourers. A child labour vigilance officer in each taluk will monitor the implementation of the plan of action.

Child abuse. The act has taken into consideration the increasing number of child sexual abuse cases in the State of Goa. For the past few years there has been a major increase in the case of child sexual abuse. Goa is also a tourist attraction, and many pedophiles come to Goa with the aim of sexually abusing children. Due to this, the Goa Children's Act has concentrated on child sexual abuse and covered it quite thoroughly.

In India there is no separate law for child sexual abuse. In fact it is barely recognized. There are a few sections in the Indian Penal Code that can be used in cases of child sexual abuse. Unless rape has taken place, the offence is not considered to be very traumatic to the child. There is also no definition of child sexual abuse. The Goa Children's Act, 2003, has very clearly defined child sexual abuse and categorized it into three types:

(1) *Grave sexual assault.* This covers different types of intercourse: vaginal, oral, anal, use of objects, forcing minors to have sex with each other, deliberately causing injury to sexual organs, making children pose for pornographic photos or films.
(2) *Sexual assault.* This covers sexual touching with the use of any body part or object, voyeurism, exhibitionism, showing pornographic pictures or films to minors, making children watch others engaged in sexual activity, issuing of threats to sexually abuse a minor, verbally abusing a minor using vulgar and obscene language.
(3) *Incest.* This is the commission of a sexual offence by an adult or a child who is a relative or is related through ties of adoption.

The punishment for grave sexual assault is imprisonment for not less than seven years but which may extend to ten years and fine of ₹ 2,00,000, and for sexual assault the punishment is imprisonment for a term that may extend to three years and fine of ₹ 1,00,000. The punishment for incest is however laid down as imprisonment for the term of one year plus fine of ₹ 1,00,000. Tourism has proved to be an area of concern in Goa. For this reason, two new sections have been introduced in the act.

Onus on person. All persons who keep children who are not related to them by blood will have to inform this fact immediately to the director as per the prescribed form. The post of director has been established under this act. Goa has a problem with tourists who "keep" children with them in hotels and other establishments. There is no logical explanation as to how a child spends the night in a hotel room with a tourist without suspicion being attached to the situation. It is now mandatory for persons with children who are not related to them to make a report to the director.

Onus on establishment. All hotels and other establishments that provide boarding or lodging or any similar facility shall ensure that children are safe and are not at risk of child abuse within their premises, including all adjoining beaches, parks, and so on.

Apart from the above-mentioned sections, some other important sections are prohibition of children for the purpose of commercial sexual exploitation, internet pornography, organ trafficking of children, sexually obscene photographs, sale of children under the garb of adoption, Victim Assistance Units, child sensitization training, and a child-friendly tourism code for Goa. In all the above matters, the consent or willingness of the child to be a party to sexual abuse will not be a consideration.

Child sexual trafficking. There is nothing really new as far as child sexual trafficking is concerned in the act. The act prohibits the trafficking of children for commercial sexual exploitation and also condemns the Devadasi system. Severe punishment has been mentioned in relation to the parent/guardian of a child who is dedicated. The state has been given the responsibility to come up with a comprehensive plan of action, which shall include education and livelihood skills for the children who have been exploited for the purposes of prostitution.

Children in difficult circumstances. The children mentioned in this section are street children. The state government is supposed to establish and maintain shelters for children, either by itself or in association with voluntary organizations, for the care, treatment, education, training, development, and rehabilitation of street children.

Girl child. The act has recognized the girl child as an especially vulnerable section of society and has a plan of action for the survival, protection, development, and advancement of the girl child. The act also mentions gender sensitization programmes at all levels and to eliminate degrading and violent portrayals of the girl child. The act also encourages educational institutions and the media to adopt and project non-stereotyped images of girls and boys. The last point is extremely important because children at a very young age adopt stereotyped images of gender due to the environment they are raised in and the image that the media portrays in advertisements, magazines, books, and so on.

Differently-abled children. The act endeavours to ensure that children with disabilities are provided with appropriate initiatives like counselling to the parents of disabled children, early detection, vocational training, and institutional and community-based programmes.

Other provisions. This provision contains the State Children's Fund, State Commission for Children, Steering Committees, Village Child Committees, awareness campaigns, child-friendly police stations, computer training for children, and special provisions for children of prisoners and commercial sex workers. All these provisions, if implemented correctly by the state, could have a very positive and progressive impact on the lives of children in Goa.

Violation and penalties. Non-adherence or violation of all the above-mentioned provisions could result in the imposition of a fine ranging from ₹ 100–50,000 on every occasion. The Department of Women and Child Development will be the competent authority for the purpose of this act and their decision will be final and binding.

Thus, we see that the he Goa Children's Act, 2003 (hereafter, the act) is an act to protect, promote, and preserve the best interests of children in Goa and to create a society that is child-friendly. It is the first comprehensive act which has taken into account not just the welfare and best interests of the child but also the rights of the child as per the principles of UNCRC.

Immoral Traffic (Prevention) Act, 1956

In 1986, the Government of India amended the erstwhile Suppression of Immoral Traffic in Women and Girls Act, 1956, renamed as the Immoral Traffic (Prevention) Act (ITPA) to widen the scope of the law to cover both the sexes exploited sexually for commercial purposes and provided enhanced penalties for offences involving children and minors. "Child" under ITPA means a person who has not completed the age of 16 years and "prostitution" means the sexual exploitation or abuse of persons for commercial purposes. The ITPA prescribes stringent action and punishment for keeping a brothel or allowing premises to be used as a brothel (Section 3), living on the earnings of prostitution (Section 4), procuring, inducing or taking a person for the sake of prostitution (Section 5).

The act further provides that where any person is found with a child in a brothel, it shall be presumed, unless the contrary is proved, that he has committed an offence of detaining a person in the premises where prostitution is carried on (Section 6). Similarly, when a child or minor found in a brothel, on medical examination, detected to have been sexually abused, it shall be presumed unless the contrary is proved that the child or minor has been detained for purposes of prostitution or, as the case may be, has been sexually exploited for commercial purposes.

The punishment consists of imprisonment of either description for a term which shall not be less than seven years but which may be for life or for a term, which may extend to ten years and shall also be liable for fine, with a provision for less than seven years under special circumstances. Besides contemplating specialized machinery for its enforcement, the act envisages a comprehensive scheme for rescue, protection, and corrective treatment of prostitutes. Section 21 deals with the establishment of protective homes by the state government.

The Ministry of Women and Child Development is in the process of amending the act with a view to making the law victim-friendly and, at the same time, making punishment for traffickers more stringent and putting greater criminal culpability on them.

Child Labour (Prohibition and Regulation) Act, 1986

The Child Labour (Prohibition and Regulation) Act, 1986, was formulated with a view to eliminating child labour from various hazardous occupations and processes. It defines a "Child" as a person who has not completed 14 years of age; Section 3 of the act deals with prohibition of employment of children in certain occupations and processes.

Section 14 deals with the following penalties:

1. Whoever employs any child or permits any child to work in contravention of the provisions of Section 3 shall be punishable with imprisonment for a term which shall not be less than three months but which may extend to one year or with fine which shall not be less than 10,000 rupees but which may extend to 20,000 or with both.
2. Whoever, having been convicted of an offence under Section 3, commits a like offence afterwards, he shall be punishable with imprisonment for a term which shall not be less than six months but which may extend to two years.

Children working in the unorganized sector (comprising almost 90% of the child labour force), according to the act, are not within the purview of law. Only about 10% of the children working in the organized or formal sector or within specified occupations and processes are covered under the act. The rest of the working children are subjected to the worst forms of exploitation and abuse. The law has not been able to meet its objective of eliminating child labour in totality primarily for this reason and needs to be modified to include all categories of working children (Mohsin, 2002[1]). The law provides very limited coverage in terms of the protection, care, and rehabilitation, with NCLP being the only related scheme to cover just about a miniscule out of the millions of unrecognized and un-enumerated child labour in the country.

Moreover, there is ambiguity with regard to the concept of child work and child labour, due to which it has been difficult to undertake a complete enumeration of the number of children in workforce. Rodgers and Standing (1981)[2] divided children's activities into four categories: domestic, non-monetary work, usually within the family; non-monetary and non-domestic work usually found in the poor agrarian/rural economies; children working in the non-agrarian environment; and children working as bonded labourer and are pledged by their parents in lieu of debt.

The Ministry of Labour, Government of India, only through a notification issued on July 10, 2006, has broad-based the scope of the Child Labour (Prohibition and Regulation) Act, 1986, by including within the purview of the act child domestic workers and children working in *dhabas* (roadside eateries) aged up to 14 years of age. Although this widens the scope of the act, it poses serious challenges to all civil society organizations and the government machinery to reach out to children, especially in domestic work, since most of these children are invisible, working within the four walls of the employers' homes.

These children are deprived of their right to education, health, play, security, protection, equal opportunity, participation, and development. This further increases their vulnerability to exploitation and abuse. With no official statistics available, it is difficult to estimate their actual numbers. Also, majority of child domestic workers fall in the age category of 15–18 years, and, in the absence of any law for them it is difficult to wean them out of work.

Child Marriage Restraints Act, 1929

The Child Marriage Restraint Act, 1929, as amended in 1979, is an act to restrain the solemnization of child marriages. The act prescribes a minimum age of 21 years for males and 18 years for females for marriage. This law is applicable to all Indians. The act provides for punishment of simple imprisonment which may extend to three months and shall also be liable to fine for solemnizing a child marriage (Section 5). It also provides for punishment of simple imprisonment which may extend to three months and shall also be liable to fine the parent or guardian, if they marry off their children/wards before the permissible age (Section 6).

Under the act, any man who marries a minor girl is liable to the punishment of simple imprisonment which may extend to 15 days or with fine which may extend to 1,000 rupees or with both in case the man is below 21 years of age, and a person above 21 years shall be punishable with simple imprisonment which may extend to three months and shall also be liable to fine (Sections 3 and 4). No woman can be punished under this law.

Considering the shortcomings in the Child Marriage Restraint Act and its implementation, the Government of India has proposed an improved legislation—The Prevention of Child Marriage Bill, 2004. The National Commission for Women and the National Human Rights Commission played an important role in the preparation of the draft bill, which was introduced in the Rajya Sabha on December 20, 2004. The bill aims at:

1. providing for declaration of all child marriages void
2. making a provision for declaring the child marriage as void in certain circumstances
3. requiring the husband, or if he is a minor at the material time, his guardian to pay maintenance to the minor girl until her remarriage
4. providing for legitimization of children born of a child marriage even if the marriage has been annulled, including providing for the custody and maintenance of the children born of child marriages
5. empowering the district court to add to, modify, or revoke any order relating to the maintenance of the female petitioner and her residence and custody or maintenance of her children, and so on
6. empowering the courts to issue injunctions prohibiting solemnization of marriages in contravention of the provisions of the proposed legislation
7. making the offences under the proposed legislations to be cognizable for the purpose of investigations and for other purposes

8. providing for appointment of child marriage prevention officers by the state government
9. empowering the state governments to make rules for effective administration of the legislation.

The parliament constituted a standing committee to receive written and oral evidence from several experts in the civil society to get their comments and suggestions on the proposed legislation. At present the bill is still under discussion. In February 2006, the Supreme Court of India ruled that all marriages, existing and future, would have to be registered. The central government, state governments, and union territories were accordingly directed by the Supreme Court to frame a uniform set of rules and procedures for registration of marriages.

Government's Recent Initiatives on Girl Child Protection

Initiatives Taken by the Ministry of Women and Child Development

India has taken a proactive stand on the issue of child protection. Recent developments in this direction give clear signals about government's intention to bring the issue of women and child development to the forefront of all major developmental activities. The setting up of an independent Ministry of Women and Child Development is not only the result of consolidation of earlier sporadic efforts toward the issue of childcare and protection but also an indication toward effective convergence. Women and Child Development, previously a department under the Ministry of Human Resource Development, Government of India, has made some remarkable achievements during the past few months. The National Plan of Action for Children was formulated by the department in 2005. It aims at ensuring all rights to children up to the age of 18 years.

The plan affirms government's commitment toward ensuring all measures and creating an enabling environment for the survival, growth, development, and protection of all children so that they realize their inherent potential and grow up to be healthy and productive citizens. The National Commission for the Rights of Children was also set up by the department in the same year.

Furthermore, with a view to dealing with the incidence of offences against children, the Ministry of Women and Child Development has proposed the Offences against Children's Bill, 2006. The bill aims at identifying incidence of offences against children and protecting them from offences, punishing persons who committed offence against children and setting up rules to fulfil its objectives. The bill has been sent to all the states for comments, after which it will be passed by the parliament. A new initiative of the ministry is the formulation of the Integrated Child Protection Scheme, on the lines of the Integrated Child Development Scheme, which has one of the largest outreach in the country.

National Charter for Children, 2003

Underlying the National Charter for Children adopted in 2004 is the intent to secure for every child its inherent right to be a child and enjoy a healthy and happy childhood, to address the root causes that negate the healthy growth and development of children, and to awaken the conscience of the community in the wider societal context to protect children from all forms of abuse, while strengthening the family, society, and the nation. This charter has the following sections on child protection:

1. Survival, life, and liberty
2. Protection from economic exploitation and all forms of abuse
3. Protection of the girl child
4. Care, protection, welfare of children of marginalized and disadvantaged communities
5. Ensuring child-friendly procedures.

National Plan of Action for Children, 2005

The National Plan of Action for Children commits itself to ensure all rights to children up to the age of 18 years. The government shall ensure all measures and an enabling environment for survival, growth, development, and protection of all children, so that each child can realize his or her inherent potential and grow up to be a healthy and productive citizen. This calls for collective commitment and action by all the organs of government and partnership with families, communities, voluntary sector, civil society, and the children themselves.

The plan will be implemented throughout the country through national measures and through State Plans of Action for Children. In all actions for children, whether undertaken by public or private institutions, courts of law, quasi-judicial bodies, and executive or legislative bodies, the best interests of the child shall be a primary consideration. In recognition of the fact that 41% of India's population is below 18, constituting a significant national asset, this plan reaffirms the nation's commitment to wisely, effectively, and efficiently invest its national resources to fulfil its commitments to children. The National Plan of Action for Children is divided into the following four sections and all categories of rights apply to all age groups, including before birth.

1. Child survival
2. Child development
3. Child protection
4. Child participation

Commissions for the Protection of Child Rights Act, 2005

The commission shall have the powers to uphold child rights and to take suo moto cognizance of child rights violations. Similar powers shall also vest in state commissions. For providing speedy trial of offences against children or violations of child rights, a state government may, with the concurrence of the Chief Justice of the State High Court, by notification, specify at least a court in the state or specify, for each district, a Court of Session to be a Children's Court to try the said offences: provided that nothing in this section shall apply if (1) Court of Session is already specified as a special court, or (2) a special court is already constituted, for such offences under any other law for the time being in force. For every children's court, the state government shall, by notification, specify a public prosecutor or appoint an advocate who has been in practice as an advocate for not less than seven years, as a Special Public Prosecutor for conducting cases in that court.

Offences against Children's Bill, 2005

Although India has the second largest child population in the world, there is no separate legislation to deal with offences against children, and hence, this enactment. In addition to child-related provisions within the Indian Penal Code (1860) and several other central and state, local, and special laws, the basic legislation for children, namely, The Juvenile Justice (Care and Protection) Act. 2000, deals primarily with the "juveniles in conflict with law" and "children in need of care and protection"; however, it does not separately cover the persons who commit crimes against children and some other categories of children under various circumstances of abuse, exploitation, and neglect. In view of this, it is considered essential that the

Government of India enact a separate law for the children under the title "Offences against Children," 2006.

The act says that every child is entitled to the rights, freedoms, and guarantees as enumerated in the Constitution of India and the statutes, in addition to the UNCRC provisions and other international instruments ratified by the Government of India. The children have inherent rights to survival, protection, development, and participation, including right to shelter, food, clothing, education, and protection from physical, emotional, and sexual abuse and exploitation, within the overarching provisions of equal and inalienable rights, without distinction on the basis of race, colour, sex, language, religion, property, political or other opinion, nationality or social origin, and birth or other status that go with it. The children, meaning persons who have not completed 18 years of age, deserve the fulfilment of their basic rights that are also deemed to be their basic needs.

It is expedient to enact a law to protect children from violation of their rights and to provide them holistic justice with the following objectives:

1. To identify offences against children, protect them, and provide legal remedy.
2. To provide for punishment against persons who have committed offences against children.
3. To safeguard the best interest of children while providing support to child victims of crimes, abuse, exploitation, and neglect.
4. To set in place rules and create legal mechanisms to fulfil the objectives of this act.

The bill proposes to address the legitimate rights of children against sexual abuse, neglect, exploitation, torture, or any form of cruelty and aims at

1. identifying offences against children and protecting children from offences
2. providing for punishment against persons who have committed offences against children
3. setting the rules to fulfil the objectives of the proposed bill.

In order to ensure that procedures and practices prescribed are child-friendly, the draft bill is based on eight principles:

1. Best interest of the child
2. "Protection" of the child

3. Equality and non-discrimination—"Leave No Child Behind"
4. Individuality and participation
5. Privacy and confidentiality
6. Non-stigmatizing semantics, decisions, and actions
7. Avoidance of harm
8. Non-criminalization of the child.

Integrated Child Protection Scheme, 2006

The Integrated Child Protection Scheme concretizes the government/state responsibility for creating a system to protect children. Such a system is influenced by many aspects, including regulatory frameworks, structures, resources, professionals, and the relationships between them. When the child protection system functions in the best interest of the child then adequate state and voluntary institutions, services, and structures are put in place and backed strongly by policies, laws, and regulations.

Professionals providing services for children are competent and bound by professional standards. Children's views are taken into account. The Integrated Child Protection Scheme is based on the cardinal principles of "protection of child rights" and "best interests of the child." The ICPS aims to promote the best interests of the child and prevent violations of child rights through appropriate punitive measure against perpetrators of abuse and crimes against children and to ensure rehabilitation for all children in need of care and protection. It aims to create a protective environment by improving regulatory frameworks, strengthening structures, and professional capacities at national, state, and district levels so as to cover all child protection issues and provide child-friendly services at all levels.

The target groups of this scheme are as follows.

Child in need of care and protection means a child who

1. is found without any home or settled place or abode and without any ostensible means of subsistence;
2. resides with a person (whether a guardian of the child or not) and such person has threatened to kill or injure the child and there is a reasonable likelihood of the threat being carried out, or has killed, abused, or neglected some other child or children and there is a reasonable likelihood of the child in question being killed, abused, or neglected by that person;

3. is a mentally or physically challenged or ill child or a child suffering from terminal diseases or incurable diseases and/or having no one to support or look after him or her
4. has a parent or guardian and such parent or guardian is unfit or incapacitated to care for or exercise control over the child;
5. does not have a parent/parents and no one is willing to take care of him or her, or whose parents have abandoned him or her or who is a missing and/or runaway child and whose parents cannot be found after reasonable inquiry;
6. is being or is likely to be grossly abused, tortured, or exploited for the purpose of sexual abuse or illegal acts;
7. is found vulnerable and is likely to be inducted into drug abuse or trafficking;
8. is being or is likely to be abused for unconscionable gains;
9. is a victim of any armed conflict, civil commotion, or natural calamity.

Children in conflict with the law are the ones who are alleged to have committed an offence.

Children in contact with law are the ones who have come in contact with the law either as a victim or a witness or due to any other circumstance.

Any other vulnerable child, including but not limited to the following categories, would also be covered under the scheme: Children of potentially vulnerable families and families at risk, children of socially excluded groups like migrant families, families living in extreme poverty, lower-caste families, families subjected to or affected by discrimination, minorities, children infected and/or affected by HIV/AIDS, orphans, child drug abusers, children of substance abusers, child beggars, trafficked or sexually exploited children, children of prisoners, and street and working children.

In spite of such efforts at the international and the national level, the conditions of children in various spheres have not substantially changed. They are often subjected to cruelty, exploitation, and deprivation. There is a plethora of laws to deal with these problems and to provide adequate care, protection, and growth opportunity to the child in need. However, these laws could not be implemented properly partly due to paucity of funds and adequate infrastructures and partly to the inertia and lack of zeal and motivation on part of the authorities and the public in general.[3]

Initiatives by the Department of Social Welfare, Government of NCT of Delhi

As reported in the website of Department of Social Welfare, Delhi Government, the department has already taken the following initiatives for implementing the Juvenile Justice (Care and Protection of Children) Amendment Act, 2006:

1. Delhi Juvenile Justice Care and Protection Rules, 2002, have been notified on August 19, 2002 under Section 68 of this act.
2. One juvenile justice board as per Section 4 of Juvenile Justice (Care and Protection of Children) Act, 2000, has been notified on April 10, 2003, vide Notification No. F.61 (SC)/DO-I/DSW/2003-04/3709-727. After the completion of the term of the Juvenile Justice Board for three years a fresh notification dated April 10, 2006, has been issued.
3. Four child welfare committees have been notified under Section 29 of the act. The offices of the committees are located at Kasturaba Niketan, Lajpat Nagar; Nirmal Chhaya, Jail Road; Sewa Kutir, Kingsway Camp; and NPS, Mayur Vihar.
4. Three observation homes have been notified under Section 8 of the act for the juveniles in conflict with law. One of the observation homes at Delhi Gate is being managed by an NGO, Prayas, under an agreement with the Delhi state government. One observation home under Section 8(1) for boys is being run by the Delhi state government at Sewa Kutir, Kingsway Camp, and one special home under Section 9(1) is being run at 1 Magazine Road, Delhi, and observation home for girls is being run at Nirmal Chhaya Complex, Jail Road, Delhi.
5. (i) Eleven children homes have been established by the government for the care and protection of children during pendency of inquiry and subsequently for their care, protection, education, development, and rehabilitation vide Notification No. F.61 (NOH)/DO-I/DSW/2002/5218-236 dated June 6, 2003, under Sections 66 and 56 of Juvenile Justice (Care and Protection of Children) Act, 2000. In these homes apart from boarding and lodging the children are provided vocational training, recreation, and counselling facilities, which are required for their emotional, social, and psychological development. (ii) Out of these 11 homes, three are exclusively for the mentally challenged children. In the case of girls, after attaining

the age of 18 and if they are not restored, they are sent to After Care Institution for their rehabilitation and when marriage is possible to be arranged, the same is also organized.

6. Ten district-level visiting committees have been constituted vide Notification No. F.61 (NOH)/DO-I/DSW/2002/5358 dated June 12, 2003, for all the districts to inspect the children homes and provide advice and guidance for their improvement and development.
7. Six homes run by NGOs have been notified as shelter homes to provide immediate care and protection to the children in need of care and protection.
8. Eleven NGOs are recognized as adoption agencies. Foster care services are carried out by the department itself. The department is also managing two aftercare homes: one for girls at Nirmal Chhaya Complex, Jail Road, and another for boys at Narela, Delhi.
9. Juvenile Justice Fund under Section 61 has been created recently with a corpus of ₹ 10 lakh. This fund shall be administered by the state-level advisory board, which has been notified under Section 62 of the act vide Notification No. 61(AB)/DO-I/DSW/2002/11901-956 dated December 24, 2003, for a period of three years.

It is incumbent upon the department to provide a child-friendly environment and also ensure rehabilitation of children in conflict with law and those requiring protection and care by providing vocational training and restoration to the family. The proposed vocations are in electronic trade (e.g. TV repairing), electric trade (e.g. house wiring), mechanical trade (e.g. auto repair), stenography, typing/computer, cutting and tailoring, phone repairing, DTP, candle making, plumbing, and so on.

The act contemplates two distinct kinds of proceedings against the different categories of children. The Juvenile Justice Board has powers to deal exclusively with all proceedings relating to juveniles in conflict with law, and child welfare committees have the final authority to dispose of the cases for the care protection, treatment, development, and rehabilitation of the children as well as to provide for their basic needs and protection of human rights.

Although one juvenile justice board and four child welfare committees are already functioning, regular posts and necessary infrastructure have not yet been created. The salary of the presiding magistrate is being drawn against the post of deputy director (technical) in the scale of ₹ 10,000–15,200. The ministerial staff posted there is on diverted capacity from other sections of the department. The honorarium of the members of child welfare committees is being paid from the budget of Probation Services.

Future Plan of Action of the Delhi Government to Implement Childcare and Rehabilitation Measures under the Provisions of Juvenile Justice (Care and Protection of Children) Act, 2000

1. Identification of sites and purchase of suitable land in nine districts for the creation of observation homes, special home, children homes, juvenile justice boards, child welfare committees, place of safety, and aftercare homes.
2. Construction of buildings for observation homes, special home, children homes, juvenile justice boards, child welfare committees, and place of safety.
3. Expenses on salaries, honorarium of members of the juvenile justice board, child welfare committees, and staff/manpower required for the all the statutory homes.
4. Expenses on purchase of vehicles (ambulance), office equipment, computers, furniture/fixtures, stationery items, electricity, water charges, telephones charges, day-to-day maintenance charges, and conveyance charges.
5. Expenses on food, clothing, education, vocational training, medical care, rewards/awards, sports materials, security, and so on.
6. 2007–2008: Identification and purchase of sites and construction of new observation homes. Improvement/renovation of existing observation homes, special homes, and existing juvenile justice boards.
7. 2008–2009: Construction and operation of new observation homes, special home, place of safety, and children's homes.
8. 2009–2010: Creation of new juvenile justice board and child welfare committees in the new setup of observation homes for boys, special homes and places of safety and children's homes. The operationalization of the new observation homes for boys and juvenile justice boards will be subject to the need assessment.

Other Initiatives by the Delhi Government

Delhi Ladli Scheme, 2008

The state government of Delhi has launched the "Laadli Scheme" with an aim to curb female feticide and enhance the social status of the girl child by promoting their education and protecting them from discrimination and deprivation. The government has been quite successful in achieving what it aimed when the scheme was launched. In the first year of its implementation, more than 1 lakh girl students registered themselves under the scheme in the government-aided schools of the capital. MCD schools also witnessed an increase in the number of girl students.

"The scheme has got a tremendous response from the government schools. What is encouraging is that the schools run by the MCD have also seen an increase in the intake of girl students," said an official from the social welfare department. The news has come in at a time when the capital is struggling with a dwindling gender ratio. As per the last census, there are 886 girls per 1,000 boys in the capital against a national average of 927 girls per 1,000 boys.

Under this programme, the government deposits ₹ 10,000 in the name of girl child at the time of her birth and subsequently deposits an amount of ₹ 5,000 each at the time of her admission to Class 1, 6, 9, 10, and 12. An accumulated amount of approximately ₹ 1 lakh becomes eligible to girl child on attaining the age of 18 years and at least passing out Class 10. The scheme is being implemented in association with the State Bank of India (SBI) which serves as an authorized agency for the secure maintenance of money deposited in phases by the government.

Girl Child Protection Scheme

The scheme envisages building awareness among society for changing attitudes considering girl child as an asset and not as liability; to ensure proper education and all-round development of girl child; to ensure better rehabilitation and economic security for a girl child and to protect the girl child from discrimination and deprivations. The benefit of the scheme will be open to all. An amount of ₹ 5,000 will be deposited in the name of each girl child born in the government hospitals/local bodies. The said amount can be drawn after the girl's attaining 18 years of age and upon her completing school education up to Class 10.

Notes

1. Mohsin, N. (2002), *Lost Innocence*, New Delhi, Common Wealth Publishers, p. 73.
2. Rodgers, G. and Standing, G. (1981), *Child Work, Poverty and Underdevelopment*, Geneva, International Labour Office, pp. 2–11.
3. Bhattarcharya, S.K. (2002), *Juvenile Justice: An Indian Scenario*, New Delhi, Regency Publications, Preface, vii.

9

Conclusion

Preventing Delinquency

The term "Delinquency" is used to denote a wide range of acts of youthful behaviour that are considered deviant. As the notion of deviance itself varies in space and time, juvenile delinquency does not provide a precise, universally acceptable meaning. Undoubtedly, the concept is closely related to cultural norms prevalent in a society and the perception of the type of behaviour designated as such. There is also a tendency in every society to bring within the ambit of delinquency prevention strategies even such patterns of juvenile maladjustment as would not be deemed as antisocial when committed by adults.

Thus, delinquency prevention efforts centre around a wide range of activities and programmes for the welfare of children and young persons, not merely ones specifically designed to forestall conditions responsible for the causation of the problem or the services initiated for the recovery, reeducation, and rehabilitation of those in conflict with law but also the measures that tend to protect and promote their interests and general well-being. Such a perspective naturally requires the prevention of juvenile delinquency to be considered as an integral component of the national planning for human resources development, with various social services, including health, education, and social welfare, becoming critically important.

However, to think that a well-developed and integrated approach toward delinquency prevention, catering to the requirements of various categories of children in need of care and protection, whether recognized as delinquents or found endangered, would solve the problem may be highly unrealistic. Furthermore, to think that an overall improvement in living conditions through steps taken to alleviate situations of stark deprivation contributing most to the causation of delinquency would eliminate the societal maladies that children face is just as unrealistic. While socio-economic development might prevent delinquency, delinquency in certain forms like, truancy, vagrancy, and begging children will likely generate several new dimensions, more intense and volitional in nature.

Although a planned development balancing both its economic and social aspects considerably minimizes the chances of personal disorganization, development per se could not be taken either as a remedy or a precursor of delinquency. A rational thinking, rather than hoping for eradicating problem, has to rely on a full range of preventive programmes, thoughtfully conceived and implemented as part of social action consonant with the existing level of socio-economic development in a particular country.

A comprehensive strategy for delinquency prevention inevitably extends beyond the juvenile justice operations and gets into the system in which the child is born and grows. In this process, the immediate environment of the child, consisting of the family, school, and neighbourhood, is of profound significance. In the wake of industrialization, urbanization, and modernization, the role of family as the principal transmitter of social values and instrument of social control appears to have weakened considerably in many countries.

In India, deviance among children is still largely tackled through informal means of social control; however, the socio-economic transition resulting in large-scale migration from rural to urban areas, mostly in search of gainful vocations, tends to disrupt and undermine the stability of the institution of family. The deteriorating nature of interpersonal relationships within the family, weakening of religious and conventional values to maintain its sanctity, and changing social attitudes toward sex and morality can be seen as some of the factors contributing to the rise in juvenile delinquency. An analysis of conditions associated with delinquency would clearly reveal that broken homes, lack of parental care, discordant relationship between parents, antisocial family influence, and so on are the most potent issues and causal factors. It is, therefore, universally realized that efforts to prevent juvenile delinquency, both by way of social justice to children in need of care and protection and specialized services to wean them away from criminogenic situations, can be most effective if provided through the family.

Next to family, educational system plays a dominant part in determining the quality of development of children and young persons. The school environment can influence children either way. It can help them to realize their full potential and maximize their talents, and, in the eventuality of their being unable to do so, can also be a cause of conflict, frustration, and social maladjustment. The significance of educational system can be realized from the fact that, despite its faith in its socialization function, it is sometimes accused of being a possible source of juvenile delinquency.

In view of the impact of school relationship on the emotional and social maturation of children and young persons, there is a widespread awareness to induct delinquency prevention measures within the general framework of the educational system. However, educational system in developing countries is often caught in a kind of dilemma. On one hand, education is considered as a vital sector of national development, and on the other, inadequacy of resources, shortage of manpower, and lack of educational material often lead to substandard institutions not fully capable of meeting the needs of children and young persons in the background of a changing social scene.

There is no dearth of material exhorting the need of community participation in the prevention and control of juvenile delinquency. What is really lacking is the knowledge of the manner in which the community can be most purposefully involved in this sphere. The effectiveness of family and school as agencies for control and socialization of children is considerably dependent on the support and assistance of the community as a whole. When the family atmosphere is not fully equipped to deal with the special problems of children, community has to assume a basic responsibility to provide mechanisms for the mainstreaming of erring children.

In various countries, diverse community groups, including professional organizations, academic bodies, public and private agencies, and so on, make valuable contributions to delinquency prevention at the community level. The community service systems are certainly found to be more beneficial when administered without invoking legal sanctions and in a manner that enhances the central role of the family. The government has, however, a duty to ensure that only such modalities of community participation are fostered and developed that are socially protective and not socially disruptive.

The juvenile justice system in India reflects many of the social characteristics of the Indian society. Juveniles in families, schools, and in justice institutions are still handled harshly for their deviant and illegal misconduct and even for their failure to measure up to adult expectations and demands. Physical abuse of children is very common in juvenile justice correctional institutions. The police and officials of the custodial and correctional institutions often cover up their abuses.

The general public has become accustomed to occurrences of such abuses to both juveniles and adults and has come to tolerate them. There is a great danger if the police, who desire the legal system to become more inquisitorial, have their way, especially in the context of growing democratic fervour. This would thwart efforts at making the juvenile justice system fair and just. The higher-level legal institutions, such as the courts, need to provide the leadership in facilitating the training of the police and other juvenile justice personnel and to process complaints made against them diligently and quickly.

Before the British rule, Hindu and Mohammedan laws were in force in India. None of those laws has any specific reference to juvenile delinquents. There were, of course, certain ethical codes concerning treatment and training of children. During the Moghul period, the Koranic precepts were mainly followed in dealing with any kind of antisocial behaviour.

In the beginning of the latter half of the nineteenth century, the Government of India felt the need of enacting laws pertaining to children. In 1850, the Apprentices Act was passed as an all-India measure. It provided for dealing with children between the ages of 10 and 18 years who had committed petty offences or were destitute. This act authorized magistrates to commit such children as apprentices to employers with provisions for controlling the relationships between them. The objective of the act was to divert the misdirected energies of juvenile offenders toward learning of some trades so that they might eke out a living on their own after completion of training.

Then, the Indian Penal Code, 1860, the first important codified law of the land, was introduced. Sections 82 and 83 of the code relate to juvenile offenders by defining the lower age limit for criminal responsibility and the operation of the concept of discernment in the case of juvenile offenders. These sections provide that under the age of seven years no infant can be guilty of an offence as under that age an infant is, by presumption of law, cannot be endowed with rationalizing capacities to determine the right from wrong. Similarly, if the accused is aged above 7 years but below 12, and he has not attained sufficient maturity or understanding to judge the nature and consequences of his misconduct or committing offence, he cannot be guilty of such an offence. Furthermore, the Criminal Procedure Code was enacted in 1861 and later modified in 1884 and 1898. Sections 29(B), 399, and 562 of this code related to the treatment of juvenile delinquents. These sections of the code carried with them the lofty principles of socialized treatment of juvenile offenders and provided for a progressive approach toward them.

Section 29(B) provided for the trial of any person under 10 years of age for any offence not punishable with death or transportation by a district magistrate or any magistrate empowered under the Reformatory Schools Act, 1897. This section restricted trial of juvenile delinquents. Section 399 provided that when any person under the age of 15 years was sentenced by any criminal court to imprisonment for any offence, the court might direct that such person, instead of being imprisoned in a criminal jail, should be confined to any reformatory established by the state government as a fit place for confinement in which there were means of suitable discipline and training in some branch of useful industry. Section 562 also made a specific provision for offenders under 21 years of age for release on probation of good conduct under certain conditions, instead of sentencing such persons to imprisonment.

The first special law dealing directly with the treatment of juvenile delinquents was the Reformatory Schools Act, 1876, which was modified later in 1897. It was an all-India enactment to deal with young offenders. It provided that youthful offenders might, at the discretion of the sentencing court, be ordered to be detained in such a reformatory for a period of three to seven years instead of undergoing a sentence of imprisonment. Under Section 18 of the act, the superintendent of a reformatory might, with the sanction of the committee of visitors, by license under his hand, permit the transfer of any youthful offender to reformatory school, who has attained the age of 14 years to live under the charge of any trustworthy and respectable person or any officer of government or a municipality, being an employer or labour and willing to receive and take charge of him on the condition that the employer shall keep such youthful offenders employed at some trade, occupation, or calling, Thus, the Indian Penal Code, the Criminal Procedure Code, and the Reformatory Schools Act had played an important role in evolving special legislation for juvenile offenders in India.

In the first half of the nineteenth century in England very severe punishments used to be awarded to children even for petty offences. This led to the establishment of separate institutions for juvenile offenders and the enactment of the Reformatory Schools Act for separate treatment of juvenile delinquents and the Industrial Schools Act for neglected children who might be prone to antisocial activities. Numerous other acts were also brought into being for separate institutional treatment of juvenile delinquents during the latter part of the nineteenth century.

At the beginning of the twentieth century, a movement was gradually gaining ground in the correctional field. Subsequently, the Society for the Protection of Children was established in western India in 1917. Another landmark took place almost simultaneously with the setting up of the Indian Jails Committee by the Government of India in 1919. This committee emphasized the importance of separate treatment of youthful offenders for their rehabilitation. In pursuance of this recommendation, Madras, Bengal, and Bombay passed their Children Acts in 1920, 1922, and 1924, respectively.

The main purpose of these acts was to provide for the custody, treatment, and training of children who fell foul with laws. After independence, Punjab, Uttar Pradesh, and Hyderabad also passed their Children Acts. In the meantime, the Constitution of India came into force. The Directive Principles of State Policy of the Constitution provide under Article 39(F) that "the state shall, in particular, direct its policy towards securing that childhood and youth are protected against exploitation and moral and material abandonment." In consonance with this principle, the Government of India enacted the Children Act, 1960, with some novel features for enforcement in the union territories.

One of the most important provisions of the Children Acts was the creation of the juvenile courts exclusively for dealing with the youthful offenders. This provision aimed at separate arrangement for trial, treatment, and training of a child who was of immature understanding and is at an impressionable age. Till the end of the nineteenth century, juvenile offenders were tried and convicted in the same manner as adult criminals. Consequently, the juvenile court movement started with the establishment of the first juvenile court in the world at Chicago, United States, in 1899.

In the words of Roscoe Pound, "It was the greatest advance in the judicial history since the Magna Carta." It was realized that the old punitive and retaliatory methods of the criminal law has failed to check juvenile delinquency. A new principle was, therefore, adopted to treat maladjusted juveniles individually through social and protective process. Thus, with the establishment of juvenile courts, an entirely new procedure was initiated. The basic idea behind the juvenile court is that of guardianship, the state acting for the welfare of children. The juvenile offender is not treated as a criminal but as a ward of the state and receives care and protection. Thus, the fundamental principles of the juvenile court is not to determine whether a child has committed a specific offence but to discover whether he is in a condition requiring the special care and protection of the state.

The Central Children Act, 1960, and some other states' Children Acts provided for the first time that the children's court magistrates should be conversant with the subjects of child welfare and juvenile delinquency. Another novel feature of these acts was that they made provisions for two agencies at the trial level to deal with the delinquent and the destitute separately. The children's court was to deal with juvenile delinquents and the Child Welfare Board was concerned with neglected children who were in crime-prone situations. The aim of this provision was to segregate the neglected from the delinquent and to provide for treatment and training to the different categories of children separately. This process helped not only in preventing contamination but also minimized the problem of institutional management and discipline.

The police as the primary law enforcement agency had a special role in the enforcement of the Children Acts. In accordance with the provisions of all the Children Acts the police had to report to the nearest juvenile court immediately after apprehending a child who could not be detained in the police custody for more than 24 hours. Some Children Acts went a step further to provide that the police should appear in the juvenile court in plain dress so that the child might not have any fear in his mind and feel at ease. Under the provisions of the Children Acts, a police officer or a person authorized in that behalf was empowered to bring before a juvenile court any person who, in his opinion, was a child and had no home, a destitute or was known to associate or live with any prostitute or person or persons of criminal or drunken habits or was likely to fall into bad association or exposed to moral danger.

For detention of the child, the Children Acts provided for remand/observation homes as places of safety. After apprehension, a child was detained in such a home pending disposal of his case by the juvenile or children's court. It provided for safe accommodation and served as an observation centre for a detailed study about the child. Its main function, apart from its detention and custodial functions, was that it would alleviate pressures under which a child was living before his coming to the centre and provide him opportunity to mobilize his inner strength and capacity. The Children Acts provided for the release of a delinquent child on bail with or without sureties. However, he could not be so released if there were reasonable grounds for believing that the release was likely to jeopardize his safety and normal development or defeat the ends of justice. The juvenile court might also make an order directing the child to be sent to an institution as provided under different Children Acts. Such institutions, besides providing good physical care, had arrangements for case work and psychological services, literacy classes, and training in various crafts. The nomenclatures of such institutions, however, varied from state to state.

For arriving at a decision in respect of treatment and training of the child, the juvenile court utilized the services of the probation officer to get a detailed report regarding the child on various sociological factors and if his home conditions were found congenial for healthy development of the child, the court applied its discretion and released him under the supervision of the probation officer for a period not exceeding three years. In fact, the probation officer had a vital role to play under the Children Act programmes.

The Children Acts provided for setting up aftercare organizations to take necessary measures for the rehabilitation of the discharged inmates of institutions. Aftercare organizations established either by the government of voluntary agencies rendered invaluable assistance in solving rehabilitative problems of children discharged from institutions and provided follow-up services till they were rehabilitated. The Central Children Act as amended in 1978 emphasized that a comprehensive aftercare programme might be pursued by aftercare agencies for enabling discharged inmates of institutions to lead an honest, industrious, and useful life.

Children Acts provided that a child apprehended and committed to an institution might, with the consent of the state government, be transferred to such an institution in another state to which he belonged. The aim of the provision was that the child would have an opportunity to be treated, trained, and brought up in an atmosphere to which he was accustomed since infancy. The climate, food, language, and customs differ from state to state. The child should, as far as practicable, be allowed to grow in a familiar atmosphere. If he lived at a place with unfavourable surroundings, his spontaneous growth might be stunted and his psychological development might also be defective. The framers of juvenile legislation had taken into consideration this aspect of child development. The importance of the interstate transfer of children was aptly highlighted under the provisions of the Children Acts.

The United Nations has been playing a prominent role to bring about improvements in child development services at the international level. The Standard Minimum Rules for the Administration of Juvenile Justice, 1985 (The Beijing Rules), were framed and approved by the United Nations for adoption by the member-states. Close on the heels of this development at the international arena came the reenactment of existing laws in this regard by the Government of India, in keeping with the juvenile justice provisions adopted by the UN. Thus, the Juvenile Justice Act was enacted in 1986, as the common law in force for the entire country, replacing all the other existing state and union territory laws and Children Acts, for the care, protection, treatment, development, and rehabilitation of neglected and delinquent children. The main objectives of the act were:

1. to have a uniform law for juvenile justice in the country so as to ensure that no child under any circumstances is lodged in a jail or police lockup;
2. to introduce a specialized approach toward the prevention and treatment of juvenile delinquency in keeping with the developmental needs of the maladjusted child;
3. to establish norms and standards for the administration of juvenile justice in terms of investigation, adjudication disposition, care, treatment, and rehabilitation;
4. to develop appropriate linkages and coordination between the formal system of juvenile justice and voluntary agencies engaged

in the welfare of neglected and socially maladjusted children and to specifically define the areas of their responsibilities;

5. to bring the operation of the juvenile justice system in the country in conformity with the United Nations Standard Minimum Rules for the Administration of Juvenile Justice.

Some progressive features were also incorporated in the Juvenile Justice Act, 1986, to make it more effective in keeping with the changing dynamics in the social scenario. The Juvenile Justice Act was a landmark in the history of care and protection of children in India. It provided inter alia for the active participation of governmental and nongovernmental agencies, individual social workers, and philanthropic groups.

Every individual in the community had the opportunity to contribute for the welfare of the child. The police as the law enforcement agency were to assume a more responsible and enlightened role in dealing with both categories of children, that is, neglected and delinquent, to render assistance in the best interest of the child. The new provision for creating a fund to be utilized for the welfare and rehabilitation of children was indeed a unique source of resource mobilization for all the functionaries working for the welfare of children.

Subsequently, further developments took place in juvenile correctional facilities. The Convention on the Rights of the Child was adopted by the United Nations (UNCRC) on November 26, 1989. It is a milestone in the history of human progress in respect of child welfare and development. It is based on the principle of the best interest of the child. The member-countries are directed to take appropriate social and legal measures to ensure the protection of the rights of the child. Moreover, the UNCRC has specifically prescribed a set of standards to be adhered to by all the state parties in securing the best interests of the child. It has also emphasized social reintegration of child victims, to the extent possible, without resorting to judicial proceedings. The Government of India has ratified the convention on December 11, 1992. In view of all these momentous developments at the international level, the Government of India thought it expedient to reenact the existing laws relating to juvenile justice (Beijing Rules), the United Nations Rules for the Protection of Juveniles Deprived of Their Liberty, 1990, and all other relevant international instruments.

The overall objective of this act, unlike earlier acts relating to juveniles, is to make the law more child-friendly. The expression "juvenile in conflict with law" instead of "delinquent juvenile" as specified in earlier acts, has been used to do away with the stigma attached to the term "delinquent." This act also provides for the involvement of local authorities like Panchayats at the village level and Zilla Parishads at the district level, municipal committees/corporations in metropolitan regions, and so on, in the implementation of the act. It becomes easier to gain community support for implementing such programmes if the local authorities representing various sections of people are actively involved.

The Children Acts and, subsequently, the Juvenile Justice Act, 1986, provided for the creation of juvenile courts. The new act provides for establishing "Juvenile Justice Boards," named so with the intention to do away with the fear and consternation associated with the term "Court" and thus make its provisions more child-friendly. Although the functions and procedures of the board continue to be the same under the new act, the change of the term has instilled some level of informality in dealing with juveniles in conflict with law. There was no clear demarcation between the observation homes for delinquent and neglected juveniles in the previous Juvenile Justice Act, 1986.

The Juvenile Justice Act of 1986 was replaced by the Juvenile Justice Act of 2000 which serves as a laudable instrument that provides for openness in the juvenile justice system. The Juvenile Justice (Care and Protection of Children) Act, 2000, has been enforced in the entire country except the state of Jammu and Kashmir with effect from April 1, 2001. It calls for the involvement of private and public agencies and officials and citizens. There also many human rights watch groups, juvenile advocacy and activist organizations, and children's organizations, which are playing important roles in raising consciousness that delinquents and unfortunate children should be treated with dignity and care.

If the act is disregarded the prevailing mistrust of the justice system could increase, especially toward the police, its front organization. Police–juvenile and police–community relations could suffer greatly. Even after passage of the act, information from the media about juvenile abuse incidents in India abounds. The plethora of statements by nongovernmental, child-centred organizations, opinion pieces, and letters to the editors of newspapers reveal that there is a wide range of voices that call for drastic changes in the juvenile justice system. People's active interventions, dialogues, and discussions should continue, which could help the system function more as parens patriae.

The Juvenile Justice (Care and Protection and Children) Act, 2000, lays emphasis on the speedy disposal of cases and provides that an inquiry in respect of juvenile in conflict with law shall be completed within four months from the date of its commencement. Simultaneously, a number of dispositional alternatives have been introduced in the act to cater to the needs of different categories of juveniles processed under its provisions. As new measures, the board may, inter alia, direct the juvenile to participate in group counselling or similar activities or order the juvenile to perform community service. Although there is a provision for the release of a juvenile on probation of good conduct, the fact remains that juvenile probation as such has been relegated to the fringes in the current Juvenile Justice (Care and Protection of Children) Act.

This act does not provide for appointment of a separate cadre of probation officers as stipulated in the previous act, to exclusively concentrate on matters relating to the release of juveniles on probation supervision and their rehabilitation back into the community. The probation officers appointed under the Probation of Offender Act, 1958, are now to look after the cases of juveniles as well under the purview of Juvenile Justice (Case and Protection of Children) Act. As a result, the probation programme, which is already lagging behind, will suffer setbacks due to paucity of personnel and funds. As regards institutionalization, the board may, as a last resort, make and order directing the juvenile to be sent to a special home in the case of those aged above 17 years but below the age of 18 for a period of not less than two years, and in the case of any other juveniles, for a period until he ceases to be a juvenile.

The new act provides for the Constitution of the child welfare committees which were earlier known as juvenile welfare boards to handle neglected juveniles. The juvenile justice board has been introduced for handling or disciplining the child in conflict with law, whereas the child welfare committee's job is to provide care and protection. Any child in need of care and protection may be produced before the committee by specific categories of persons like a public servant, a recognized voluntary organization such as child line, and social worker or public-spirited citizen authorized by the state government or the child himself. Thus, the scope of the procedure to produce the neglected child has been widened to avoid any delay in this respect.

There is also provision for the establishment of children's homes by the state government for children in need of care and protection both for the reception during the pendency of any enquiry and subsequently for their care and rehabilitation. With a view to constantly monitoring and supervising the functioning of these institutions in the state, the act provides for the Constitution of inspecting committees at various levels. However, a new provision has been made for social auditing of these institutions by both central and state governments for the proper evaluation of the functions of these institutions. There is also a provision for the establishment of shelter homes by reputed and capable voluntary organizations recognized by the state government as drop-in-centres for the children who are on the streets without family care and support. These shelters are meant not only for care protection but also for providing rehabilitation.

Like earlier acts, this act also provides for the transfer of the child to the competent authority having jurisdiction over the place of residence of the child so that he may be brought up in a familiar atmosphere. As a matter of fact, efforts through institutions are made for the ultimate rehabilitation and social reintegrating of the child in the community. With this end in view, various alternatives such as adoption, foster-care, sponsorship, and so on, in conformity with the UNCRC, have been provided. The main purpose of this provision is to make available a congenial family atmosphere to the child to facilitate his spontaneous psychosocial development. In consonance with the provisions of the previous Juvenile Justice Act, 1986, this act also provides for the transfer of a juvenile or a child of unsound mind or child suffering from leprosy or addicted to drugs to mental health institutions, treatment centres, places of safety, as may be applicable case to case, for such period not exceeding the period for which he is required to be kept under the order of the competent authority.

This act also provides for the creation of a fund to be exclusively utilized for the welfare and rehabilitation of juveniles in conflict with law and children in need of care and protection dealt with under the act. This fund may be raised from voluntary donations, contributions, or subscriptions from benevolent individuals or organization. It has opened up an effective juvenile justice system in the country. Another provision of the act which is of utmost importance is that the state government have to constitute advisory boards to advise on various matters relating to the establishment and maintenance of institutions, mobilization of resources, facilities for education, training and rehabilitation of juveniles in conflict with laws, and children in need of care and protection. The main objective of these provisions is to garner public support and to mobilize enlightened public opinion for proper implementation of the juvenile justice programme.

Theoretical Perspective on Control of Juvenile Delinquency

Modern ideas of equality and individualism are influencing the youth, slowly vitiating the traditional power and control of parents, teachers, community elders, and the police, and thereby contributing to challenges to authority, and to delinquency. In addition, extreme poverty, economic inequalities, and growing economic desires are also creating large-scale discontent, which under circumstances of weakened social controls could result in increasing crime and delinquency. Currently, there's an increasing tendency among both politicians and the general public to see economic problems as a result of competition among castes and religious minorities to improve their economic conditions. Advancement of lower castes and minorities are often resented, as this weakens traditional status arrangements. Hence, the current discontent is largely expressed in inter-caste and inter-religious/communal strife, violence, and riots; these are often perpetrated by juveniles and young adults who ignore the peacemaking directives of elders in their families and communities. As affiliations with groups decline under modern, democratic influences, discontent expressed now in the form of group protests and violence may give way to more individual forms of delinquency.

Various other modern trends will also have an impact on juvenile delinquency. Modern conditions of family life, such as career parents, breakdown of extended family, and lack of child supervision, may also contribute to delinquency and child neglect. On the other hand, some modern trends may have positive consequences. As the sense of personhood develops for children and is socially recognized, young people will increasingly demand to be treated with dignity, and others will increasingly treat them accordingly. These developing attitudes could raise the worth of children and help reduce their victimization and ill treatment that occur today in families, schools, and the juvenile justice system.

In reality, the denial of the role of family as the cornerstone of adolescent stability will continue to maintain and sustain the tribulations inherent in the juvenile justice system. Following radical criminologists' insistence that criminology examines the root causes of crime, this chapter takes the position that delinquency is rooted in problems prevalent typically in dysfunctional families, such as those characterized by teenage pregnancies, teens raising babies, single-parent households, higher rate of school dropouts, and lack of respect for authority, as the definite precursors of teen problems.

Patrick Pagan[1] argues that criminologists have begun to accept the premise that youth raised in broken families are more inclined than other young people to engage in law-breaking behaviours. He contends that criminological and sociological literature supports the idea that the breakdown of family systems in American society is the authentic basis of delinquency. Indeed, the family stands as the fundamental agent of social control. A child's initial contact with the world and his or her socialization process begins with the family. It is the family—not schools or churches—that initiates adolescents to societal moral codes. Therefore, families are important in controlling juvenile delinquency. In addition to upholding the moral standards of society, families constitute the basis of the economic stability that ensures the well-being of youth. Low-income families may drastically affect the future direction of the life course of their children.

An appropriate education goes a long way in the development and maintenance of law-abiding lifestyles. Although official social control agencies play significant roles in socializing and educating the youth, the family is equally vital in introducing children to the benefits of education. Many scholars have suggested that learning begins from birth and includes the interfacing of various characteristics of pupils' experiences such as ability to learn, inspiration, family support, impact of social conditions, and the "channeling effects of social organizations."[2]

At the other end of the spectrum, in affluent societies where individuals are taught that financial success is available to all, governments can provide certain incentives to help families. Elliot Currie[3] suggested that the government should provide certain services for all children, particularly in healthcare, domestic violence, child abuse, and funding for treatment facilities.

Social control theorists have also proposed relevant policy directions for crime and delinquency prevention, including those involving school-based programmes that are aimed at keeping children engaged in positive activities that would decrease the idleness leading to delinquent behaviour. Indeed, recreational programmes, physical events, social groups, community clubs, boy scouts and girl scouts, and similar programmes are all byproducts of involvement. Gottfredson and Hirschi authoritatively assert that "policies directed toward enhancement of the ability of familial institutions to socialize children are the only realistic long-term state policies with potential for substantial crime reduction."[4] Such state-supported programmes must include instructions in parenting, imparting discipline in children, and training them in accountability.

The labelling perspective, for example, has led to major changes in the operation of the juvenile justice system. Most notable in this regard are policy directions in areas such as diversion, due process, decriminalization, and deinstitutionalization.[5] Regarding punitive aspects of policy influences, three-strike laws are a result of classic and neoclassic emphases placed on deterrence and retribution. The positivist revolution and the current biosocial implications place emphasis on rehabilitation and treatment.

According to Barbara Sims and Pamela Preston (2006)[6] although most of the research about delinquency among girls focuses on the extent and type of offences they commit, more recently, researchers have begun investigating and identifying developmental pathways most likely to lead girls to delinquency. By focussing specifically on girls, researchers are gaining a better understanding of female adolescent development and factors that put girls at risk of delinquency as well as identifying protective measures. More recent empirical studies that include findings on adolescent girls and boys suggest that significantly different risk factors exist for girls. Results of these studies also suggest that early predictors of male conduct disorder and delinquency are not as reliable when applied to females.

When other risk factors are added to the already daunting developmental tasks of female adolescence, the results can be overwhelming, pushing some girls into delinquency. Although research about delinquency among girls is still scarce, some researchers are focussing on the developmental pathway to delinquency. Just as girls and boys develop in different ways physically and emotionally during adolescence, so do their pathways to delinquency emerge often in a gender-specific manner.

The problems faced by girls and young women can be viewed as part of a developmental continuum linking early problems (such as family dysfunction, abuse, loss of a primary caregiver, and other traumas) to later behavioural problems. During the teen years, when girls are transitioning to adulthood, unresolved issues from earlier stages of development may come to a head. Incomplete bonding in infancy, sexual abuse in childhood, failed relationships with adults, and other problems can result in an inability to form positive relationships, lack of self-respect, ignorance of physical health and sexuality issues, and low self-image. Substance abuse at a young age can also interrupt a girl's psychosocial development.

Researchers have recommended the development of several types of female-specific programmes, these include[7]:

1. Programmes that include treatment for neglect and sexual abuse and physical victimization;
2. Crisis intervention programmes that provide short-term shelter, family mediations, and conflict resolution;
3. Programmes that engage girls in healthy relationships and provide social skills training;
4. Programmes that provide medical care for pregnant teens;
5. Programmes for unwed mothers, including parent training and childcare relief time;
6. Programmes that build and preserve the teen mother–child bond;
7. Programmes for sexually active females;
8. Programmes that include peer mediation to deal with conflicts concerning boyfriends and peer status.

International Initiatives for Preventing Juvenile Delinquency

Violence against children endangers their fundamental human rights. It is therefore imperative to convince individuals and institutions to commit the time, money, expertise, and other resources needed to address this global problem.[8] A number of UN instruments and directives reflect a preference for social rather than judicial approaches to controlling juvenile delinquency. The Riyadh Guidelines assert that the prevention of juvenile delinquency is an essential part of overall crime prevention in society,[9] and the UN Standard Minimum Rules for the Administration of Juvenile Justice (Beijing Rules) recommend instituting positive measures to strengthen a juvenile's overall well-being and reduce the need for state's intervention.

It is widely believed that early-phase intervention represents the best approach to preventing juvenile delinquency. Prevention requires individual, group, and organizational efforts aimed at keeping adolescents from breaking the law. Methods implemented to discourage delinquent and criminal behaviour vary widely across the globe. Some focus on punitive prevention intended to frighten potential offenders by making sure they understand the possibility of severe punishment, and others focus on taking preventive action to curtail recurrent crime, which includes explaining the negative aspects of an offence to a delinquent and attempting to reconcile offenders and their victims.

Early preventive work is being carried out in several areas in many countries. Some of the most promising approaches, programmes, and initiatives are described in some detail in the following sections. Within the *economic sector*, professional development programmes are being set up to provide legal alternatives for income generation. Supplying adolescents and young people with increased economic opportunities, professional training and education, new workplaces, and assistance in organizing businesses can help prevent youth involvement in delinquent activities.

Educational programmes are helping young people learn how to engage in positive self-appraisal, deal with conflict, and control aggression. The programmes debunk the myth of gang glamour and help young people find alternatives to illegal behaviour. Some work with troubled youth to help them develop the social and cognitive skills necessary to avoid conflict and control aggression. Children raised in strong families, quality schools, and healthy communities typically develop these skills as a matter of course. In the United States law enforcement agencies, schools, local communities, and parents of adolescents are involved in these programmes. Recreation and youth development activities are directly encouraged in the Riyadh Guidelines: "A wide range of recreational facilities and services of particular interest to young persons should be established and made easily accessible to them."[10] In a number of towns in the United States the establishment of basketball programmes for adolescents led to a 60% decrease in crime rates.

Recently, greater attention has been given to the role and responsibility of local communities in dealing with juvenile delinquency. There are programmes designed to train groups and individual representatives of local communities in which juvenile delinquency has increased to informally control youth and include young people in constructive activities.[11] The idea that young people can and should work in partnership with adults to improve conditions in their communities has gained currency in the past decade.

A promising development in efforts to prevent juvenile delinquency and crime is the involvement of NGOs and volunteers (students and pensioners, along with well-known and authority figures such as sportsmen, politicians, and public figures) in social work with adolescents. Generally, programmes for preventing gang delinquency should endeavours to integrate children and youth into organized group activities. This can be achieved through social service agencies or organizations such as the YMCA, YWCA, Girl Guides, and Boy Scouts, as well as independent boys' and girls' clubs and community centres; local government recreational activities also serve this purpose.

Cooperation between various agents of prevention work is becoming increasingly important. Multi-sectoral prevention initiatives designed and implemented by entire communities are the most effective, in particular those that build on the strengths and interests of youth rather than focussing only on their problems or deficits.

The family, as the primary institution of socialization, appears to play the most important role in the prevention of child and juvenile delinquency. The most impressive prevention efforts focus on the families of troubled youth, including those with serious behaviour problems. In this connection special attention must be given to street children and to children and adolescents who have lost their families (or their ties to them) during armed conflicts and have thus had no appropriate family surveillance. The majority of programmes serving street children are remedial in nature, as they operate on an ad hoc basis, providing food, clothing, and occasionally shelter and health services. These initiatives, which provide symptomatic treatment, have to be complemented by programmes that also address the causes of "streetism."[12] Special programmes are needed to tackle the problem of unaccompanied and homeless children, including rehabilitation schemes that take children off the streets.

The UNCRC provides a framework for improving the living conditions of children, focussing on the following four broad areas:

1. *Survival rights*. Articles 6.1, 6.2, and 24.1 deal with the basic needs that must be met for children to enjoy good health,

adequate growth, including medical care, nutrition, shelter, and clothing. For street children most of these needs are not satisfied.

2. *Development rights*. Articles 6, 26, and 28 relate to the opportunities and means for providing children with access to education, skills, training, recreation and rest, information, parental care, and social security.
3. *Protective rights*. Articles 2, 19.1, 19.2, 32.1, 33, 34, 36, and 37 focus on the legal and social provisions that must be made by each country to protect children from exploitation, drug abuse, sexual abuse, cruelty, separation from family, discrimination, and the effects of all types of man-made or natural disasters.
4. *Participation rights*. Articles 12, 13, 14, and 17 focus on the opportunities and means provided to children to enable them to express opinions on matters affecting their lives, including freedom of worship, access to information about oneself, and freedom to give evidence (where applicable). Children are knowledgeable about their situations and can devise innovative solutions to their problems if consulted. Street children, in particular, have already learned to make important decisions regarding their daily lives without the assistance of adults.[13]

Many countries still have "punitive" prevention programmes that try to suppress juvenile and youth offences, as well as gang recruitment, expansion, and criminal behaviour by means of surveillance (continuous police observation) and prosecution. Suppression is a form of active intervention wholly legitimized by the state because this approach is believed to be inherently "right"; it requires no special justification or evaluation of results.[14] This type of approach generally precludes efforts to promote proper behaviour, focussing instead on preventing unwanted behaviour. However, aggression on the part of authorities can in many cases contribute to the further integration of youth into delinquent groups.

Purely preventive (or suppressive) efforts are not very effective for youth already in trouble. The majority of crimes are committed by a relatively handful of repeat offenders who typically display serious behaviour problems in early childhood. For them, more intensive, individualized treatment is likely required.

Prevention of recurrent crime is best achieved through "restorative justice," which is usually carried out by nongovernmental remedial organizations and local communities. Restorative justice is regarded as an alternative mode of criminal justice. It involves a process whereby all the parties with a stake in a specific offence come together and collectively determine how best to deal with the aftermath of the offence and its implications for the future.[15]

The offender, through interaction with the victim, must understand the seriousness of the incident and together with the victim and social workers develop a series of steps toward reconciliation, arranging reparations for damages and providing whatever remedial assistance the victim might require. If successful resolution occurs, the juvenile is not placed in a correctional facility or labelled a delinquent, thereby avoiding the influence of an environment (jail) that can reinforce delinquent behaviour. The reconciliation process must be carried out very carefully so that the offender does not consider it a "deal" with the victim—a risk emphasized by various researchers.

One of the key elements of restorative justice is reconciliation between the offender and the victim, a process necessary not only for the correction of the offender but also for the restoration of justice for the victim. The protection and support of victims and witnesses is recognized as an important basic element of overall crime prevention and crime control strategies. Support measures reduce the impact of crime on those most directly affected and are essential for preserving and protecting the role of victims and witnesses in the criminal justice process. It also aids the investigation and prosecution of crime by facilitating cooperation between victims, witnesses, and law enforcement and prosecution agencies.[16]

Generally, a crime prevention system will be effective if only (i) the contents and framework of prevention efforts are clearly defined and the functional opportunities of all agencies included in that system are appropriately utilized; (ii) all of the subjects and targets of prevention work (including adolescents themselves and their relations in different spheres of society) are covered and the specific characteristics of each are taken into consideration; and (iii) the mechanisms of administration, control, and coordination for this type of prevention work have been developed.

Prevention initiatives are not always easily transferred from one sociocultural environment to another. Programmes that work effectively in one country may be totally inadequate in others; for example, an approach to restorative justice developed and successfully applied in one country may be implemented in another with poor results. There is a need to factor the subcultural specifics of a particular group of juvenile delinquents into programme development and to clearly define the target group at which preventive measures will be directed.

A proactive but carefully considered approach to the development and implementation of prevention and rehabilitation programmes is needed, with care taken to apply those lessons learned through direct experience. Significant public investment is warranted to both strengthen and expand the youth-oriented prevention agenda and to intensify efforts to refine and improve upon the promise of prevention. However, it must be acknowledged that the thoughtless expenditure of money, time, or effort for spontaneous or poorly developed measures will do little to solve the problem; research and evaluation must therefore be integrated into all prevention efforts.

Juvenile delinquency develops and manifests within a complex constellation of factors. Therefore, the prevention and intervention efforts should be based on these complex multiple factors. Emphasis should be based on empirically supported programmes that have identified key malleable risk factors in children, family, schools, and neighbourhood, especially drug abuse, delinquency, and violence. Relevant preventive and remedial interventions in the juvenile justice system, families, peer groups, schools, and neighbourhoods should be done making a case important in the integration of the services for juvenile delinquents. The juvenile justice system was also created because it was recognized that youth offenders are needed to be managed differently from the adults. They should receive habilitation services instead of punishment because adolescent brain does not fully develop before 18 years of age and children do not have the same emotional and mental capacity as adults do.

Preventing Delinquency in India

In India, a variety of community service projects have been experimented within bigger cities. The Tamil Nadu Government has set up Juvenile Guidance Bureau under Department of Social Defence, which is functioning under the Department of Social Welfare and Nutritious Meal Programme of the state government. Juvenile Guidance Bureau[17] has been set up to provide delinquency prevention services, including case work assistance, counselling and guidance, organized recreation, educational activities, nutrition, medical aid, and psychiatric and mental health referrals.

In several states, the juvenile aid units have been created in the police, to handle cases under the Children Acts as well as to organize boys' clubs for recreational and reading facilities for youngsters with a view to channelizing their energies on constructive lines. In Mumbai, community centres offer pre- and post-natal services, medical and nutritional services, family case work, temporary shelter to needy families, and organized recreation and educational activities. The family service centre is geared to screening destitute, neglected, and other unwanted children to find for them foster homes, adopting, guardianship, and sponsorship as a means of protection from social maladjustment. By providing counselling and guidance to the family as a whole community centres seek to avert the possible deviance among younger family members.

In Hyderabad, a non-institutional programme for the prevention of truancy, vagrancy, and juvenile delinquency has been successfully launched, with organized recreation, counselling and guidance, and training as its main components. In a few cities, a major voluntary organization has established family life institutes to deal with the problems of interpersonal relationships within the family.

The role of the state in preventing delinquency is inherent in its commitment for social justice to all children in need of care and protection. In India, the policy in this regard clearly enunciates that while the children and youngsters coming in conflict with law have to be treated within a specialized legal framework, only such socially handicapped children are dealt with through the juvenile justice system that, in the interest of such children, need stronger support from statutory measures.

The National Policy for Children, adopted by the Government of India in 1974, declares that "the nation's children are a supremely important asset. Their nurture and solicitude are our responsibility." It further enjoins that "children who are socially handicapped, who have become delinquent or have been forced to take to begging or are otherwise in distress, shall be provided facilities for education, training and rehabilitation and will be helped to become useful citizens."

The National Plan of Action for the International Year of the Child (1979) had visualized a package of integrated community services covering various aspects of physical, social, and educational welfare of needy children. It aptly aimed at securing the basic rights of children and protecting them against neglect, cruelty, and exploitation through the effective implementation of existing legislations and enactment of new ones where necessary. In pursuance of this, a number of schemes for the welfare of children, as far as possible within their families, have been initiated in the country and are being implemented and monitored by the Union Ministry of Social Welfare. Such programmes function as a filter for the juvenile justice system to concentrate on those who cannot be treated outside its purview.

There is, however, a growing awareness that preventive services programmes against juvenile delinquency need comprehensive planning at various levels. This planning necessarily requires a thorough assessment of the needs and resources and gaps and cleavages in existing services. The services offered through the juvenile justice system have to be purposefully linked with other sectors of social development which aim at improving the quality of life in the whole society. The various community organs have to be involved in the planning process from the very beginning so as to ensure that public cooperation is readily available at various stages of the implementation of plans. Evaluation of performance has to be built within the process of programme development itself, so that the schemes could be modified and reinforced, as found necessary, at various stages without wastage of time and scarce resources. A total dependence on the juvenile justice system to prevent delinquency may prove futile because, besides the limitations of the system itself, it is often too late for the damage to be repaired. The question of preventing juvenile delinquency is essentially one of protecting children's right as guaranteed in the Constitutional provisions and as specifically identified in the National Policy for Children.

Similarly, a concerted action to enforce laws relating to the care and protection of children and youngsters in trouble is equally imperative. Besides the safeguards provided in the substantive law against the exploitation of children by antisocial elements, there are numerous enactments to protect the rights of children in various spheres, including marriage, legitimacy, guardianship, maintenance, property, adoption, criminal law, health, education, labour, and welfare. Children, being the supreme national asset for human resource development, have aptly been accorded highest priority in social welfare planning, for there is no greater purpose of investment than investing in the future of a society. It is quite appropriate that in laying down framework for the prevention of juvenile delinquency, the Children Acts not only contemplate a specialized procedure for the treatment and rehabilitation of juveniles in conflict with law but also envisage a protective umbrella to those in circumstances of neglect, destitution, and exploitation. In this respect, experience has shown that it is often difficult to draw a line between a delinquent and a potential delinquent. Juvenile delinquency, in the Indian setting, is generally preceded by various phases of truancy and vagrancy that arise from conditions of insecurity and cruelty toward children. A well-rounded programme of delinquency control would, therefore, necessarily call for an integration of various formal and informal approaches in which protective legislation has a vital role to play.

Crime and delinquency are social phenomena that change and vary in space and time. The advancement of social sciences and behavioural disciplines has only partly discovered the nature and genesis of deviant behaviour. Repeated attempts by social thinkers to establish a causal relationship have failed to offer a wholly satisfactory theoretical framework. The early notions of evil effect or inmate depravity, the doctrine of "free will,"[18] and the philosophy of "hedonism"[19] as explanations for deviance have long been discredited. The later probe into the personal characteristics of the individual offender, with specific reference to the probable role of various cartographic, biological, constitutional, psychiatric, and anthropological factors did not succeed in unravelling the whole mystery.

The concepts propounded by modern social scientists, including Merton's emphasis on anomy[20] and Sutherland's focus on differential association,[21] and the later conceptual models developed along similar lines of thoughts have also not provided a complete answer. As a result, the concept of causation has itself been replaced by that of probability in modern criminology. Even the popular theory of multi-causation has, of late, been criticized as one with little practical value for efficient planning and effective social action. Nevertheless, it is generally accepted that the behaviour of the individual is influenced by the system with which he or she constantly interacts. Therefore, the protective measures implemented for women and children who are likely easy preys to the structural defects in the system have to be seen as, and be made, an integral part of social defence.

In the face of such complexities, social defence approach cannot afford to confine itself to the individual who violates the law; it has to reach people at the grassroots level to counteract tendencies for crime among them. A thoughtfully devised multipronged strategy for crime control would include, among various statutory measures, a vigorous enforcement of protective legislation, with a focus on vulnerable sections. Most laws in this sphere seem to have remained rather dormant, primarily for want of suitable implementation machinery. In order to provide the desired thrust, a mechanism to ensure close scrutiny of relevant laws and assess regularly the extent of their enforcement is a dire need. Active interest and cooperation of public is a prerequisite for policy formulation and programme development. In this context, voluntary welfare agencies that represent the concern and conscience of the community can be appropriately tapped and utilized as partners in the common social cause. A fuller use of mass communication media can go a long way in moulding public opinion and generating awareness about the objectives of protective legislation and how such objectives are sought to be achieved. On the basis of such a thorough reappraisal of the felt needs and welfare resources, government should consider developing and implementing well-thought-out plans of action to enforce legislation for women and children, with supportive services like legal aid, counselling and guidance, and social assistance to those requiring care and protection.

Researchers indicate that delinquency is an acquired trait, and it is the product of various socio-economic and environmental factors. Truly, treatment of delinquency is inherently a very limited concept. If prevention is to be effective, there must be early detection of maladjustment in children. Remedies must be found for any causes present in the family or society and which lead to delinquency. The following are some important preventive measures for delinquency acts.[22]

Family System and Well-Adjusted Home

Rapid urbanization and scientific advancement have also weakened the family, affecting vitally important relationships that constitute the core of the society, such as those between the husband and the wife and the parent and the child. The social change that came about as a result has a decisively adverse effect on the unified life constituting harmonious, healthy relationships that only a family can provide. In our tradition-loving society, the family is the sole agency for handing down the cultural heritage. The behaviour of the individual is regulated by social control groups to which he or she belongs. In big cities, the sense of isolation is common because people keep themselves to themselves and are wary of others in the public space. They have no group security. No doubt, the adult world is governed by human emotions such as breaking down of homes and the intricate network of human relationships, resulting in frequent splits and forging of new alliances among individuals, groups, and nations. Research reveals that the different psychological disorders, antisocial tendencies, rising crime rates, and a clear lack of empathy witnessed in the general society as well as in adult criminals can be easily traced to maladjustment and other issues that occur typically during childhood; thus, it is clear that juvenile delinquency and adult crime are intimately related. Therefore, more attention should be paid to the emotional life of a child.

Another powerful operative factor is the breakup of the joint family system. Older traditions are on the way out, with newer traditions fast-replacing the old ones. This means marked changes in family life. Simultaneously, old values of character and personality need to be revived by constant efforts to bring harmony between the old and the new. One potent factor affecting harmony in family life is the understanding, or the lack of it, between men and women.

In man–woman relationship, three factors such as ascendancy, submission, and equality play the main role. The idea that man and woman are complementary to each other has also not been accepted in its entirety. In our male-dominated society, typical chauvinistic views abound, entertaining the notion that a female is less rational and more emotional compared to a male, who is viewed as more level-headed and rational. With such flawed age-old ideas perpetrated through "traditions" in the institution of "marriage," a harmonious family life will continue to remain a dream if man–woman relationship is not reconstituted or better understanding is not fostered.

If we consider these facts minutely, the causes of delinquency become more complex and variable. Still a well-adjusted home provides a solid band of affection between the parents and their children. Improvement of family life is considered to be an important preventive measure. Young parents should be educated for adequate motherhood and fatherhood. They must know how to deal with their children. Working women should find time to remain with their children as long as they can within the course of the day.

Parents should not quarrel in front of their children, and they must demonstrate the norms of good conduct and restraint. They should be impartial and just to all the children. In addition, parents must be aware of the interests of their children. Children should be made to realize that their parents are always there to help them whenever they face any problems.

Again, parents must remember that children acquire disobedience, obstinacy, quarrelsome behaviours as they grow up. These are not inborn qualities. Children's nature, interest, habits, and so on are dependent on the treatment which they receive from their parents. Thus, it is necessary to see and observe these habits and their reasons. Besides that, parents should have complete knowledge about the upbringing of their children. They may receive some training from child guidance centres. While pocket money should be given for children, parents must make sure children spend it for right purposes. Children may develop bad habits if they get pocket money frequently. A strict vigil should be kept on the friends of the child. It is very important to note what type of friends the child has. Parents should keep in touch with the parents of children's friends and try to learn about their habits, interest, and so on. Another important fact is that the attitude of parents toward sexual awareness of children should be educational and proper. Any immoral and unwanted behaviour of other members of the family should be stopped at the earliest. Parents must isolate these family members who exercise bad influence on the children.

Adequate Schooling

Adequate schooling can contribute a great deal toward prevention and control of delinquency and make children understand the need for them to play a more responsible role. Personality development of children is largely influenced by schooling. That is why, in many affluent societies, attempts are being made to make the school an extension of home with the same atmosphere of informality and freedom. First, schools need trained teacher with a high moral character. They must be prepared to solve the problems of students though psychological guidance and motivation. Education must be imparted according to the child's interest and abilities. Besides this the school must have library and recreational facilities. Children must be encouraged to read and motivated by teachers. Furthermore, coordination and regular communication between homes and schools should be maintained. Teachers and parents should inform each other about the problems of the child.

Recreational Activities

Research shows that recreational activities play an important role in preventing delinquency. In rural areas, lack of healthy recreation and a community centre may induce youth to seek pleasure in bad places and in the company of antisocial elements, such as gamblers, prostitutes, drug sellers, and other dubious acquaintances. Poor children living in slums do not have facilities for any healthy recreation. In most cases, it is necessary to take the child away from unhealthy surroundings. It is wise to institute active guidance, allowing the child to establish new emotional bonds with healthy people. Improper use of leisure time is another primary cause of delinquency in children. Properly organized and supervised play and recreation can not only prevent delinquency among children but also improve their physical and mental health. Organized recreation has therapeutic values. The provision of adequate broad-based recreation services may make a substantial, measurable contribution in mitigating the problems associated with juvenile delinquency.

Role of State and Social Agencies

The state and the social agencies can play important roles in preventing delinquency. First, the state and the social agencies must establish good schools where children can receive proper education. Poor parents and impoverished families should be taken care of by the state. The censor board must work strictly on films and motion pictures. The movies having open sexual acts and violence must be strictly censored. Orphan children and illegitimate children should be facilitated with homely environment. They should not feel that they are unwanted in this world.

The Role of Police

In our state, the duty of the police is to control violation of the law and to enforce regulations. Thus, the activity of the police is both preventive and protective. The juveniles pose special problems for the police because of the generally held view that the antisocial acts of children should be treated as behaviour problems rather than as crimes. Truly speaking, the control of delinquency is a precautionary measure. In controlling delinquency, the police department has a pivotal role to play as the law enforcement agency. It is not the number but the quality of the police that is essential for the control of delinquents. All the agencies working for the prevention of delinquency should work in liaison with the police, which is critically necessary for the control of delinquency.

Creation of Social Responsibility in Children

For impoverished families, because of low income it is almost impossible for parents to take care of, or nurture, the health of their children. Many children are thus exposed to the hazards of dangerous diseases. In addition, there are other factors that are as important as health. The young and tender minds of children should be protected from any negative influences prevailing outside their homes in unhealthy surroundings. Consequently, in an unhealthy atmosphere the children are more likely to imbibe all the wrong traits and become delinquent even before they complete teen years. Parents must work at instilling morality and spiritual strength in children. Such qualities will encourage children to lead a purposeful life and acquire a sense of greater responsibility and strengthen their will to fight against all odds to succeed in their endeavours when faced with the stresses and strains of life outside their homes. In all, with parents' help and demonstrative moral leadership children can acquire noble qualities that make them conscious of the social circumstances and their responsibility towards the betterment of the society. Indirectly it prevents them from remaining idle or becoming destructive elements in society. Therefore, parents and teachers must plan in a dynamic way to inculcate positive qualities in children. Cooperation among teachers, parents, and social organizations and between teacher and parents, as well as coordinated work among individuals, are the essentials for the success of the programmes discussed here.

Specific Recommendations for Preventing Girl Child Delinquency

The state should establish a statewide task force to address the needs of girls in the juvenile justice system and work to implement gender services. This task force could closely examine each county and identify areas where success is occurring as well as areas where changes are needed. It is essential that this task forced comprise key community and state leaders, without whose presence and power it will be difficult to bring about the changes envisaged. It is important to involve key juvenile court leaders as well, as they have an important role in the implementation of changes brought about.

Furthermore, this task force should specifically examine the issues facing girls of lower castes in the society and determine what changes are necessary to make the system culturally more responsive. In addition to working to eliminate the casteism inherent in the system, it is important for the task force to identify areas rampant with institutionalized sexism. There needs to be a new sense of accountability for the system itself to eradicate these problems, problems plaguing the civil society since it came into being.

In addition to convening a task force, the state should work toward developing a training programme specifically designed for anyone working with girls in the juvenile justice system. This training should be available to legal practitioners, police, child welfare committees, juvenile justice boards, educators, and NGOs. Individuals at all levels of the system must understand the unique needs of girls before this problem can be solved. The training should also disseminate guidelines on how to build successful collaborations across agencies and programmes.

Because of current budget constraints, it is unlikely that many individual programmes will have enough funding to meet girls' needs by themselves. It is much more likely that strong partnerships will need to be built. Collaboration is difficult as it involves bridging and smoothing out differences between the working style and culture of different agencies, and often training is necessary to help concerned people to sharpen their skills in dealing and interacting with people from different agencies involved in the programmes. And it is this task that the state has to complete successfully.

Programming Recommendations

The following programming recommendations are offered for girls:

1. Recognize the uniqueness and difference in female juvenile offenders' lives and create individualized, more flexible plans sensitized to the specific needs of female juveniles;
2. Provide a safe forum for girls to openly discuss their experiences with abuse and victimization and personal safety issues;
3. Provide opportunities for girls to develop trusting and healthy relationships within their peer group;
4. Provide a safe forum to address family dynamics and problems that might contribute to delinquency pathways;
5. Include education on female health, along with opportunities for girls to understand and define healthy sexuality and to develop positive body images;
6. Offer appropriate treatment for depression, suicidal ideation and attempts, and self-injurious behaviours;
7. Provide education on and treatment for substance abuse, especially ice dependence;

8. Engage mentors, better if they are reformed past delinquents themselves, who enjoy working with girls, who share common experiences with female juvenile offenders, and who have led successful lives (perhaps despite a delinquent past);
9. Create programmes that assist girls in living independently and in building career options;
10. Provide opportunities for girls to make changes that positively affect themselves and their communities.

Limitations of the Study

The present study, like most studies, produced promising results but had some limitations that possibly affected the outcomes. One such limitation was the lack of contact with the parents of the respondents, which eliminated possibilities of knowing, for example, how the guardians viewed their child-rearing strategies and whether or not they perceived these strategies to be an overt factor in juvenile delinquency. These parents could not be contacted because most of the residential addresses given by the girls are wrong or they do not know the addresses. The only thing they remembered was either the name of the state or district. It is also because of this that most of the girls have not been able to go back home.

This study has also not been able to analyse and know about those girls who have been integrated back with their families. The effect and impact of various juvenile justice interventions in their lives could not be assessed. The main reason behind this was that we did not contact the families of those girls who had been repatriated to their families, which was done to avoid taboo and further labelling of these girls.

Another limitation was that since the girls were interviewed within the boundaries of the institutions, at times we felt as they weren't being frank and forthright in expressing their views probably due to fear and anxiety that they might be overheard by the staff. We believe that this fear is the reason for their hesitation in disclosing information at times about their plight and difficulties about their life in and outside the care homes. However, we still managed to gather a lot of information with constant interaction with the inmates. Along with this, non-participant observation also helped to elicit actual information about the children regarding the subject of the study. The analysis of the official records and files of some of the girls also helped in getting a broader picture regarding the family background of the inmates and the reasons behind their interface with the juvenile justice system.

Relevance of the Study

The present study was conducted as part of my PhD research work and is an attempt to find out the factors and conditions that cause abuse and victimization of the girl child and her induction into criminogenic culture. For this purpose, 200 girls were interviewed, who were living in government-recognized homes and were below the age of 18 years.

The girls interviewed during the study felt it was the circumstances that forced them to indulge in acts which the society calls as antisocial and delinquent. Keeping all this in mind the present research topic was chosen in order to understand the disparities between what the society considers as delinquent and the meaning attached to delinquency by the girl child herself. The study also highlights the effect on the child accused of being delinquent. Hopefully, this research, besides contributing to knowledge related to this subject, will have implications for policy development and policymakers.

Philosophical Debate of the Study

As discussed earlier, the limited studies that are there are mostly of Western countries whose sociocultural conditions are vastly different from the Indian situations. Since all the definitions of juvenile delinquency are based on Western theories it may have very serious ramifications. It needs to be understood that in the Indian context most of the juvenile girls enter into delinquency because of abusive situations at home. These situations force them to run away, as a result of which the society labels them delinquent. The delinquent girls in the Western countries are mostly violent and vagrant, but an Indian delinquent girl is often abused and neglected. Western theories have very limited practical utility in Indian scenario. This study also reveals that most of the respondents did not consider their act to be delinquent. Therefore, most of the interventions for prevention of female juvenile delinquency that are based on Western concepts need to be made more specific to the circumstances and situations faced by a female delinquent in India.

Another important aspect that needs to be stressed here is that the cases of juvenile delinquency among girls are not individual occurrences. The approach of the society about blaming the juvenile delinquent girls for their situation rather than blaming the system needs to be revised and revisited. Their problems are not theirs alone; these problems are rooted in the sociocultural conditions of the society where they live. This insight also formed the main basis of C. Wright Mills' *Sociological Imagination*. The sociocultural circumstances such as the role of the family, unprotected environment, discrimination, and social structure that were seen to be reasons for girls taking up delinquent acts have been discussed at great length in some of the chapters. In order to understand delinquency we need to focus on the structural basis for the individual's problem. Delinquency among girls needs to be analysed in its own cultural context. As discussed earlier, its meaning in one society may differ from another society. It is a culturally relative term; therefore, while analysing the research findings the sociocultural context and the meaning attached to delinquency by the respondents themselves were duly recorded and represented.

Further Research

A variety of strategies may strengthen future research involving juvenile delinquents. One approach that might yield promising results would be by conducting a thorough examination of the family, for example, by interviewing juvenile offenders and their legal guardians. Another important approach would be to conduct a longitudinal study of files of the juveniles, possibly following these juveniles over a span of ten years. It would be useful to see whether these individuals will enter an adult correctional facility. Third, research could be done to explore the correlation between delinquency and mental health issues, substance abuse, aggression, peer group dynamics, and family stressors.

Notes

1. Fagan, P. (2001), *The Real Root Causes of Violent Crime*, Guildford, CT, McGraw-Hill, pp. 61–63.
2. Dauber, S.L., Alexander, K.L., and Entwisle, D.R. (1996), Tracking and Transitions through the Middle Grades: Channeling Educational Trajectories, *Sociology of Education*, 69(10), 290–307.
3. Currie, E. (1989), Confronting Crime: Looking toward the 21st Century, *Justice Quarterly*, 6(1), 5–25.
4. Gottfredson, M. and Hirschi, T. (1990), *A General Theory of Crime*, Stanford, CA, Stanford University Press, p. 272.

5. Empey, L.T. (1982), *American Delinquency: Its Meaning and Construction*, Chicago, Dorsey Press, p. 491.
6. Sims, B. and Preston, P. (2006), *Handbook of Juvenile Justice: Theory and Practice*, Boca Raton, FL, CRC, p. 101.
7. Howell, J.C. (2003), *Preventing and Reducing Juvenile Delinquency: A Comprehensive Framework*, Thousand Oaks, CA, Sage, p. 302.
8. United Nations Department of Economic and Social Affairs (2004), *Juvenile Delinquency, World Youth Report 2003: A Global Situation of Young People*, New York, United Nations Publication, p. 200.
9. Ibid., p. 200.
10. United Nations Guidelines for Prevention of Juvenile Delinquency (The Riyadh Guidelines).
11. Division of Law Enforcement (1993), *Gang 2000: A Call to Action: The Attorney General's Report on the Impact of Criminal Street Gangs on Crime and Prevention by the Year 2000*, Sacramento, CA, State of California, Department of Justice.
12. United Nations (2003), *World Youth Report: The Global Situation of Young People*, New York, United Nations Publications, pp. 202–203.
13. Ochola, Lynette and Andre Dzikus (2000), Street Children and Gang in African Cities: Guidelines for Local Authorities, Working Papers Series 18, UMP Publications, pp. 26–37.
14. Klein, M. (1995), *The American Street Gang: Its Nature, Prevalence, and Control*, New York, Oxford University Press, pp. 138–139.
15. United Nations, *Draft Plans of Action for the Implementation during the Period 2001–2005 of the Vienna Declaration on Crime and Justice: Meeting the Challenges of the Twenty-First Century: Report of the Secretary-General*, Tenth Session of the Commission on Crime Prevention and Criminal Justice, Vienna, Austria, May 8–17, 2001 (E/CN.15/2001/5).
16. United Nation, *Global Situation of Young People*, p. 204.
17. Department of Social Defence, Tamil Nadu.
18. Vold, G.B. and Bernard, T.J. (1979), *Theoretical Criminology* (2nd ed.), New York, Oxford University Press, pp. 19–34.
19. Bainbridge, W.S. (1997), *The Sociology of Religious Movements*, London, Routledge, p. 280.
20. Merton, R. (1957), *Social Theory and Social Structure*, New York, Free Press, p. 154.
21. Sutherland, E. (1939), *Principles of Criminology* (3rd ed.), Philadelphia, Lippincott, pp. 75–77.
22. Kara, C. (1992), *Exceptional Children: Their Psychology and Education*, New Delhi, Sterling Publishers, pp. 154–158.

Annexure

Ethical Guidelines

Four well-known moral principles constitute the basis for ethics in research. They are:

1. Principle of non-maleficence: Research must not cause harm to the participants in particular and to people in general.
2. Principle of beneficence: Research should also make a positive contribution towards the welfare of people.
3. Principle of autonomy: Research must respect and protect the rights and dignity of participants.
4. Principle of justice: The benefits and risks of research should be fairly distributed among people.

The following ethical guidelines should be kept in mind while conducting any research involving children.

1. In case of studies on child abuse, one has to consider whether participation might increase a child's vulnerability.
2. Covert research, where participants do not know that they are being observed or having their words recorded, is unacceptable. One of the many reasons for this is that a researcher may not know what risks he or she may expose research "subjects" to, if children are not consulted about their participation.
3. All attempts should be made to minimize distress caused to children. While privacy may be valuable, it can make children feel safer to be interviewed along with a friend or to work in groups.
4. Further victimization of the child should be avoided. For example, children who have been violated/abused in any

obvious way should not be singled out. Also, children who are victims of violence and abuse should not be repeatedly interviewed.

5. While children may want to tell about their experiences of abuse, recalling the details may well cause them pain. Researchers need to be ready to respond appropriately during interviews. They should think about how they would react if told of shocking experiences. It may be useful to ask children how they have felt to talk about something pleasant at the end of an interview, so that children are not left focussed on abusive experiences with no time to adjust.
6. Situations where one adult and one child are in a closed room should be avoided.
7. No participant should be made to participate without having first given informed consent.
8. It will be important to explain both how the research process will be conducted and what use the research will be put to when it is completed. The researcher needs to positively "sell" his or her research to the adults and children.
9. It is essential that the identities of respondents be protected.
10. One needs to take care never to write respondents' names on the same sheet as the data they give and to keep data in a secure place.
11. Confidentiality should be observed.
12. It will be best that women researchers work with girls and women and that men researchers work with boys and men.

Child Protection Code of Conduct

Don'ts

1. Have any expectations about helping to heal the child.
2. Hit or otherwise physically assault or physically abuse children.
3. Develop physical/sexual relationship with children.
4. Develop relationships with children which could in any way be deemed exploitative or abusive.
5. Behave physically in a manner which is inappropriate or sexually provocative.
6. Act in ways intended to shame, humiliate, belittle, or degrade children, or otherwise perpetrate any form of emotional abuse.
7. Discriminate against, show differential treatment, or favour particular children to the exclusion of others.

8. Spend excessive time alone with children away from others.
9. This is not an exhaustive or exclusive list.

Do's

1. Plan and organize the work and the workplace so as to minimize risks.
2. As far as possible, be visible in working with children.
3. Ensure that a culture of openness exists to enable any issues or concerns to be raised and discussed.
4. Empower children—discuss with them their rights, what is acceptable and unacceptable, and what they can do if there is a problem.

Checklist

1. Assess the risks of harm to participants through your research and plan to minimize these.
2. Seek informed consent of children, ensuring that they know they can withdraw their consent at any point.
3. Be prepared to deal with any distress children may express during the research process.
4. Make arrangements for further ongoing support to any individual child who needs it.
5. Seek consent from parents and caretakers.
6. Ensure that information about the research is given in such a way that it is understandable and attractive to children and includes information about their rights as respondents and about how the data they provide will be handled.

Sources

1. So You Want to Involve Children in Research? A Toolkit Supporting Children's meaningful and Ethical participation in research relating to violence against children; *Save the Children*, 2004.
2. *Researching Violence against Children Using Participatory Assessments: A Handbook*; UNICEF, March 2005.
3. *Ethical Guidelines for Social Science Research in Health*, National Committee for Ethics in Social Science Research, Indian Council of Medical Research.
4. *Study on Child Abuse: India*, 2007.

Bibliography

Adler, F. (1992), *New Directions in Criminological Theory*, Piscataway, NJ, Transaction Publishers, pp. 381–398.

Arnot, M.L. and Usborne, C. (1999), *Gender and Crime in Modern Europe*, London, Taylor and Francis, pp. 77–84.

Arulselvam, M. (2002), *Law Relating to Juveniles and Probation*, Chennai, Marathi Publications, pp. 226–246.

Bainbridge, W.S. (1997), *The Sociology of Religious Movements*, London, Routledge, p. 280.

Baines, M. and Alder, C. (1996), Are Girls More Difficult to Work with? Youth Workers' Perceptions in Juvenile Justice and Related Areas, *Crime and Delinquency*, 42, 467–485.

Bartol, C.R. (2004), *Introduction to Forensic Psychology*, London, Sage, pp. 102–103.

Barton, J.H., Gibbs, J.L., Li, V.H., and Merryman, J.H. (1983), *Laws in Radically Different Cultures*, St Paul, MN, West Publishing, pp. 5–6.

Becker, H.S. (1963), *Outsiders: Studies in the Sociology of Deviance*. New York: Free Press, pp. 9–10.

Belknap, J. (1996). *The Invisible Woman: Gender, Crime and Justice*. Belmont, CA: Wadsworth, pp. 3–21.

Bergsmann, I.R. (1989), The Forgotten Few: Juvenile Female Offenders. *Federal Probation*, 53(1), 73–78.

Beteille, A. (1964), Family and Social Change in India and South Asian Countries, *Economic Weekly*, 16, 239.

Bhattacharyya, C.D. (1972), *Sociology*, Calcutta, Vidyodaya Library, pp. 628.

Bhattarcharya, S.K. (2002), *Juvenile Justice: An Indian Scenario*, New Delhi, Regency Publications, Preface, vii.

Bhushan, B. (1989), *Dictionary of Sociology*, New Delhi, Anmol, p. 74.

Borgatta, E. and Borgatta, M. (1991), *Encyclopedia of Sociology* (Vol. 2), New York, Maxwell Macmillan, pp. 1031–1032.

Bose, A.B. (1992), *The Disadvantaged Urban Child in India* (UNICEF: Innocenti Occasional Papers: The Urban Child Series, 1), Florence, Italy, pp. 56–73.

Bottoms, A. (1996), *Sexism and the Female Offender*, Gower, Sydney, p. 1.

Bowlby, J. (1952), *Maternal Care and Mental Health*, Geneva, World Health Organization, p. 47.

Burfeind, J.W. and Bartusch, D.J. (2005), *Juvenile Delinquency: An Integrated Approach*, London, John and Bartlett, pp. 380–386.

Burt, C. (1915), *The Young Delinquents*, London, London University Press, p. 15.

Cain, M. (ed.). (1989), *Growing up Good: Policing the Behavior of Girls in Europe*, London, Sage, pp. 96–113.

Carmichael, M. (2004), No Girls Please, *Newsweek*, January 26, p. 50.

Cavan, R.S. (1961), The Concept of Tolerance and Contra-culture as Applied to Delinquency, *Sociological Quarterly*, 2, 243.

Chaffin, M., Kelleher, K., and Hollenberg, J. (1996). Onset of Physical Abuse and Neglect: Psychiatric, Substance Abuse, and Social Risk Factors from Prospective Community Data. *Child Abuse and Neglect*, 20(3), 191–203.

Chambliss, W. and Seidman, R. (1971), *Law Order and Power*, Reading, MA, Addison Wesley, p. 268.

Chesney-Lind, M. (1988), Girls and Status Offenses: Is Juvenile Justice Still Sexist? *Criminal Justice Abstracts*, 20(1), 144–165.

Chesney-Lind, M. (1995), Girls, Delinquency and Juvenile Justice: Toward a Feminist Theory of Young Women's Crime. In *The Criminal Justice System and Women* (ed. B.R. Price and N.J. Sokoloff), New York, McGraw-Hill, pp. 71–88.

Chesney-Lind, M. (1997), *The Female Offender: Girls, Women, and Crime*, London, Sage, p. 10.

Chowdhary, S. (2003), Keeping Them at Bay, *The Hindu*, May 14, http://www.thehindu.com/thehindu/mp/2003/05/14/stories/20033051400360200.htm

Clough, P., Garner, P., Yuen, F., and Pardeck, J.T. (2005), *Handbook of Emotional and Behavioural Difficulties*, London, Sage, pp. 175–176.

Cloward, R. and Ohlin, L. (1960), *Delinquency and Opportunity*, New York, Free Press, pp. 31–47.

Cohen, A. (1955), *Delinquent Boys*, New York, Free Press, pp. 24–32, 121–140.

Colvin, M. and Pauly, J. (1983), A Critique of Criminology: Towards an Integrated Structural-Marxist Theory of Delinquency Production. *American Journal of Sociology*, 89(3), 512–552.

Cooley, C.H. (1902), *Nature and the Social Order*, New York, Scribners, p. 152.

Corbett, J. (1999), Women Lash Out More Readily: Crime Stats, *The New Zealand Herald*, August 21, http://www.fact.on.ca/newpaper/nz990821.htm.

Currie, E. (1989), Confronting Crime: Looking Toward the 21st Century, *Justice Quarterly*, 6(1), 5–25.

Datesman, S.K., Scarpitti, F.R., and Stephenson, R.M., (1975), Female Delinquency: An Application of Self and Opportunity Theories, *Journal of Research in Crime and Delinquency*, 12, 120.

Dauber, S.L., Alexander, K.L., and Entwisle, D.R. (1996), Tracking and Transitions through the Middle Grades: Channeling Educational Trajectories, *Sociology of Education*, 69(10), 290–307.

Davis, C., Tang, C., and Ko, J. (1998), Exploring Current Behaviors and Social Service Needs for Chinese Juvenile Delinquents in Hong Kong, *Children and Youth Services Review*, 20(8), 733–745.

Dube, S.R., Anda, R.F., Felitti, V.J., Croft, J.B., Edwards, V.J., and Giles, W.H. (2001), Growing up with Parental Alcohol Abuse: Exposure to Childhood Abuse, Neglect and Household Dysfunction. *Child Abuse and Neglect*, 25(12), 1627–1640.

Dumont, L. (1970), *Homo Hierarchicus*, Chicago, University of Chicago Press, p. 9.

Durkheim, E. (1950), *The Rules of Sociological Methods* (trans. and ed. S.A. Solovay and J.H. Mueller), New York, Free Press, p. 71.

Durkheim, E. (1951), *Suicide*, New York, Free Press, p. 248.

Dutta Gupta, B. (1964), *Contemporary Social Problems in India*, Calcutta, Vidyodaya Library, p. 122.

Empey, L.T. (1982), *American Delinquency: Its Meaning and Construction*, Chicago, Dorsey Press, p. 491.

Epstein, I. (1987), Psychological and Behavioral Attributes of Juvenile Delinquents in the People's Republic of China, *Asian Thought and Society*, 12, 267–268.

Erikson, E. (1979), Report to Vikram: Further Perspectives on Life Cycle. In S. Kakar (ed.), *Identity and Adulthood*, Delhi, Oxford University Press, p. 25.

Fagan, P. (2001), *The Real Root Causes of Violent Crime*, Guildford, CT, McGraw-Hill, pp. 61–63.

Feinman, C. (1994), *Women in the Criminal Justice System*, Westport, CT, Praeger, pp. 22–28.

Female Infanticide Alarming in Dharmapuri. (1998, August 2), *The Hindu*, p. 1.

Fischer, C. (1995), The Subcultural Theory of Urbanism: A Twentieth Year Assessment, *American Journal of Sociology*, 101(3), 543–577.

Flowers, R.B. (1987), *Women and Criminality: The Women as Victim, Offender and Practitioner*, Westport, CT, Greenwood Press, pp. 68–70.

Frank, L.K. (1937), *The Fundamental Needs of the Child*. Paper presented at the Conference of the National Association for Nursery Education, October 22, Nashville, TN.

Freud, S. (1924), *The Dissolution of the Oedipus Complex: Standard Editions of Freud's Works*, London, Hogarth Press, pp. 320–321.

Friday, P.C. and Ren, X. (2006), *Delinquency and Juvenile Justice Systems in the Non-Western World*, New York, Criminal Justice Press, p. 30.

Friday, P.C. and Ren, X. (ed.). (2006), *Delinquency and Juvenile Justice System in the Non-Western World*, New York, Criminal Justice Press, pp. 37–38.

Garkinkel, H. (1956), Conditions of Successful Degradation Ceremonies, *American Journal of Sociology*, 61, 420–424.

Garrison, K.C. (1959), *Growth and Development*, New York, Longmans, p. 420.

Geismar, L.L. and Wood, K.M. (1986), *Family and Delinquency: Re-socializing the Young Offender*, New York, Human Sciences Press, pp. 131–134.

Gelsthorpe, L. (1986) Towards a Sceptical Look at Sexism, *International Journal of the Sociology of Law*, 14, 125–152.

Ghosh, S.K. (1984), The Aiders and Abettors of Crime. In *Women in Changing Society*, New Delhi, Ashish Publishing, pp. 95–96.

Gibbens, T.C.N. and Ahrenfeldt, R.H. (1966), *Cultural Factors in Delinquency*, London, Tavistock, p. 170.

Gibbons, D.C. (1968), *Society, Crime and Criminal Careers*, Upper Saddle River, NJ, Prentice Hall, pp. 104–105.

Gottfredson, M. and Hirschi, T. (1990), *A General Theory of Crime*, Stanford, CA, Stanford University Press, p. 272.

Haberfeld, Y., Menaria, R.K., Sahoo, B.B., and Vyas, R.N. (1999), Seasonal Migration of Rural Labour in India, *Population Research and Policy Review*, 18(4), 73–89.

Hagan, J., Gillis, A.R., and Simpson, J. (1987), Class in the Household: A Power-Control Theory of Gender and Delinquency, *American Journal of Sociology*, 92, 788–816.

Hartjen, C.A. and Kethineni, S. (1996), *Comparative Delinquency: India and the United States*, London, Taylor and Francis, pp. 149–150.

Heiland, H.G., Shelley, L.I., and Katō, H. (1992), *Crime and Control in Comparative Perspectives*, New York, Walter de Gruyter, p. 194.

Herman, N.J. (1995), *Deviance: A Symbolic Interactionist Approach*, Dix Hill, New York, p. 36.

Hirschi, T. (1969), *Causes of Delinquency*, Berkeley, CA, University of California Press, pp. 162–186.

Hirschi, T. (author) and Laub, J.H. (ed.). (2002), *The Craft of Criminology, Selected Papers*, Piscataway, NJ, Transaction Publishers, p. 76.

Howell, J.C. (2003), *Preventing and Reducing Juvenile Delinquency: A Comprehensive Framework*, Thousand Oaks, CA, Sage, p. 302.

Hoyt, S. and Scherer, D.G. (1998). Female Juvenile Delinquency: Misunderstood by the Juvenile Justice System, Neglected By Social Science. *Law and Human Behavior*, 22, 81–107.

India Pleads: Adopt Our Orphan Girls: British Couples Urged to Aid "Lost" 11. (2007, April 8). *Sunday Times*.

Joseph, J. (1995), *Black Youths, Delinquency, and Juvenile Justice*, Westport, CT, Greenwood Publishing, pp. 12–13.

Kadushin, A. and Martin, J.A. (1988), *Child Welfare Services*, New York, MacMillan, pp. 11–17.

Kanth, A. (1993), Neglected Juvenile (or Neglected Children): Need for a Concept and Definition. in A. Kanth and R.M. Varma, *Neglected Child: Changing Perspectives*, Delhi, Prayas Juvenile Aid Centre, pp. 93–101.

Kapur, P. (1995), Girl Child Abuse: Violation of Her Human Rights. *Social Change*, 25, (2–3), 3–18.

Khan, M.Z. and Dassi, A. (1997), Children in Urban Blight in Delhi: Problems and Social Intervention, *Contemporary Social Work*, 14, 39–50.

Klein, D. (1973), The Etiology of Female Crime: A Review of Literature, *Issues in Criminology*, 8, 6.

Klein, M. (1995), *The American Street Gang: Its Nature, Prevalence, and Control*, New York, Oxford University Press, pp. 138–139.

Komorosky, M. (1953), *Women in the Modern World*, San Francisco, Jossey-Bass, pp. 67–76.

Lane, T.W. and Davis, G.E. (1987), *Child Maltreatment and Juvenile delinquency: Does a Relationship Exist?* In Burchard, D. John and Burchard N. Sara, Prevention of Delinquent Behaviour, Newbury Park, California, Sage Publications, pp. 122–138.

Lemert, E. (1951), *Social Pathology*, McGraw-Hills, New York, pp. 76–78.

Lemert, E. (1967), *Human Deviance, Social Problems, and Social Control*. Englewood Cliffs, NJ, Prentice Hall, p. 40.

Lipsey, M.W. and Derzon, J.H. (1998), Predictors of Violent or Serious Delinquency in Adolescence and Early Adulthood: A synthesis of Longitudinal Research. In R. Loeber and D.P. Farrington (eds), *Serious and Violent Juvenile Offenders: Risk Factors and Successful Interventions*, Thousand Oaks, CA, Sage, pp. 86–105.

Madhava Menon, N.R. and Banerjea, D. (2002), *Criminal Justice India Series: National Capital Territory of Delhi*, New Delhi, Allied Publishers, p. 8.

Mahoney, A. (1974), The Effect of Labeling upon Youths in the Juvenile Justice System: A Review of the Evidence, *Law and Society Review*, 8, 583–614.

Mann, C.R. (1984), *Female Crime and Delinquency*, Tuscaloosa, AL, University of Alabama Press, p. 57.

Marx, Karl. (1867), *Capital* (Vol. 1), London, Lawrence and Wishart, p. 734.

McIvor, G. (2004), *Women Who Offend*, London, Jessica Kinsley, p. 24.

Meclellan, S.G. (1956), *Juvenile Delinquency*, New York, Wilson Publishers, p. 47.

Menon, S. (2000), *Young Criminals: Crime and Punishments in Juvenile Delinquency*, New Delhi, Kanishka, pp. 6–7.

Merton, R. (1938), Social Structure and Anomie, *American Sociological Review*, 3, 672–682.

Merton, R. (1957), *Social Theory and Social Structure*, New York, Free Press, pp. 154–160.

Miller, W. (1958), Lower Class Culture as a Generating Milieu of Gang Delinquency, *Journal of Social Issues*, 14, 5–20.

Miller, W. (1959), Implications of Urban Lower-Class Culture for Social Work, *Social Service Review*, 33, 219–236.

Mines, M. (1988), Conceptualizing the Person: Hierarchical Society and Individual Autonomy in India, *American Anthropologist*, 90, 568–579.

Mohsin, N. (2002), *Lost Innocence*, New Delhi, Common Wealth Publishers, p. 73.

Moore, J. and Hagedorn, J. (2001), *Female Gangs: A Focus on Research*, Washington, DC, Office of Juvenile Justice and Delinquency Prevention, pp. 2–6.

Morash, M. and Chesney-Lind, M. (1991), A Reformulation and Partial Test of the Power Control Theory of Delinquency, *Justice Quarterly*, 8, 347–377.

Moretti, M.M., Odgers, L.C., and Jackson, A.M. (2004), *Girls and Aggression: Contributing Factors and Intervention Principles*, New York, Kluwer, p. 170.

Nagla, B.K. (1991), *Women, Crime and Law*, Jaipur: Rawat Publications, p. 120.

National Crime Records Bureau. (2002), *Crime in India 2000*, New Delhi, Author.

Ochola, Lynette and Andre Dzikus (2000), Street Children and Gang in African Cities: Guidelines for Local Authorities, Working Papers Series 18, UMP Publications, pp. 26–37.

Piers, B. (ed.). (2004), *The Chicago School of Criminology 1914–1945: The Gang: A Study of 1,313 Gangs in Chicago by Frederic Milton Thrasher*, London, Taylor and Francis, pp. 224.

Pinheiro, P.S. (2005), *World Report on Violence against Children*, New York, United Nations Publications, pp. 185–186, 195–196.

Poe-Yamagata, E. and Butts, J.A. (1996), *Female Offenders in the Juvenile Justice System: Statistics Summary*, Washington, DC, Diane Publishing, pp. 2–8.

Pollock, J. (1978), Early Theories of Female Criminality. In Lee H Bowker, *Women, Crime and the Criminal Justice System*, Lanham, MD, Lexington Books, p. 45.

Ponnaian, M. (1992), *Criminology and Penology*, New Delhi, Pioneer Books, pp. 67–68.

Prescott, L. (1998), *Adolescent Girls with Co-occurring Disorders in the Juvenile Justice System*. New York, Policy Research, pp. 2–6.

Quay, H.C. (1987), *Handbook of Juvenile Delinquency*, Toronto, ON, Canada, John Wiley, pp. 216–243.

Ramachandran, V. (2004), *Gender and Social Equity in Primary Education: Hierarchies of Access*, New Delhi, Sage, pp. 44–48.

Reiss, A.J. (1960), Sex Offences: The Marginal Status of the Adolescent, *Law and Contemporary Problems*, 25, 309–333.

Reynolds, L.T. and Herman-Kinney, N.J. (2003), *Handbook of Symbolic Interactionism*, Lanham, MD, Rowman and Littlefield, pp. 696–697.

Richie, B.E., Tsenin, K., and Widom, C.S. (2000), *Research on Women and Girls in the Justice System: Plenary Papers of the 1999 Conference on Criminal Justice Research and Evaluation—Enhancing Policy and Practice through Research* (Vol. 3), Washington, DC, NIJ Publications, p. 29.

Robinson, S.M. (1961), *Juvenile Delinquency: Its Nature and Control*, New York, McGraw-Hills, p. 11.

Rodgers, G. and Standing, G. (1981), *Child Work, Poverty and Underdevelopment,* Geneva, International Labour Office, pp. 2–11.

Roland, A. (1988), *In Search of Self in India and Japan: Towards a Cross-Cultural Psychology*, Princeton NJ, Princeton University Press, p. 211.

Rosenheim, M.K. (ed.) (2002), *A Century of Juvenile Justice*, Chicago, University of Chicago Press, p. 192.

Ross, M. (1992), Reflecting Appraisals, Parental Labeling and Delinquency: Specifying a Symbolic Interactionist Theory, *American Journal of Sociology*, 57, 1577–1611.

Sagade, J. (2005), *Child Marriage in India: Socio-legal and Human Rights Dimension*, New Delhi, Oxford University Press, p. 257.

Sandhu, H.S. (1977), *Juvenile Delinquency: Causes Control and Prevention*, New York, McGraw-Hills, p. 2.

Sarkar, C. (1987), *Juvenile Delinquency in India*, Delhi, Daya Publishing, p. 21.

Schur, E.M. (1971), *Labeling Deviant Behavior: Its Sociological Implications*, New York, Harper and Row, p. 8.

Schwartz, I.M., Barton, W.H., and Orlando, F. (1991), Keeping Kids Out of Secure Detention: The Misuse of Juvenile Detention Has a Profound Impact on Child Welfare, *Public Welfare*, 49(2), 20–26.

Sharma, R.K. (1996), *Fundamentals of Sociology*, London, Atlantic, pp. 241–242.

Sharp, C. and Simon, J. (2004), *Girls in the Juvenile Justice System*, Washington, DC, Child Welfare League of America Publications, p. 4.

Siddique, A. (1978), *Criminology Problems and Perspectives*, Lucknow, UP, India, Eastern Book Company, pp. 129–130, 138.

Siegel, L. (1992), *Criminology* (4th ed.), St. Paul, MN, West Publishing, p. 270.

Siegel, L.J. and Welsh, B.C. (2008), *Juvenile Delinquency Theory, Practice and Law* (10th ed.), Belmont, CA, Wadsworth, p. 95.

Sims, B. and Preston, P. (2006), *Handbook of Juvenile Justice: Theory and Practice*, Boca Raton, FL, CRC, p. 101.

Singh, R. (1990), *The Womb of Mind: A Sociological Exploration of the Status-Experience of Women in Delhi*, New Delhi, Vikas Publishing, pp. 45–50, 109.

Snyder, J. and Patterson, G. (1987), Family Interaction and Delinquent Behaviour. In H.C. Quay, *A Handbook of Juvenile Delinquency*, Toronto, ON, Canada, John Wiley, pp. 216–243.

Srinivasan, P. (2002), At Home Yet Alone, *The Hindu*, August 29, http://www.the hindu.com/thehindu/mp/2002/08/29/stories/2002082900010100.htm

Stumphauzer, J.S. (1986), *Helping Delinquents Change: A Treatment of Social Learning Approaches*, New York, Haworth, pp. 67–74.

Sutherland, E. and Cressey, D.R. (1939), A Sociological Theory of Criminal Behavior. In P. Bean, *Crime Critical Concepts in Sociology*, London, Taylor and Francis, pp. 151–158.

Sutherland, E. and Cressey, D.R. (1966), *Principles of Criminology* (7th ed.), Philadelphia, PA, Lippincott, p. 43.

Sutherland, E. (1939), *Principles of Criminology* (3rd ed.), Philadelphia, PA, Lippincott, pp. 75–77, 157.

Sutherland, E. (1974), *Criminology*, Philadelphia, PA, Lippincott, pp. 75–77.

Tannenbaum, F. (1938), *Crime and the Community*, Boston, MA, Ginn, p. 17.

Tappan, P.W. (1949), *Juvenile Delinquency*, New York, McGraw-Hills, p. 30.

Temin, C.E. (1973), Discriminating Sentencing of Women Offenders, *American Criminal Law Review*, 11, 353–372.

Thilagaraj, R. and Priyamvadha, M. (2000), Deviance among Street Children, *Indian Journal of Criminology*, 28(1), 41–44.

Thomas, W.I. (1923), *The Unadjusted Girl with Cases and Standpoint for Behavior Analysis*, Boston, MA, Little Brown and Co., pp. 38–37.

Thornberry, T.P. (1987), Towards an Interactional Theory of Delinquency, *Criminology*, 25, 863–892.

United Nations Department of Economic and Social Affairs. (2004), *Juvenile Delinquency, World Youth Report 2003: A global Situation of Young People*, New York, United Nations Publications, pp. 189–204.

United Nations. (2001), Draft Plans of Action for the Implementation during the Period 2001–2005 of the Vienna Declaration on Crime and Justice: Meeting the Challenges of the Twenty-First Century: Report of the Secretary-General, *10th Session of the Commission on Crime Prevention and Criminal Justice*, May 8–17, 2001, Vienna, Austria (E/CN.15/2001/5).

Vicentnathan, S.G. (2006), Juvenile Justice in India. In P.C. Friday and X. Ren (eds), *Delinquency and Juvenile Justice System in the Non-Western World*, New York, Criminal Justice Press, pp. 28–32.

Vincentnathan, S.G. (1985), *Caste, Class and Crime: India and the United States, Comparative Social Research. Vol. 3: Deviance*, Greenwich, CT, Jai Press, p. 114.

Vincentnathan, S.G. (1992), The Social Construction of Order and Disorder in Two South Indian Communities, *Journal of Legal Pluralism*, 32, p. 86.

Vold, G. (1958), *Theoretical Criminology*, New York, Oxford University Press, p. 211.

Vold, G. and Bernard, T.J. (1979), *Theoretical* Criminology (2nd ed.), New York, Oxford University Press, pp. 19–34.

Wasserman, G.A. and Seracini, A.M. (2001), *Family Risk Factors and Interventions*. In R. Loeber and D.P. Farrington (eds), *Child Delinquents: Development, Intervention and Service Needs*, Thousand Oaks, CA, Sage, pp. 165–169.

Wattenberg, W. and Saunders, F. (1954), Sex Differences among Juvenile Offenders, *Sociology and Social Research*, 39 (September–October), 24–31.

Wilson, J.Q. and Herrenstein, R.J. (1985), *Crime and Human Nature*, New York, Simon and Schuster, pp. 59–67.

Zezulka-Mailloux, G. and Gifford, J. (2003), *Culture + The State*, Edmonton, AB, Canada, CRC, p. 153.

Index